GRAMMAR
AND BEYOND

Randi Reppen
with Deborah Gordon

2B

CAMBRIDGE
UNIVERSITY PRESS

CAMBRIDGE
UNIVERSITY PRESS

University Printing House, Cambridge CB2 8BS, United Kingdom

One Liberty Plaza, 20th Floor, New York, NY 10006, USA

477 Williamstown Road, Port Melbourne, VIC 3207, Australia

314–321, 3rd Floor, Plot 3, Splendor Forum, Jasola District Centre, New Delhi – 110025, India

79 Anson Road, #06–04/06, Singapore 079906

Cambridge University Press is part of the University of Cambridge.

It furthers the University's mission by disseminating knowledge in the pursuit of education, learning and research at the highest international levels of excellence.

www.cambridge.org
Information on this title: www.cambridge.org/9780521143127

First published 2012
20 19 18 17 16 15 14 13 12 11 10 9 8

Printed in Malaysia by Vivar Printing

A catalogue record for this publication is available from the British Library

ISBN 978-0-521-14296-0 Student's Book 2
ISBN 978-0-521-14310-3 Student's Book 2A
ISBN 978-0-521-14312-7 Student's Book 2B
ISBN 978-0-521-27991-8 Workbook 2
ISBN 978-0-521-27992-5 Workbook 2A
ISBN 978-0-521-27993-2 Workbook 2B
ISBN 978-1-107-67653-4 Teacher Support Resource 2
ISBN 978-0-521-14335-6 Class Audio 2
ISBN 978-1-139-06186-5 Writing Skills Interactive 2

Art direction, book design, and layout services: Adventure House, NYC
Audio production: John Marshall Media

Contents

Appendices

Introduction to *Grammar and Beyond*

Grammar and Beyond is a research-based and content-rich grammar series for beginning- to advanced-level students of North American English. The series focuses on the grammar structures most commonly used in North American English, with an emphasis on the application of these grammar structures to academic writing. The series practices all four skills in a variety of authentic and communicative contexts. It is designed for use both in the classroom and as a self-study learning tool.

Grammar and Beyond Is Research-Based

The grammar presented in this series is informed by years of research on the grammar of written and spoken North American English as it is used in college lectures, textbooks, academic essays, high school classrooms, and conversations between instructors and students. This research, and the analysis of over one billion words of authentic written and spoken language data known as the *Cambridge International Corpus*, has enabled the authors to:

- Present grammar rules that accurately represent how North American English is actually spoken and written

- Identify and teach differences between the grammar of written and spoken English

- Focus more attention on the structures that are commonly used, and less attention on those that are rarely used, in written and spoken North American English

- Help students avoid the most common mistakes that English language learners make

- Choose reading and writing topics that will naturally elicit examples of the target grammar structure

- Introduce important vocabulary from the Academic Word List

Grammar and Beyond Teaches Academic Writing Skills

Grammar and Beyond helps students make the transition from understanding grammar structures to applying them in their academic writing.

In the Student's Books

At Levels 1 through 3 of the series, every Student's Book unit ends with a section devoted to the hands-on application of grammar to writing. This section, called Grammar for Writing, explores how and where the target grammar structures function in writing and offers controlled practice, exposure to writing models, and a guided but open-ended writing task.

At Level 4, the most advanced level, the syllabus is organized around the academic essay types that college students write (e.g., persuasive, cause and effect) and is aimed at teaching students the grammar, vocabulary, and writing skills that they need in order to be successful at writing those kinds of essays.

Online

Grammar and Beyond also offers *Writing Skills Interactive*, an interactive online course in academic writing skills and vocabulary that correlates with the Student's Books. Each unit of the writing skills course focuses on a specific writing skill, such as avoiding sentence fragments or developing strong topic sentences.

Special Features of *Grammar and Beyond*

Realistic Grammar Presentations

Grammar is presented in clear and simple charts. The grammar points presented in these charts have been tested against real-world data from the *Cambridge International Corpus* to ensure that they are authentic representations of actual usage of North American English.

Data from the Real World

Many of the grammar presentations and application sections in the Student's Book include a feature called Data from the Real World, in which concrete and useful points discovered through analysis of corpus data are presented. These points are practiced in the exercises that follow.

Avoid Common Mistakes

Each Student's Book unit features an Avoid Common Mistakes section that develops students' awareness of the most common mistakes made by English language learners and gives them an opportunity to practice detecting and correcting these errors in running text. This section helps students avoid these mistakes in their own work. The mistakes highlighted in this section are drawn from a body of authentic data on learner English known as the *Cambridge Learner Corpus*, a database of over 35 million words from student essays written by nonnative speakers of English and information from experienced classroom teachers.

Academic Vocabulary

Every unit in *Grammar and Beyond* includes words from the Academic Word List (AWL), a research-based list of words and word families that appear with high frequency in English-language academic texts. These words are introduced in the opening text of the unit, recycled in the charts and exercises, and used to support the theme throughout the unit. The same vocabulary items are reviewed and practiced in *Writing Skills Interactive*, the online writing skills course. By the time students finish each level, they will have been exposed several times to a carefully selected set of level-appropriate AWL words, as well as content words from a variety of academic disciplines.

Series Levels

The following table provides a general idea of the difficulty of the material at each level of *Grammar and Beyond*. These are not meant to be interpreted as precise correlations.

	Description	TOEFL IBT	CEFR Levels
Level 1	beginning	20 – 34	A1 – A2
Level 2	low intermediate to intermediate	35 – 54	A2 – B1
Level 3	high intermediate	55 – 74	B1 – B2
Level 4	advanced	75 – 95	B2 – C1

Components for Students

Student's Book

The Student's Books for Levels 1 through 3 teach all of the grammar points appropriate at each level in short, manageable cycles of presentation and practice organized around a high-interest unit theme. The Level 4 Student's Book focuses on the structure of the academic essay in addition to the grammar rules, conventions, and structures that students need to master in order to be successful college writers. Please see the Tour of a Unit on pages xiv–xvii for a more detailed view of the contents and structure of the Student's Book units.

Workbook

The Workbook provides additional practice of the grammar presented in each unit of the Student's Book. The exercises offer both discrete and consolidated practice of grammar points and can be used for homework or in class. Each unit also offers practice correcting the errors highlighted in the Avoid Common Mistakes section in the Student's Book to help students master these troublesome errors. Self-Assessment sections at the end of each unit allow students to test their mastery of what they have learned.

Writing Skills Interactive

This online course provides graduated instruction and practice in writing skills, while reinforcing vocabulary presented in the Student's Books. Each unit includes a vocabulary review activity, followed by a short text that builds on the theme presented in the Student's Book and provides an additional context for the vocabulary. The text is followed by an animated interactive presentation of the target writing skill of the unit, after which students have the opportunity to practice the target skill in three different activities. Each unit closes with a quiz, which allows students to assess their progress.

Teacher Resources

Teacher Support Resource Book

This comprehensive book provides a range of support materials for instructors, including:

- Suggestions for applying the target grammar to all four major skill areas, helping instructors facilitate dynamic and comprehensive grammar classes

- An answer key and audio script for the Student's Book

- A CD-ROM containing:

  - Ready-made, easily scored Unit Tests

  - PowerPoint presentations to streamline lesson preparation and encourage lively heads-up interaction

Class Audio CDs

The class audio CDs for each level provide the Student's Book listening material for in-class use.

Teacher Support Website

www.cambridge.org/grammarandbeyond

The website for *Grammar and Beyond* contains even more resources for instructors, including:

- Unit-by-unit teaching tips, helping instructors plan their lessons

- Downloadable communicative activities to add more in-class speaking practice

- A monthly newsletter on grammar teaching, providing ongoing professional development

We hope you enjoy using this series, and we welcome your feedback! Please send any comments to the authors and editorial staff at Cambridge University Press, at grammarandbeyond@cambridge.org.

About the Authors

 Randi Reppen is Professor of Applied Linguistics and TESL at Northern Arizona University (NAU) in Flagstaff, Arizona. She has over 20 years experience teaching ESL students and training ESL teachers, including 11 years as the Director of NAU's Program in Intensive English. Randi's research interests focus on the use of corpora for language teaching and materials development. In addition to numerous academic articles and books, she is the author of *Using Corpora in the Language Classroom* and a co-author of *Basic Vocabulary in Use*, 2nd edition, both published by Cambridge University Press.

Deborah Gordon, creator of the Grammar for Writing sections, has more than 25 years' experience teaching ESL students and training ESL teachers in the United States and abroad. She is currently an ESL instructor at Santa Barbara City College and a TESOL Certificate instructor at the University of California, Santa Barbara Extension. Deborah is coauthor of *Writers at Work: From Sentence to Paragraph*, published by Cambridge University Press, among many other titles.

Corpus Consultants

Michael McCarthy is Emeritus Professor of Applied Linguistics at the University of Nottingham, UK, and Adjunct Professor of Applied Linguistics at the Pennsylvania State University. He is a co-author of the corpus-informed *Touchstone* series and the award-winning *Cambridge Grammar of English*, both published by Cambridge University Press, among many other titles, and is known throughout the world as an expert on grammar, vocabulary, and corpus linguistics.

Jeanne McCarten has over 30 years of experience in ELT/ESL as a teacher, publisher, and author. She has been closely involved in the development of the spoken English sections of the *Cambridge International Corpus*. Now a freelance writer, she is co-author of the corpus-informed *Touchstone* series and *Grammar for Business*, both published by Cambridge University Press.

Advisory Panel

The ESL advisory panel has helped to guide the development of this series and provided invaluable information about the needs of ESL students and teachers in high schools, colleges, universities, and private language schools throughout North America.

Neta Simpkins Cahill, Skagit Valley College, Mount Vernon, WA

Shelly Hedstrom, Palm Beach State College, Lake Worth, FL

Richard Morasci, Foothill College, Los Altos Hills, CA

Stacey Russo, East Hampton High School, East Hampton, NY

Alice Savage, North Harris College, Houston, TX

Acknowledgments

The publisher and authors would like to thank these reviewers and consultants for their insights and participation:

Marty Attiyeh, The College of DuPage, Glen Ellyn, IL

Shannon Bailey, Austin Community College, Austin, TX

Jamila Barton, North Seattle Community College, Seattle, WA

Kim Bayer, Hunter College IELI, New York, NY

Linda Berendsen, Oakton Community College, Skokie, IL

Anita Biber, Tarrant County College Northwest, Fort Worth, TX

Jane Breaux, Community College of Aurora, Aurora, CO

Anna Budzinski, San Antonio College, San Antonio, TX

Britta Burton, Mission College, Santa Clara, CA

Jean Carroll, Fresno City College, Fresno, CA

Chris Cashman, Oak Park High School and Elmwood Park High School, Chicago, IL

Annette M. Charron, Bakersfield College, Bakersfield, CA

Patrick Colabucci, ALI at San Diego State University, San Diego, CA

Lin Cui, Harper College, Palatine, IL

Jennifer Duclos, Boston University CELOP, Boston, MA

Joy Durighello, San Francisco City College, San Francisco, CA

Kathleen Flynn, Glendale Community College, Glendale, CA

Raquel Fundora, Miami Dade College, Miami, FL

Patricia Gillie, New Trier Township High School District, Winnetka, IL

Laurie Gluck, LaGuardia Community College, Long Island City, NY

Kathleen Golata, Galileo Academy of Science & Technology, San Francisco, CA

Ellen Goldman, Mission College, Santa Clara, CA

Ekaterina Goussakova, Seminole Community College, Sanford, FL

Marianne Grayston, Prince George's Community College, Largo, MD

Mary Greiss Shipley, Georgia Gwinnett College, Lawrenceville, GA

Sudeepa Gulati, Long Beach City College, Long Beach, CA

Nicole Hammond Carrasquel, University of Central Florida, Orlando, FL

Vicki Hendricks, Broward College, Fort Lauderdale, FL

Kelly Hernandez, Miami Dade College, Miami, FL

Ann Johnston, Tidewater Community College, Virginia Beach, VA

Julia Karet, Chaffey College, Claremont, CA

Jeanne Lachowski, English Language Institute, University of Utah, Salt Lake City, UT

Noga Laor, Rennert, New York, NY

Min Lu, Central Florida Community College, Ocala, FL

Michael Luchuk, Kaplan International Centers, New York, NY

Craig Machado, Norwalk Community College, Norwalk, CT

Denise Maduli-Williams, City College of San Francisco, San Francisco, CA

Diane Mahin, University of Miami, Coral Gables, FL

Melanie Majeski, Naugatuck Valley Community College, Waterbury, CT

Jeanne Malcolm, University of North Carolina at Charlotte, Charlotte, NC

Lourdes Marx, Palm Beach State College, Boca Raton, FL

Susan G. McFalls, Maryville College, Maryville, TN

Nancy McKay, Cuyahoga Community College, Cleveland, OH

Dominika McPartland, Long Island Business Institute, Flushing, NY

Amy Metcalf, UNR/Intensive English Language Center, University of Nevada, Reno, NV

Robert Miller, EF International Language School San Francisco – Mills, San Francisco, CA

Marcie Pachino, Jordan High School, Durham, NC

Myshie Pagel, El Paso Community College, El Paso, TX

Bernadette Pedagno, University of San Francisco, San Francisco, CA

Tam Q Pham, Dallas Theological Seminary, Fort Smith, AR

Mary Beth Pickett, Global-LT, Rochester, MI

Maria Reamore, Baltimore City Public Schools, Baltimore, MD

Alison M. Rice, Hunter College IELI, New York, NY

Sydney Rice, Imperial Valley College, Imperial, CA

Kathleen Romstedt, Ohio State University, Columbus, OH

Alexandra Rowe, University of South Carolina, Columbia, SC

Irma Sanders, Baldwin Park Adult and Community Education, Baldwin Park, CA

Caren Shoup, Lone Star College – CyFair, Cypress, TX

Karen Sid, Mission College, Foothill College, De Anza College, Santa Clara, CA

Michelle Thomas, Miami Dade College, Miami, FL

Sharon Van Houte, Lorain County Community College, Elyria, OH

Margi Wald, UC Berkeley, Berkeley, CA

Walli Weitz, Riverside County Office of Ed., Indio, CA

Bart Weyand, University of Southern Maine, Portland, ME

Donna Weyrich, Columbus State Community College, Columbus, OH

Marilyn Whitehorse, Santa Barbara City College, Ojai, CA

Jessica Wilson, Rutgers University – Newark, Newark, NJ

Sue Wilson, San Jose City College, San Jose, CA

Margaret Wilster, Mid-Florida Tech, Orlando, FL

Anne York-Herjeczki, Santa Monica College, Santa Monica, CA

Hoda Zaki, Camden County College, Camden, NJ

We would also like to thank these teachers and programs for allowing us to visit:

Richard Appelbaum, Broward College, Fort Lauderdale, FL

Carmela Arnoldt, Glendale Community College, Glendale, AZ

JaNae Barrow, Desert Vista High School, Phoenix, AZ

Ted Christensen, Mesa Community College, Mesa, AZ

Richard Ciriello, Lower East Side Preparatory High School, New York, NY

Virginia Edwards, Chandler-Gilbert Community College, Chandler, AZ

Nusia Frankel, Miami Dade College, Miami, FL

Raquel Fundora, Miami Dade College, Miami, FL

Vicki Hendricks, Broward College, Fort Lauderdale, FL

Kelly Hernandez, Miami Dade College, Miami, FL

Stephen Johnson, Miami Dade College, Miami, FL

Barbara Jordan, Mesa Community College, Mesa, AZ

Nancy Kersten, GateWay Community College, Phoenix, AZ

Lewis Levine, Hostos Community College, Bronx, NY

John Liffiton, Scottsdale Community College, Scottsdale, AZ

Cheryl Lira-Layne, Gilbert Public School District, Gilbert, AZ

Mary Livingston, Arizona State University, Tempe, AZ

Elizabeth Macdonald, Thunderbird School of Global Management, Glendale, AZ

Terri Martinez, Mesa Community College, Mesa, AZ

Lourdes Marx, Palm Beach State College, Boca Raton, FL

Paul Kei Matsuda, Arizona State University, Tempe, AZ

David Miller, Glendale Community College, Glendale, AZ

Martha Polin, Lower East Side Preparatory High School, New York, NY

Patricia Pullenza, Mesa Community College, Mesa, AZ

Victoria Rasinskaya, Lower East Side Preparatory High School, New York, NY

Vanda Salls, Tempe Union High School District, Tempe, AZ

Kim Sanabria, Hostos Community College, Bronx, NY

Cynthia Schuemann, Miami Dade College, Miami, FL

Michelle Thomas, Miami Dade College, Miami, FL

Dongmei Zeng, Borough of Manhattan Community College, New York, NY

Tour of a Unit

Grammar in the Real World presents the unit's grammar in a **realistic** context using **contemporary** texts.

Notice activities draw students' attention to the **structure**, guiding their own **analysis** of form, meaning, and use.

UNIT

4

Simple Past

Entrepreneurs

1 Grammar in the Real World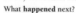

A What is the best way to find information today? Read the article from a technology magazine. How did Google start?

The Story of Google

Who started Google?
Sergey Brin and Larry Page **started** the company. Sergey **came** from Moscow, Russia. He **moved** to the United States as a young child and later **studied** mathematics and computer science. Larry **was** born in Michigan and **became** interested in computers as a child.

How did they meet?
They **met** in 1995 at Stanford University, in California, where they **were** both computer science students. They **did not get along** at first, but they soon **became** friends.

What happened next?
They **designed** a new Internet search engine. At first, they **worked** in their rooms in college. Then they **rented** a friend's garage because Sergey's roommate **complained** about the noise from his computers. Three years later, they **started** Google.

Was it an immediate success?
The company **was** an immediate success. Before Google, **there were** other search engines, but Google soon **became** the most popular one. The company **grew** quickly. They **did not stop** at just one product. Very soon, **there were** other Google products, like Google Maps and Gmail. Ten years later, Google **earned** over $10 billion and **had** about 20,000 employees.

So what did people do before Google?
Before Google, people **went** to libraries. They **got** information from books. These days, they just "google" for information.

40

Simple Past

B *Comprehension Check* Answer the questions.

1. Where did Larry Page and Sergey Brin meet?
2. Why did they work in a garage?
3. What other products did Google start?
4. How many people worked at Google after 10 years?

C *Notice* Look at the article. Find the simple past forms of these verbs.

Group A		Group B	
1. start	_____	5. come	_____
2. move	_____	6. be	_____, _____ (two forms)
3. study	_____	7. become	_____
4. happen	_____	8. meet	_____

How are the two groups of verbs different?

2 Simple Past

▶ **Grammar Presentation**

You can use the simple past to talk about completed events in the past.	*Brin and Page **started** Google in 1998.* *They **did not get along** at first.*

2.1 Affirmative Statements

Subject	Verb + -ed (Regular Verbs)		Subject	Irregular Verb
I You He / She / It We They	**started** in 1998. **employed** 20,000 people.		I You He / She / It We They	**grew** quickly. **became** successful.

▶ Spelling Rules for Regular Verbs in Simple Past: See page 403.   ▶ Irregular Verbs: See page 402.

Data from the Real World

Research shows that these are six of the most common **regular** simple past verbs.	work	worked		live	lived
	start	started		try	tried
	call	called		plan	planned
Research shows that these are eight of the most common **irregular** simple past verbs.	have	had		go	went
	get	got		come	came
	do	did		take	took
	say	said		make	made

Entrepreneurs   41

The *Grammar Presentation* begins with an **overview** that describes the grammar in an **easy-to-understand** summary.

xiv

2.5 Using Simple Past

a. Use the simple past to talk or write about:

• a single action that started and ended in the past.	They **started** Google in 1998. ✕ past ——————→ now
• a repeated action or habit in the past.	They **worked** in their rooms every day. ✕ ✕ ✕ past ——————→ now
• a state, situation, or feeling in the past.	They **didn't get along**. ▬▬ past ——————→ now

b. Time expressions can come at the start or end of a statement. Examples: *last week / month / year, 10 years ago, in 1998, yesterday*

Last year, I joined a new company.
I joined a new company *last year*.
Two years ago, I graduated.
I graduated *two years ago*.

c. Remember to use a comma when the time expression comes at the beginning of the sentence.

In 1998, they started Google.
They started Google *in 1998*.

d. Adverbs of frequency often come before the main verb in simple past statements. Some examples of adverbs of frequency are *never, rarely, sometimes, often, usually*, and *always*.

They *often had* meetings at a pizza parlor.
They *sometimes worked* in their room.

Data from the Real World

Research shows that *didn't* is not common in formal writing. Use *did not* instead. Writers sometimes use *didn't* in quotes of people speaking.

Use *didn't* in conversation and informal writing. In conversation, *did not* can sound formal, emphatic, or argumentative.

Formal writing
didn't ▬
did not ▬▬▬▬▬

Conversation
didn't ▬▬▬▬▬▬▬
did not ▮

▶ ## Grammar Application

Exercise 2.1 Statements and Questions

A Complete the article with the simple past form of the verbs in parentheses.

Ben Cohen and Jerry Greenfield _grew up_ (grow up) (1) in Merrick, Long Island. They _____ (2) (meet) in middle school, and they _____ (3) (graduate) from high school together. Their connections to ice cream _____ (4) (begin) at an early age. Ben _____ (5) (drive) an ice cream truck in high school. Jerry _____ (6) (work) in his college cafeteria as an ice cream scooper.

Ben _____ (7) (try) different colleges, but he _____ (8) (not graduate). At one time, he _____ (9) (teach) crafts in a school. At the school, he sometimes _____ (10) (make) ice cream with his students. Jerry _____ (11) (want) to be a doctor. After he _____ (12) (graduate) from college, he _____ (13) (apply) to medical school, but he was not successful. During those years, Ben and Jerry _____ (14) (stay) friends.

After a few years, Ben and Jerry _____ (15) (go) into the food business together. At first, they _____ (16) (think) about making bagels, but the equipment was expensive. So they _____ (17) (choose) ice cream and _____ (18) (take) a $5 class on ice-cream making.

Ben and Jerry _____ (19) (see) an opportunity in Burlington, Vermont. This college town _____ (20) (not have) an ice cream shop. They _____ (21) (find) an old gas station, and in 1978 they _____ (22) (open) the first Ben & Jerry's store.

Ben & Jerry's quickly _____ (23) (become) popular because it _____ (24) (have) great ice cream and a caring approach to the community. On their first anniversary, they _____ (25) (give) everyone free ice cream as a "thank you." They still give away free ice cream every year on their anniversary.

C *Over to You* Write six sentences about your own life. Use the ideas in B or your own ideas. Compare sentences with a partner. Ask your partner for more information.

A *My family moved here in 1998.*
B *Really? Where did you live before that?*

Exercise 2.3 Questions and Answers

A Complete the article with the simple past form of the verbs in parentheses.

Today Oprah Winfrey is one of the most successful broadcasters, publishers, and entrepreneurs in the world. However, she did not have an easy start in life. Oprah __had__ (have) a difficult childhood. She _____ (2) (not have) a lot of opportunities as a child, but she was very intelligent. She _____ (3) (learn) to read before the age of 3. Her broadcasting career _____ (4) (begin) in high school. In 1971, she _____ (5) (go) to Tennessee State University. During high school and college, she _____ (6) (work) on a radio show. She also _____ (7) (work) at a TV station in Nashville as a student. At the age of 19, she _____ (8) (become) the first African-American woman news anchor[1] at the station.

In 1976, she _____ (9) (graduate) from college. That year, she _____ (10) (move) to Baltimore. There she _____ (11) (host) a TV talk show called *People Are Talking*. Eight years later, she _____ (12) (start) working on a morning show in Chicago. It _____ (13) (become) *The Oprah Winfrey Show*. Oprah's popularity _____ (14) (grow) quickly, and in 1986, it _____ (15) (become) a national show.

[1] **anchor:** a person who reports the news

B *Pair Work* Complete the questions about Oprah Winfrey. Use the information in the article. Then ask and answer the questions with a partner.

1. What kind of childhood _____ ?
2. What _____ before the age of 3?
3. Which university _____ ?
4. What _____ during high school and college?

Exercise 3.2 Questions with *Be* and Other Verbs

A *Pair Work* Write the simple past questions. Then interview a classmate. Ask for more information as you talk.

1. What / be / your first job
   What was your first job?
2. be / it / a good job
   _____
3. What / be / your co-workers like
   _____
4. What / you / do there
   _____
5. Why / you / leave _____
6. What / be / your best job _____
7. Why / you / like it _____
8. Where / be / your worst job _____

B *Pair Work* Write a short work history of your classmate.
Luis's first job was in a hotel in San Diego. He worked there from 2008 to 2009.

4 Avoid Common Mistakes ⚠

1. **Use the simple past, not the simple present, when you write about the past.**
   started
   I start my first job in 2008.

2. **After *did not* or *didn't*, use the base form of the verb, not the past form.**
   They didn't earned a lot of money.

3. **Put time expressions at the beginning or end of a statement, not between the subject and the verb, and not between the verb and the object.**
                                       yesterday
   I bought yesterday a computer.
      OR
   Yesterday
   I bought yesterday a computer.

4. **Use *there were* with plural nouns. Use *there was* with singular or noncount nouns.**
      were   *was*
   There was a lot of people. There were no information.

Editing Task

Find and correct nine more mistakes in the blog.

> *moved*
> My family move from Mexico City to the United States in 1998. I went to Hamilton High School in Los Angeles. I did not knew anybody, and I did not had any friends here. I in 1999 met Jun. He became my first friend.
>
> We in 2001 graduated. I got a job at a nice restaurant, but I did not enjoyed my job. Jun drove a taco truck, but he did not liked the food. I wanted to be my own boss, and I always liked food and cooking. Jun wanted his own business, too. Jun saw an opportunity. There was hungry office workers downtown at noon, but there weren't a nice place to eat. We bought a food truck and we start Food on the Move in 2003. Today, we have 5 trucks and 15 employees.

5 | Grammar for Writing

Using Simple Past

Writers use the simple past to describe single actions, repeated actions, or states in the past. In a story about a person's life, the verbs that tell about past events, actions, or states should be in the past.

STATE STATE SINGLE ACTION
He *wanted* his own business, but he *did not have* the money for it. He *went* to the bank to ask for a loan.

Writers often use the simple present at the end of a story to say what is different now.

PRESENT
...Today my uncle *has* a successful business.

Remember:

Check the spelling of irregular verbs.
got   *paid*
He *getted* a loan from the bank. Then he *payed* a lot of money to start the business.

Pre-writing Task

1 Read the paragraph below. Notice how the writer uses the simple past to describe the single actions, repeated actions, and states in a person's life.

My Boss Missolle

My boss, Missolle, came to the United States from Haiti 12 years ago. When she came here, she was very sad because her children were still in Haiti. She wanted them to come here, so she worked very hard. She practiced her English all the time. She worked during the day in a hair salon, and at night she cooked for people. She always thought about her children. When I met her five years ago, she was always happy and enthusiastic. I did not know her life was difficult. She told me that she did not want to show her true feelings. Now she is very happy because her children are here, and her life is good.

2 Read the paragraph again. Circle the verbs in the simple past, and underline the verbs in the simple present.

Writing Task

1 *Write* Use the paragraph in the Pre-writing Task to help you write about the life events of a person you know. What are some important past events in this person's life? How is this person's life different today?

2 *Self-Edit* Use the editing tips to improve your paragraph. Make any necessary changes.

1. Did you use the simple past for all single actions, repeated actions, and states?
2. Did you use the correct form for irregular verbs?
3. Did you avoid the mistakes in the Avoid Common Mistakes chart on page 51?

Future (1)

Life Lists

1 Grammar in the Real World

A What exciting things do you want to do someday? Read the blog about a "life list."
What does the writer hope to do someday?

My Life List

September 23
posted by: Lisa Sanchez

Welcome to a new feature of my blog – my life list.
What is a life list? It's a list of things that you **are going
to do** before you die, if you can. Here are some things
on my life list:

5 • I**'m going to ride** in a hot-air balloon.
• I**'m going to live** in Spain.
• I**'m going to write** a poem.
• I**'m going to travel** to all 50 states in the
United States.

10 Psychologists[1] agree that life lists are motivating. They encourage people to try new
things. However, to achieve the goals on your list, you need to be realistic[2] and have
a plan. For example, I**'m not visiting** all 50 states this year. I don't have the money!
First, I**'m going to make** a plan to save money for each trip, and I**'m going to do**
research on the places I want to visit. That is the point of a life list. It motivates you to
15 work toward your goals. I**'m going to have** to work to accomplish my life list!

Are you **going to create** a life list, too? Here are some tips:

1. Make a list that reflects the direction you want for your life. For example,
I want to understand more about the world, so travel is a big part of my
life list.

20 2. Understand that it **is going to take** time to accomplish the things on your list –
maybe a lifetime!

If you follow these simple steps, you **aren't going to be** disappointed. Your life **is
going to be** full of new adventures and new accomplishments.

[1]**psychologist:** someone who studies the mind and emotions and their relationship to behavior | [2]**realistic:** showing an
understanding of how things really are

B *Comprehension Check*   Answer the questions.

1. What is a life list?
2. What is one reason to create a life list?
3. What are two tips to help you create a life list?

C *Notice*   Find the sentences in the article and complete them.

1. I _____ ride in a hot-air balloon.
2. I _____ travel to all 50 states in the United States.
3. _____ you _____ create a life list, too?
4. Understand that it _____ take time to accomplish the things on your list.

Are the sentences about the present or the future?

2 | Be Going To, Present Progressive, and Simple Present for Future Events

▶ Grammar Presentation

Be going to describes future plans, predictions, and expectations. The present progressive and the simple present can also refer to the future.	I**'m going to ride** in a hot-air balloon. I**'m moving** to Spain next month. My flight **leaves** at 7:00 tomorrow morning.

2.1 *Be Going To*: Statements

STATEMENTS				
Subject	***Be***	**(Not) going to**	**Base Form of Verb**	
I	am			
You We They	are	(not) going to	live	in Spain.
He She It	is			

CONTRACTIONS		
Affirmative	**Negative**	
I**'m**	I**'m not**	
You**'re** We**'re** They**'re**	You**'re not** We**'re not** They**'re not**	You **aren't** We **aren't** They **aren't**
He**'s** She**'s** It**'s**	He**'s not** She**'s not** It**'s not**	He **isn't** She **isn't** It **isn't**

2.2 *Be Going To*: Yes / No Questions and Short Answers

Be	Subject	*Going to*	Base Form of Verb	Short Answers		
Am	I				Yes, I **am**.	No, I**'m not**.
Are	you we they	**going to**	visit Spain?		Yes, you **are**. Yes, we **are**. Yes, they **are**.	No, you **aren't**. No, we **aren't**. No, they **aren't**.
Is	he / she / it				Yes, he / she / it **is**.	No, he / she / it **isn't**.

2.3 *Be Going To*: Information Questions

Wh- Word	*Be*	Subject	*Going to*	Base Form of Verb
What	**am**	I		see?
Where **When**	**are**	you we they	**going to**	go?
	is	he / she / it		

Wh- Word	*Be*	*Going to*	Base Form of Verb
Who **What**	**is**	**going to**	visit Spain? happen?

2.4 Using *Be Going To*, Present Progressive, and Simple Present

a. Use *be going to* when future plans are *not* specific or definite.	*I'm going to visit Spain someday.* (I don't know when exactly.) *I'm going to have a baby before I'm 35.* (This is my plan, but I'm not pregnant yet.)
b. Use the present progressive when future plans are specific or definite.	*I'm visiting Spain next week.* (I have plane tickets and my plan is definite.) *I'm having a baby in June.* (I'm pregnant and I know when the baby will be born.)
c. Use *be going to* to talk about predictions, expectations, or guesses.	*You're going to have fun in Miami next week.*
d. Use *be going to* when a future event is certain to happen because there is evidence for it. Do not use the present progressive.	*Look at those clouds. It's going to rain soon.* *Look at those clouds. It is raining soon.*

2.4 Using *Be Going To*, Present Progressive, and Simple Present (continued)

e. Use the simple present, not *be going to*, for scheduled events in the future, such as class schedules, timetables, and itineraries. Some common verbs for this meaning are *arrive*, *be*, *begin*, *finish*, and *leave*.

*My flight **is** tomorrow.*
*I **leave** at 7:00 a.m.*

▶ # Grammar Application

Exercise 2.1 *Be Going To*: Statements

Complete the sentences with the correct form of *be going to* and the verbs in parentheses.

1. Lisa's blog *is going to motivate* (motivate) people to create life lists.

2. Jessica _____ (create) a life list on her blog. Here are two of the goals she wants to put on her list.

3. She _____ (not miss) the family reunion this year.

4. Jessica and her twin sister Kelly _____ _____ (attend) a twins convention someday.

5. Sam _____ (not achieve) any of his goals this year, but someday he will.

6. Here are some things that I _____ (do) someday.

7. I _____ (take) a trip to New York.

8. I _____ (learn) martial arts someday.

9. My mother and I _____ (ride) in a hot-air balloon for her birthday.

10. Remember, you _____ (not do) everything in one year!

Exercise 2.2 *Be Going To*: Questions

A Complete the conversation with the correct form of *be going to* and the verbs in parentheses.

Marco Hey, Julio. What _are_ you _going to do_ (do) now?
                              (1)   (1)

Julio I'm going to start a new job.

Marco Where _____ you _____ (work)?
                      (2)   (2)

Julio At the Central Café.

Marco Nice! What _____ you _____ (do) there?
         (3)   (3)

Julio I'm going to cook! I always wanted to be a chef – it's number 10 on my life list.

Marco That's great! _____ you _____ (get) some training?
         (4)   (4)

Julio Yes. I'm going to learn a lot on the job! And I'm also going to take a class at

         Briteway Community College.

Marco What _____ you _____ (take)?
         (5)   (5)

Julio I'm going to take a class on food safety.

Marco That's great. _____ it _____ (be) hard?
         (6)   (6)

Julio No, I don't think so.

Marco What _____ (happen) with the rest of your life list?
         (7)

Julio Oh, the trip to China?

Marco Yes. When _____ that _____ (happen)?
         (8)   (8)

Julio Well, first I'm going to earn a good salary at the Central Café. I'm going to

         save a lot of money, and then I'm going to go to China.

Marco That sounds like a plan!

B Write questions about Julio for the answers below. Use *be going to*.

1. _What is he going to do?_____
   He's going to start a new job.

2. _____
   He's going to work at the Central Café.

3. _____
   He's going to cook.

4. _____
   Yes, he's going to learn a lot on the job.

5. _____
   Yes, he's going to take a class at the community
   college.

6. _____
   He's going to take a class on food safety.

7. _____
   No, he doesn't think the class is going to be hard.

8. _____
   He's not going to visit China very soon.

Exercise 2.3 *Be Going To*, Present Progressive, or Simple Present?

A 🔊 Listen and complete the conversation with the form of the verbs that you hear: *be going to*, present progressive, or simple present.

Anne So, Jin, what __are__ you __going to do__ (do) this weekend?
$\qquad$ (1) $\qquad$ (1)

Jin I'm finally _____ (accomplish) one of my big goals:
$\qquad$ (2)

I _____ (ride) in a hot-air balloon.
$\qquad$ (3)

Anne Wow! Did you already make a reservation?

Jin Yes. I _____ (take) the flight that goes over
$\qquad$ (4)

the ocean.

Anne The ocean! You _____ (have) a great time.
$\qquad$ (5)

Jin Yeah, and I heard the weather report. It _____ (be)
$\qquad$ (6)

great this weekend. Do you want to come?

Anne When _____ you _____ (go)?
$\qquad$ (7) $\qquad$ (7)

Jin We _____ (meet) in the park at noon on Sunday,
$\qquad$ (8)

and the flight _____ (leave) at 1:00 p.m.
$\qquad$ (9)

Anne I'd love to come, but I have other plans.

Jin What _____ you _____ (do)?
$\qquad$ (10) $\qquad$ (10)

Anne I _____ (go) to the airport on Sunday
$\qquad$ (11)

afternoon. I _____ (pick up) an old friend. She
$\qquad$ (12)

_____ (stay) with me for a week, and her flight
$\qquad$ (13)

_____ (arrive) right at noon.
$\qquad$ (14)

Jin Well, it sounds like you _____ (have) a good
$\qquad$ (15)

time, too!

B 🔊 Listen again and check your answers.

Exercise 2.4 More *Be Going To*, Present Progressive, or Simple Present?

A Complete another entry from Lisa's blog. Use *be going to*, the present progressive, or the simple present and the verb in parentheses. Use contractions where possible.

Achieving #7 on My Life List

January 15
posted by: Lisa Sanchez

Finally! I *'m going to achieve* (achieve) goal
(1)
number 7 on my life list! I've bought my ticket, so it's

definite now. I _____ (move) to Spain! I
(2)

_____ (leave) on Friday, February 3rd. I
(3)

got a job, too! I _____ (work) as a tour
(4)

guide for a hotel in Barcelona. I _____
(5)

(start) on March 3rd, so I planned a little trip. I _____ (travel)
(6)

around the country for three weeks. I already bought a rail pass. I've checked the

weather, too. It _____ (be) great. It _____
(7)   (8)

(be) nice the entire time. Any advice?

_____

2 Responses   <u>leave one</u>

Robert: Lisa, you _____ (have) a fantastic time! But watch out –
(9)

I've been to Spain many times in the winter. It _____
(10)

(rain). You _____ (need) an umbrella.
(11)

Amy: Hey Lisa, I _____ (travel) in Spain at the same time!
(12)

I bought a rail pass, too! I _____ (arrive) in Catalonia
(13)

on February 11th. I _____ (stay) at the youth hostel.
(14)

I made a reservation for three days. There's a big festival in Catalonia in

February. I've heard a lot about it. It _____ (be) fun.
(15)

Do you want to meet up?

B *Pair Work*   Compare your answers with a partner. For each answer, explain the reason for the verb form you chose.

Exercise 2.5 Statements and Questions

A Think of six things to write on your life list. Begin with *I'm going to....*

I'm going to ride a horse on the beach.

1. _____
2. _____
3. _____
4. _____
5. _____
6. _____

B *Pair Work*   Compare life lists with a partner. Ask as many *going to* questions as you can about your partner's list. Then write down the six things your partner wants to do.

A *What are you going to do?*
B *I'm going to ride a horse on the beach.*
A *Where are you going to do that?*
B *I'm going to do that in Australia.*

1. _____
2. _____
3. _____
4. _____
5. _____
6. _____

3 | Avoid Common Mistakes ⚠️

1. Use *be* with *going to* to describe future plans.

　　　is
She ˄ going to write a poem someday.

2. Use the correct form of *be* with *going to*.

　　　　are
Jared and Jason ~~is~~ going to go to a twins convention next year.

3. Use *be* before the subject in *Wh-* questions with *be going to*.

　　are you
What ~~you are~~ going to do?

Editing Task

Find and correct eight more mistakes in this web interview about life lists.

Life Lists

The following is the second in a series by Alex Wu of interviews with people about their life lists.

Alex   So, Heather, what *are* you and your husband ~~are~~ going to put on your life lists?

Heather   We going to put a lot of things on our list. We going to do some things

5   together and some things separately.

Alex   What Tom is going to do?

Heather   Well, Tom is a twin. He and his brother is going to attend the International

              Twins Convention.

Alex   I've heard of that. That's right here in Ohio.

10 Heather   Right. In fact, the convention is this weekend. They going to drive there on

              Saturday.

Alex   That's usually an outdoor event, right?

Heather   Yes, and unfortunately, it going to rain this Saturday.

Alex   Too bad. What they are going to do?

15 Heather   The event is going to be inside at a hotel now.

Alex   That's good. I bet they is going to have a great time this weekend.

4 | Grammar for Writing

Using *Be Going To* and Present Progressive Together

When you talk about goals, you can use *be going to* and the present progressive in the same paragraph. Using both of the forms tells your reader which goals are things you hope to do (use *be going to*) and which goals are definite plans (use present progressive). You can also use *be going to* for definite plans, but the present progressive is more common with plans for the very near future.

Remember:

- **Use *be going to* when you hope to do something, but you don't have definite plans.**
  <u>I'm going to have</u> a big family in the future.

- **Use the present progressive when you have a definite or specific plan.**
  <u>I'm getting</u> my degree next May.

Pre-writing Task

1 Read the paragraph below. What are a lot of married couples not doing immediately? What things are they doing?

Planning for the Future

Today, more and more couples who want to get married are not starting families right after the wedding. There are many reasons for this. Some couples are graduating from school before they have children. They know they are going to be busy when they have children, so they want to finish school first. Then, after they finish school, many couples are planning to look for jobs and work for a year or two to save money. Other couples are going to travel before they settle down. If they are not having children right away, they are going to have interesting stories to tell their families later on!

2 Read the paragraph again. Underline *going to* + verb. Circle the present progressive verbs. Which describe definite plans, and which describe plans that are not definite?

Writing Task

1 *Write* Use the paragraph in the Pre-writing Task to help you write about your plans for the future. What do you hope to do a year from now? What are you going to do many years from now? Include things you don't have definite plans for as well as at least one definite plan.

2 *Self-Edit* Use the editing tips below to improve your paragraph. Make any necessary changes.

   1. Did you use *be going to* and the present progressive to talk about things you hope to do in the future?
   2. Did you use *be going to* for plans that are not definite?
   3. Did you use the present progressive for plans that are definite or specific?
   4. Did you avoid the mistakes in the Avoid Common Mistakes chart on page 199?

1 | Grammar in the Real World

A What do you think it's like to be 100 years old? Read the magazine article about centenarians. What are some of the effects of people living longer?

Centenarians[1]

In 1980, there were 15,000 people over the age of 100 in the United States. In 2000, there were 50,000. This number **will** grow, and as a result, many more people **will** live
5 to see their 100th birthday. In fact, there **will** be several million centenarians in the United States by the end of the twenty-first century. This is according to the U.S. Census Bureau. What changes **will** we see with so many
10 people over 100?

The United States **will** see many changes because of this. For example, more people **will** have illnesses such as cancer and heart conditions. According to a study by the University of Albany in New York, we **will** probably not have enough doctors to take care of them. In addition, these changes **will** affect government services. This means that there **will** be
15 less money for programs such as Social Security[2] and Medicare.[3] Many older people **will** possibly not have enough money to support themselves for a longer period of time. As a result, many **will** need to work in their 70s and even in their 80s.

On the other hand, there are some very positive aspects of aging. One is increased happiness. A study by Stanford University in California found that older people tend to be
20 happier than younger people. Why? As people age, they change their goals. They know they have less time ahead of them, and as a result, they focus on the present. They spend more time on their relationships and know themselves better. This leads to increased happiness.

As people live longer, there **will** be more of us in the world. With more people who are happier, though, perhaps the world **will** be a happier place.

---

[1]**centenarians:** people aged 100 or older | [2]**Social Security:** a U.S. government program that gives financial help to people who are old, people whose husbands or wives have died, and people who cannot work | [3]**Medicare:** a U.S. government program that pays part of the medical expenses of people 65 or older

B *Comprehension Check* Answer the questions.

1. What will happen to the population by the end of the twenty-first century, according to the U.S. Census Bureau?
2. What are two negative effects of a large number of centenarians?
3. What is one positive effect of aging?
4. Why do older people tend to be happier?

C *Notice* Find the sentences in the article and complete them.

1. There _____ be several million centenarians in the United States by the end of the twenty-first century.

2. What changes _____ we see with so many people over 100?

3. For example, more people _____ have illnesses such as cancer and heart conditions.

4. Many older people _____ possibly not have enough money to support themselves for a longer period of time.

Do we use *will* to talk about the future, the present, or the past?

2 | Future with *Will*

▶ Grammar Presentation

Will describes events that take place in the future.	*There **will** be several million centenarians in the United States by the end of the twenty-first century.*

2.1 Statements

Subject	Will (Not)	Base Form of Verb
I You He/She/It We They	**will** **will not** **won't**	help people.

2.2 *Yes/No* Questions and Short Answers

Will	Subject	Base Form of Verb		Short Answers	
Will	I you he/she/it we they	help?	Yes, I **will**. Yes, you **will**. Yes, he/she/it **will**. Yes, we **will**. Yes, they **will**.	No, I **won't**. No, you **won't**. No, he/she/it **won't**. No, we **won't**. No, they **won't**.	

2.3 Information Questions

Wh- Word	Will	Subject	Base Form of Verb		Wh- Word	Will	Base Form of Verb
How **Where** **When**	will	we they	solve the problem?		**What**	will	happen?

2.4 Using *Will*

a. Use *will* to make predictions. Predictions are things that people believe about the future.	Many people **will** live to 110. There **will** be several million centenarians by the end of the twenty-first century.
b. You can use *likely, possibly, probably, certainly, definitely,* and *undoubtedly* after *will* and before the main verb to show different degrees of certainty. In negative statements, these adverbs can usually go between *will* and *not* or before *won't*.	Humans **will possibly** live to 200 in the distant future. Technology **will undoubtedly** change the world. They **will probably not** do much physical work. They **definitely won't** do much physical work.

Maybe and *perhaps* start a sentence.

less certain		more certain
maybe		certainly
possibly	likely	definitely
perhaps	probably	undoubtedly

Maybe older people will not have enough money.
Perhaps the world will be a happier place.

c. Use the full forms (*will, will not*) in formal writing.	Increased population **will** lead to crowding. People **will not** need to work so hard in the future.
Use the contracted forms (*'ll, won't*) in informal situations.	I**'ll** live in a little house near the ocean. We **won't** have to work very hard.

Data from the Real World

Research shows that the normal position for adverbs of certainty is after *will*.	Many older people **will possibly** not have enough money to support themselves.
You can also put the adverb before *will* to add emphasis, but this is less common.	My parents didn't have to work in their 70s, but I **probably will**.

▶ Grammar Application

Exercise 2.1 *Will*: Statements

Complete the statements with *will*. Use the verbs in parentheses.

1. People _will live_ (live) longer in the future.

2. In fact, many people _____ (see) their 100th birthday.

3. This means that there _____ (be) a lot more healthy older people.

4. These healthy older people _____ (need) something productive to do.

5. Therefore, many people _____ (not retire) at the age of 60 or 65.

6. They _____ (work) in their 70s.

7. However, they _____ (not do) as much physical work.

8. This _____ (help) the economy, as it _____ (not cause) problems for government programs such as Social Security and Medicare.

Exercise 2.2 *Will*: Questions and Adverbs

A Complete the questions in an online interview with an expert on aging. Use *will* and the correct form of the words in parentheses.

Chris Zurawski's Future Blog

I recently interviewed Dr. Sam Young. Dr. Young is an expert on aging and how it will change the government and the economy. Following is our discussion.

Q Dr. Young, _will people live_ (people / live) longer in the future?
(1)

A Yes. People will live longer. Life expectancy will increase in most countries.

Q _____ (why / people / have) longer lives?
(2)

A Well, they'll have better medical care, and that will mean a healthier life.

Q _____ (people / live) longer everywhere in the world?
(3)

A I think so. A lot of countries will have more centenarians. There will be millions in countries such as the United States and Japan.

Q So, _____ (everyone / be) healthy?
(4)

A Well, no, not everyone. People will live longer, but they'll have more long-term illnesses such as cancer and diabetes.

Q I'm only 24. I'm worried about Social Security.

_____ (what / happen) to Social
(5)
Security?

In the future, people will live longer – and work longer.

A Social Security will begin to have serious problems in the future. Something will need to change.

Q But let's say it doesn't change. _____ (what / happen)?
(6)

A In that case, Social Security payments will be very low, or they won't be available at all.

Q So, _____ (how / people like me / support) ourselves?
(7)

A Even today, Social Security provides only about one-third of the average person's income. So, just like now, most people will need other sources of income as they age.

Q _____ (what other sources of income / people / have)?
(8)

A A lot of people your age will work longer. You'll keep your jobs. Some will work part-time, but many will continue to work full-time for many years.

B Add adverbs to some of Dr. Young's statements. Use the cues in parentheses to choose an adverb with the appropriate degree of certainty. Sometimes more than one answer is correct.

certainly	likely	perhaps	probably
definitely	maybe	possibly	undoubtedly

probably
1. Life expectancy will increase in most countries. (in the middle)

2. Better medical care will mean a healthier life. (more certain)

3. A lot of countries will have more centenarians. (in the middle)

4. People will have more long-term illnesses such as cancer and diabetes. (less certain)

5. Social Security will begin to have serious problems in the future. (in the middle)

6. Social Security payments will be very low. (in the middle)

7. Most people will need other sources of income as they age. (more certain)

8. A lot of people your age will work longer. (less certain)

9. Many will continue to work full-time for many years. (more certain)

Exercise 2.3 *Will*: Questions, Answers, and Adverbs

A ◀)) Listen to an informal conversation about the future. Complete the summary of Sara's ideas. Circle the correct words.

Sara thinks she probably **will** / **will not** live to be 100. She thinks
(1)

she **will probably** / **will probably not** have problems with money in old age.
(2)

B ◀)) Listen again. Circle the correct adverb.

1. Sara will **probably** / **certainly** live to be about 85 or 90.
2. Sara will **perhaps** / **undoubtedly** work in her 80s.
3. At 80, Sara will **probably** / **definitely** have the same job she has now.
4. After retirement, Sara will **possibly** / **definitely** travel or garden.
5. Sara will **perhaps** / **very likely** not have enough money to travel.
6. Sara thinks she **possibly** / **certainly** won't get Social Security.
7. Sara thinks the government will **probably** / **undoubtedly** not have any money left in the future.

Listen again and check your answers.

C *Group Work* Use *will* and adverbs of certainty to talk about your future. Discuss these questions and give your own ideas.

• How long do you think you'll live? Why do you think that?

• How long will you work? What kind of job will you have at age _____ ?

• What will you do after you retire? If you get sick, who will help you?

• Will you have enough money after you retire? Will you get Social Security? Why or why not?

A How long do you think you'll live?
B I'll probably live to be about 100.
C Perhaps I'll live to be 90. I hope so.

3 | Future with *Will, Be Going To,* and Present Progressive

▶ Grammar Presentation

Will, be going to, and the present progressive can describe future events.	Life expectancy **will** increase. I**'m going to** look for a new job. She**'s starting** a retirement account next week.

3.1 Using *Will, Be Going To,* and Present Progressive for the Future

a. Use *will* or *be going to* to talk about plans in the future. Use the present progressive for arranged events.

I**'ll open** a retirement account soon.
I**'m going to open** a retirement account soon. (This is my intention, what I want to do.)
I**'m opening** a retirement account next week. (I have an appointment at the bank at a specific time next week. It's scheduled.)

b. Use *will* or *be going to* to make predictions, expectations, or guesses about the future.

More people **will live** longer in the future.
More people **are going to live** longer in the future.

c. Use *be going to* when a future event is certain to happen because there is evidence for it.

Look at those dark clouds. It**'s going to rain**.
We have a lot of work to do. We **are not going to finish** until 6:30.

d. Use *will* for immediate decisions.

I have to go. I**'ll call** you later.
(= I just decided to call you.)

I have to go. I'm going to call you later.
I have to go. I'm calling you later.

e. Use *be going to* for intentions: things you hope or intend to do in the future.

I am healthy. I**'m going to live** to be 100 years old!
I**'m not going to retire** and sit at home.

Do not use *will* or the present progressive with intentions.

I am healthy. I will live to be 100 years old!
I am healthy. I'm living to be 100 years old!

f. Use *will* and *be going to* with adverbs to show different degrees of certainty about future events.

You can use *likely, possibly, probably, certainly, definitely,* and *undoubtedly* after *be* and before *going to* when you want to show different degrees of certainty. For negative statements, put the adverb immediately after *be*.

He **definitely won't retire this year**.
He hasn't studied. He **is probably going to fail** the exam.
People **are certainly going to work** longer in the future.
They **are probably not going to take** any English courses next year.

Maybe and *perhaps* can start sentences with *be going to*.

Perhaps the government **is going to fix** Social Security.

less certain		more certain
maybe		certainly
possibly	likely	definitely
perhaps	probably	undoubtedly

Data from the Real World

Research shows that *will* is 20 times more common in academic writing than *be going to*.	**Academic writing** — *will* ▬▬▬▬▬▬ / *be going to* ▬
	Write: *People **will be** happier in the future.*
Research shows that *be going to* is three times more common in speaking than *will*.	**Speaking** — *will* ▬▬▬ / *be going to* ▬▬▬▬▬▬▬
	Say: *"Everyone**'s going to work** to age 70 in the future."*

▶ Grammar Application

Exercise 3.1 *Will* or Present Progressive?

Complete this university press release. Circle *will* or the present progressive.
If both are possible, circle both.

FOR IMMEDIATE RELEASE
New Program at Bay City University for Senior Citizens

    Bay City, September 5 – Life expectancy **is increasing / will increase** in the future.
(1)
This means that the population of Bay City **will grow / is growing** as well, and the
(2)
number of Bay City students over the age of 60 **will increase / is increasing** someday.
(3)
Already, the number of people over 60 who want to study is growing, and it
is probably doubling / will probably double in the next 20 years. As a result, Bay
(4)
University **is needing / will need** more programs and more courses for older students.
(5)
    Therefore, Bay City University **will announce / is announcing** later this week plans
(6)
for a new department for students over 60 called Lifelong Learning. The department
will open / is opening officially next year. However,
(7)
Lifelong Learning **is holding / will hold** an orientation
(8)
event this Friday afternoon to introduce the
department. Interested students can talk to
instructors from the department about the courses
they **are teaching / will teach** next year.
(9)

Exercise 3.2 *Will* or *Be Going To?*

A Complete the conversation with *will* or *be going to* and the words in parentheses.
Sometimes, both are correct.

Lisa What _are you going to do_ (do) in your old age?
(1)

Zack Well, I've thought about this. I _____ (not retire) early.
(2)

Maybe I'll retire in my 70s, but not before. Anyway, after retirement,

I _____ (travel).
(3)

Lisa That's expensive. You aren't rich. You _____ (not have) the
(4)

money for travel.

Zack You know, you're right. I _____ (start) a savings account right
(5)

away. How about you? What _____ you _____ (do) in your old age?
(6)   (6)

Lisa Well, I _____ (go) back to school.
(7)

Zack I'm surprised. You don't like school now. You _____ (not like)
(8)

it later.

Lisa I _____ (change) my attitude. In fact, I _____ (change)
(9)   (10)

it right now! Let's go to the library and study.

Zack That's a great idea! I _____ (drive).
(11)

B *Pair Work* Compare your answers with a partner. Discuss the reason for
your choices. Which statements and questions are about immediate decisions?
Which are about intentions? Which are about future events that are certain
due to evidence?

Exercise 3.3 Adverbs

A What will life be like when you are old? Read some predictions about the future.
Add an adverb that matches the degree of certainty in parentheses.

maybe	~~likely~~	definitely
possibly	probably	undoubtedly
perhaps	certainly	

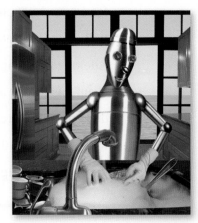

              likely
1. Robots will ˅ do all of our housework. (in the middle)

2. Computers won't have keyboards. (in the middle)

We are going to use our voices to communicate

with them. (less certain)

3. There will be no ice in the Arctic. (more certain)

4. People are not going to drive their own cars. (less certain)

   Satellites or computers will control them. (less certain)

5. Space flight is going to be available to anyone. (more certain)

   People will take vacations in space. (more certain)

B *Pair Work* Discuss the predictions with a partner. Do you agree or disagree with these predictions? Make statements with *will* and adverbs that are true for you. Give reasons for your answers.

> A *I agree with number 1. Robots will definitely do all of our housework in the future.*
> B *Why do you think that?*
> A *We already have this type of robot today. People use robots to build cars, so they will certainly use them for housework in the future.*

C *Over to You* Make predictions about your life in the future. Use *will*, *be going to*, and adverbs. Compare your predictions with a partner.

> A *What will your life be like in the future?*
> B *I'm going to make a lot of money. I'm definitely going to retire early. How about you?*

4 Avoid Common Mistakes ⚠

1. **Use *will* before the main verb in statements about the future.**

   In the future, people ˄*will* live to 110.

2. **Use *will* for predictions, not *would*.**

   Perhaps, a few years from now, I ~~would~~ *will* have a job with a good salary.

3. **Use *be* with *going to* for the future.**

   I take good care of myself. I ˄*am* going to live to be 100 years old!

4. **Use the base form of the verb after *will*.**

   People will ~~to~~ live longer in the future. He will ~~lives~~ *live* longer.

Editing Task

Find and correct eight more mistakes in this interview with an actor.

> **Pablo Percy** A lot of women actors quit around the age of 40 or 50. They say there
>   aren't good parts for older women. What ~~would~~ *will* you do in your later years?
>
> **Melanie Hinton** Well, I won't retire and sit at home. I work until I'm 90!
>
> **Pablo Percy** But there aren't many good parts for older women. How would you find work?
>
> 5 **Melanie Hinton** The entertainment business is changing. In the future, there be a lot
>   more older people making movies *and* watching movies. That means
>   there would definitely be more parts for older people, including older
>   women, in the future.
>
> **Pablo Percy** Are you sure?
>
> 10 **Melanie Hinton** Absolutely. In fact, I wouldn't wait for these
>   parts. I will to write my own scripts. I going
>   to have a script ready next year.
>
> **Pablo Percy** What is it going to be about?
>
> **Melanie Hinton** I going to write a love story about two
> 15   80-year-olds.
>
> **Pablo Percy** Sounds wonderful!

5 | Grammar for Writing

Using *Will* and *Be Going To* for Predictions

Writers use *will* and *be going to* to make predictions about how things will be in the future. They are similar in meaning. However, in writing, it is much more common to use *will*. Predictions can be positive or negative, and adverbs of certainty, such as *definitely* and *possibly*, can make them weaker or stronger.

Remember:

- **In positive statements, adverbs of certainty go after *will* and before the main verb.**
  They will <u>probably</u> see their children and grandchildren a lot more than they do now.

- **In negative statements, the adverbs can go between *will* and *not* or before *won't*.**
  They <u>definitely</u> won't run out of things to do when they retire.

> • Use *be going to* when you are certain that something is going to happen because you have evidence for it. Don't use *will* for predictions based on evidence.
>
> *My parents are going to retire soon to travel. They already have plane tickets.*

Pre-writing Task

1 Read the paragraph below. What two things do this writer's parents want to do after they retire?

When My Parents Retire

My parents are going to retire next year. When they retire, their lives will be very different. Of course they will have a lot more free time. Luckily, they will also have enough money to support themselves and try new things. My mother loves reading books, so she will probably take some literature classes. My father will possibly learn to cook. They both love to travel, so I think they are going to spend a lot of time traveling and visiting new places. They will probably see their children and grandchildren a lot more than they do now. They definitely won't run out of things to do when they retire.

2 Read the paragraph again. Underline the verbs with *will*. Circle *be going to* + verb. Which verbs make predictions based on evidence?

Writing Task

1 *Write* Use the paragraph in the Pre-writing Task and the sentence starters below to help you write about your retirement. When will you (or someone you know) retire? What are you going to do? Make some predictions and talk about some plans.

1. When I am 65, I will probably _____ .

2. I will spend a lot of time _____ .

3. I am going to / not going to live in / visit / study _____

   _____ .

2 *Self-Edit* Use the editing tips below to improve your paragraph. Make any necessary changes.

1. Did you use *will* or *be going to* to predict how things will be in the future?
2. Did you use *will* or *be going to* to talk about future plans?
3. Did you use *be going to* when you have evidence for a prediction about the future?
4. Did you avoid the mistakes in the Avoid Common Mistakes chart on page 211?

Future Time Clauses and Future Conditionals

Learning to Communicate

1 Grammar in the Real World

A What do you know about learning a language? Read the passage from a textbook. How do humans learn to communicate?

Children and Language Learning

Jake is two years old, and he is a typical American child. He plays, laughs, and cries. He also talks. He can understand about 200 English words. He uses fixed phrases. For example, he says "all gone" when
5 he finishes his food. **Until he is about four or five, Jake will talk** mostly about things around him – where he is and what he is doing at the moment. **When he is five years old, he will understand** thousands of words and will speak normally.
10 **Before he is six, he will learn** to form correct grammatical sentences.

When he starts school, he will begin to read and write. **After he starts to read, he will learn** to speak about things that are not happening right around
15 him – the past, the future, and faraway people and places. **Once he is literate,[1] Jake will learn** about a thousand words every year. **When he is 18, he will be** ready for college. He will have all the language and world knowledge he needs for his classes. Then, for the rest of his life, he will continue to learn.
20 Was Jake born with the ability to learn to speak, read, and write? Many experts say *yes*. Animals often live close to human beings, but they do not learn human language. Therefore, Jake must have a natural ability to learn his language. However, he speaks English only because his parents and the people around him use English.
25 Learning how to communicate is a combination of natural, genetic features[2] and our social environment. We need both things to be "human."

[1]**literate:** able to read and write | [2]**genetic feature:** a characteristic of living things passed on from parents to children

B *Comprehension Check* Answer the questions.

1. According to the textbook excerpt, how many words does a typical two-year-old child know?
2. What do children talk about before ages four or five?
3. What happens after children learn to read?
4. Two things make it possible for humans to learn language. What are they?

C *Notice* Find the sentences in the textbook passage and complete them.

1. _____ he is six, he _____ learn to form correct
   (a)   (b)
   grammatical sentences.

2. _____ he starts school, he _____ begin to read
   (a)   (b)
   and write.

3. _____ he starts to read, he _____ learn to
   (a)   (b)
   speak about things that are not happening right around him.

4. _____ he is literate, Jake _____ learn about
   (a)   (b)
   a thousand words every year.

Do the words in the *a* blanks refer to place or time?
Do the verbs in the *b* blanks talk about the present or the future?

2 | Future Time Clauses

▶ Grammar Presentation

Future time clauses show the time and order (first or second) of a future event.

FIRST EVENT   SECOND EVENT
Once he is literate, *he will learn about a thousand words every year.*

FIRST EVENT   SECOND EVENT
After he starts to read, *he will learn to speak about things that are not happening around him.*

2.1 Future Time Clauses

FUTURE TIME CLAUSE				MAIN CLAUSE			
Time Word	Subject	Simple Present		Subject	*Will*	Base Form of Verb	
Before **After** **When**	he	starts	school,	he	will	learn	to read.

2.1 Future Time Clauses (continued)

MAIN CLAUSE				FUTURE TIME CLAUSE			
Subject	*Will*	Base Form of Verb		Time Word	Subject	Simple Present	
He	will	learn	to read	**before after when**	he	starts	school.

2.2 Using Future Time Clauses

a. Use future time clauses to say when the event in the main clause happens. Use *after* when the event in the time clause happens first.	┌─── learns to read ───┐ **X** starts school FIRST EVENT SECOND EVENT **After she starts school, she will learn** to read.
Use *when* when two events happen at or around the same time.	**When he graduates from high school, he will go** to college.
Use *as soon as* or *once* when the event in the main clause happens immediately after the event in the time clause.	**X** **X** leaves college gets a job FIRST EVENT SECOND EVENT **As soon as he leaves college, he will get** a job. **Once he is literate, he will learn** thousands of new words.
Use *before* when the event in the main clause happens first.	SECOND EVENT FIRST EVENT **Before Anne starts school, she will learn** hundreds of words.
Use *until* to show when the event in the main clause will stop or change.	talks about ┌── immediate environment ──┐ **X** four or five years old **Until he is about four or five, Jake will talk** mostly about his immediate environment. (Jake will stop doing this when he is four or five.)
b. The time clause can come before or after the main clause. Remember to use a comma when the time clause comes first.	**As soon as he leaves college,** he will get a job. He will get a job **as soon as he leaves college**.
c. Even though the verb in the time clause is in the simple present, it refers to a future event.	He will learn more English **before he visits** California **next year**. I will stay in school **until I graduate two years from now**.

▶ Grammar Application

Exercise 2.1 Future Time Clauses

Circle the correct verb.

1. Larisa is a typical three-year-old Russian girl. Before she
   will start / **starts** school at age 5, she **learns** / **will learn**
   to print her name in the Cyrillic alphabet: Лариса.

2. Her parents **will teach** / **teach** her to read simple words
   like *cat* (Кот) before she **will start** / **starts** school, too.

3. When she **goes** / **will go** to kindergarten, Larisa
   starts / **will start** to learn to read and write more
   simple words.

4. She **will learn** / **learns** even more words as soon as she
   starts / **will start** primary school.

5. Once Larisa **gets** / **will get** to the first grade, she
   learns / **will learn** to use handwriting instead of
   printing.

6. When she **is** / **will be** about nine years old, she **will recognize** / **recognizes**
   thousands of words.

7. She **reads** / **will read** some of her textbooks in English when she **goes** / **will go**
   to college.

8. After she **will finish** / **finishes** college, she **knows** / **will know** tens of
   thousands of words.

А	Б	В	Г	Д	Е	Ё
Ж	З	И	Й	К	Л	М
Н	О	П	Р	С	Т	У
Ф	Х	Ц	Ч	Ш	Щ	Ъ
Ы	Ь	Э	Ю	Я		

Exercise 2.2 Time Words

Complete the description of a class in American Sign Language (ASL). Circle the correct time word.

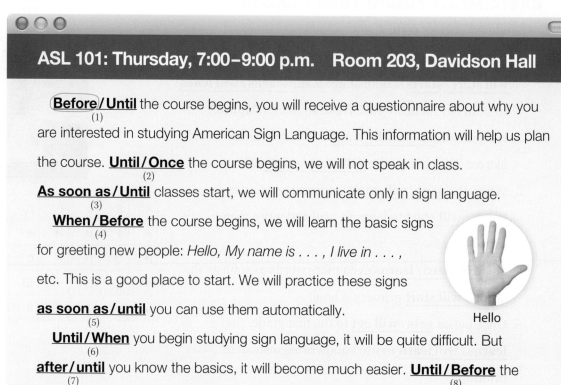

ASL 101: Thursday, 7:00–9:00 p.m.   Room 203, Davidson Hall

(**Before**)/**Until** the course begins, you will receive a questionnaire about why you
(1)
are interested in studying American Sign Language. This information will help us plan

the course. **Until/Once** the course begins, we will not speak in class.
(2)
As soon as/Until classes start, we will communicate only in sign language.
(3)
When/Before the course begins, we will learn the basic signs
(4)
for greeting new people: *Hello, My name is . . . , I live in . . . ,*

etc. This is a good place to start. We will practice these signs

as soon as/until you can use them automatically.
(5)

Hello

Until/When you begin studying sign language, it will be quite difficult. But
(6)
after/until you know the basics, it will become much easier. **Until/Before** the
(7)   (8)
course ends, you will learn to use a lot of sign language and have a lot of fun!

Exercise 2.3 More Future Time Clauses

A Dave is going to take all four levels of Spanish at Bay City College. Read the information about how many words a typical student in the program knows at each level. Complete the statements about Dave. Use the verbs in parentheses and the numbers in the chart.

	Starting Vocabulary	Ending Vocabulary
Level 1 student	about 500 words	about 1,500 words
Level 2 student	about 1,500 words	about 2,500 words
Level 3 student	about 2,500 words	about 3,500 words
Level 4 student	about 3,500 words	about 5,000 words

1. When he starts Level 1, Dave _will know_ (know) about _500_ words.

2. When he finishes Level 1, Dave _____ (know) about

   _____ words.

3. Dave will try to learn 1,000 more words before he _____ (finish) Level 2.

4. Dave will not start Level 3 until he _____ (know) about

   _____ words.

5. Once he _____ (reach) Level 4, Dave _____ (know) more

   than _____ words.

6. Once Dave _____ (read) and _____ (write) Spanish fluently,

   he _____ (apply) for a job in Spain.

B *Pair Work* Complete each sentence in a way that is true for you. Then discuss
your answers with a partner.

1. I _will continue_ (continue) to study English until I _speak the language well_ .

2. When I _____ (finish) this English course, I _____ .

3. I _____ (get) a job as soon as I _____ .

4. Before I _____ (complete) this course, I _____ .

   A *I'll continue to study English until I speak it well. How about you?*
   B *I'll continue to study English until I read and write it well.*

   A *I'll get a job as soon as I finish all the classes in this program. How about you?*
   B *I'll get a job as soon as I finish my job training course.*

C *Group Work* Tell a group member about your partner's answers in B.
Compare your answers.

   A *Mei will get a job as soon as she finishes all the courses in this program.*
   B *Rob will get a job as soon as he finishes the program, too.*

3 | Future Conditionals; Questions with Time Clauses and Conditional Clauses

▶ Grammar Presentation

Future conditional sentences describe possible situations in the future.	**If I pass all my exams,** I will go to college. **If Dave learns to read and write Spanish well, will he get** a job in Spain?

3.1 Future Conditionals: Statements

FUTURE CONDITION				MAIN CLAUSE			
If	Subject	Simple Present		Subject	*Will*	Base Form of Verb	
If	he	passes	his exams,	he	will	go	to college.

MAIN CLAUSE				FUTURE CONDITION			
Subject	*Will*	Base Form of Verb		*If*	Subject	Simple Present	
He	will	go	to college	**if**	he	passes	his exams.

3.2 *Yes / No* Questions

FUTURE CONDITION OR FUTURE TIME CLAUSE				MAIN CLAUSE			
If / Time Word	Subject	Simple Present		*Will*	Subject	Base Form of Verb	
If After When	she	learns	Spanish,	will	she	get	a job in Spain?

MAIN CLAUSE				FUTURE CONDITION OR FUTURE TIME CLAUSE			
Will	Subject	Base Form of Verb		*If* / Time Word	Subject	Simple Present	
Will	she	get	a job in Spain	**if after when**	she	learns	Spanish?

3.3 Information Questions

FUTURE CONDITION OR FUTURE TIME CLAUSE				MAIN CLAUSE				
If / Time Word	Subject	Simple Present		*Wh-* Word	*Will*	Subject	Base Form of Verb	
If After When	you	finish	this class,	what	will	you	do?	

MAIN CLAUSE				FUTURE CONDITION OR FUTURE TIME CLAUSE			
Wh- Word	*Will*	Subject	Base Form of Verb	*If* / Time Word	Subject	Simple Present	
What	will	you	do	**if after when**	you	finish	this class?

3.4 Using Future Conditional Clauses and Future Time Clauses

a. Use *if* to refer to a situation that is possible in the future but that we cannot be certain about.	*If he finishes the program, he will get a job.* (We don't know if he will finish the program.)
b. Use *when* to refer to a situation at a point in the future that is expected or likely to happen.	***When** he finishes the program, he will get a job.* (We expect him to finish the program.)
c. Use a main verb in the simple present in the conditional clause.	*If she **gets** a better job, she will be very happy.* *If she ~~will get~~ a better job, she will be very happy.*
d. Use a comma in writing when the conditional clause or time clause comes first.	***If she arrives late,** she will miss the lecture.* ***When they finish their work,** they will leave.*

Data from the Real World

Research shows that in conversation, people often use time clauses and conditional clauses alone in answers.

A   When will you start Level 3 of your course?
B   As soon as I finish Level 2.

A   Will you take another English course next year?
B   Yes, if I have time.

▶ Grammar Application

Exercise 3.1 Future Conditionals

🔊 Listen to an interview with a scientist about Edna the ape. After you listen, write the verbs in the correct form.

Bob Diaz   Edna is a mature female ape. Researchers are going to try to find out if

they can teach Edna to communicate. We asked Dr. Sheila Viss, one of the

researchers, about the study. Dr. Viss, if you _teach_ (teach) Edna, _will_
                                              (1)   (2)

she _learn_ (learn) human language?
      (2)

Dr. Viss   That is what we hope to find out. First, if we _____ (use)
                                                               (3)

American Sign Language, Edna _____ (learn) the meaning of
                                (4)

some signs. For example, we think Edna _____ (use) the sign
                                          (5)

for "more" if she _____ (want) more food.
                    (6)

Bob Diaz If Edna _____ (learn)
(7)

a sign that works in one situation,

_____ she _____ (use)
(8)   (8)

the same sign in a different situation?

Dr. Viss Yes. For example, we think Edna

_____ (make) the sign
(9)

for a toy when she _____
(10)

(want) a different toy.

Bob Diaz So, if she _____ (want) something special, _____ she
(11)   (12)

_____ (combine) the signs?
(12)

Dr. Viss We think she will. If she _____ (do) this, Edna
(13)

_____ (make) simple sentences. For example, when she
(14)

_____ (want) food quickly, she _____ (make)
(15)   (16)

the signs for "give-food-hurry."

Bob Diaz When she _____ (learn) to communicate, _____ she
(17)   (18)

_____ (learn) quickly?
(18)

Dr. Viss Well, probably not. Edna will learn slowly compared to a human child.

Exercise 3.2 More Future Conditionals

A *Pair Work* New words and expressions come into English every day. Match these new words with their definitions. They appear in most new dictionaries. Discuss with a partner how you think these expressions became popular.

1. blowback (noun) _____

2. to friend (verb) _____

3. a screenager (noun) _____

a. a young person who spends a lot of time in front of a computer

b. a bad result of a political action

c. to add someone to your list of friends on a social networking site

> **e**
> **f**
> **g**
>
> friend² /ˈfrend/ **verb** to connect with someone on a social website so that you can share information, pictures, etc.: *A lot of people from my old job have friended me.*

B Read the sentences about how a new word or expression enters the language. Combine the sentences to make future conditional sentences. If the conditional clause is first, use a comma.

1. People use new words and expressions every day. The new words survive.

   If people use new words and expressions every day, the new words will survive.

2. You have a new development in technology. You get a new word that describes it.

   _____

3. New words also enter the language. There is a big world event such as a war.

   _____

4. Someone uses the new word on the Internet. People copy it.

   _____

5. For example, you use the word. Your social networking friends use it, too.

   _____

6. A new word or expression becomes popular. A lot of people use it.

   _____

7. A person on a TV news show says the new word. It sounds important.

   _____

8. A new word appears in the dictionary. A lot of people use it in speaking and in writing.

   _____

9. People stop using the new word or expression. It dies.

   _____

C *Pair Work* Ask and answer conditional questions about the information in B.

   A *If people use a new word or expression every day, will it survive?*
   B *Yes, it will.*

Exercise 3.3 Time Clauses and Future Conditionals

A 🔊 Listen to a campus radio interview with Jawad, a student. Complete the sentences about his plans.

1. Jawad will be successful if he _____.

2. Jawad will get a good job if he _____.

3. If he does well in his English classes, Jawad _____

   _____.

4. Jawad will apply for a job when _____.

5. When he graduates and gets his certificate, Jawad _____.

B *Pair Work* Discuss your plans with a partner. Ask questions like the ones in the interview. Use time clauses and future conditional clauses where appropriate.

- Why are you here at [your school]?
- What are your plans?
- After you finish the program, what will you do?
- How will you feel when . . . ?

A *Why are you here at the community college?*
B *Well, I'm here for my career. If my English improves, I'll probably find a better job.*

4 Avoid Common Mistakes ⚠

1. Use the simple present in the conditional clause, not *will*.

If I ~~will~~ get good grades, I will go to college next year.

2. Use *will* in the main clause, not the simple present.

           will know
If she learns 1,000 words every year, she ~~knows~~ 3,000 words in three years.

3. Use the simple present in the time clause, not *will*.

    finishes
When he ~~will finish~~ this course, he will take a vacation.

4. Use *if* for something that is possible. Use *when* for something that you are certain will happen.

  If
~~When~~ I become rich, I will help poor people.

Editing Task

Find and correct nine more mistakes in this web article about how birds can learn.

Intelligent Crows

A team of scientists is doing experiments with crows to test their intelligence. This is what the scientists think will happen:

5 • When the crows ~~will be~~ *are* thirsty, they will look for water.

• As soon as they will find water, they drink it.

• If there is no water, the crows
10 search for it.

• If they don't get the water easily, the crows think of ways to get it.

For example, if the water will be in a narrow tube, it will be difficult to reach it. However, the scientists think that the crows will
15 learn the following:

• If they will drop a stone into the tube, the water level will rise.

• If they will drop more stones, the level will rise more.

• The crows drop stones into the tube until the crows reach the water.

20 • When the experiment is successful, the scientists will prove that crows are intelligent birds.

5 | Grammar for Writing ✏

Using Future Time Clauses and Conditional Clauses

Writers use future time clauses to show the order of events in a future plan or process. Future time clauses help to connect ideas in writing about a process and show how different steps fit together.

Remember:

- **Use future time clauses when you know when something will happen.**
  As soon as Elaine gets home, she will do her homework.

- **Use *if* clauses when you aren't sure if something is going to happen.**
  If Elaine is not late, she will have enough time to do all her homework.

Pre-writing Task

1 Read the paragraphs below. What is Marie's goal? What steps does she need to take to reach the goal?

Study Goals

Marie is studying English at a community college because she wants to get a better job. She is currently working at a restaurant. She likes it, but she wants to be a nurse one day.

Last week, Marie met with a career counselor at school, and they developed a plan

5 of action. First, before she begins a nursing program, she will need to complete all four levels of her English program. Once she accomplishes this, Marie will begin taking science classes at the community college. If she does well in these classes, she will apply to nursing school. If the school accepts her, she will earn a nursing degree in two or three years. Once she earns her degree, she will look for a job at a hospital. If she

10 completes all of these steps, she will accomplish her goal of becoming a nurse.

2 Read the paragraphs again. Underline the future time clauses. Circle the *if* clauses. Which things is Marie less sure of?

Writing Task

1 *Write* Use the paragraphs in the Pre-writing Task to help you write about something you want to accomplish in the future. What will you need to do to accomplish this goal? You can write about:

- a job you want

- something you want to buy

- a place you want to visit or move to

- a person you want to meet

- something you want to study

- your own idea

2 *Self-Edit* Use the editing tips below to improve your paragraph. Make any necessary changes.

1. Did you use future time clauses to show the order of events in a future plan or process?
2. Did you use future time clauses to show when events happen?
3. Did you use *if* clauses to show that you aren't sure that something will happen?
4. Did you avoid the mistakes in the Avoid Common Mistakes chart on page 224?

1 | Grammar in the Real World

A Can you think of three recent medical inventions? Read the article from a science magazine. Which invention do you think is the most interesting?

Medical Breakthroughs

Some medical problems need engineers, not doctors. Technology **can** often solve problems when doctors alone **can't** help. Here are some examples of medical
5 breakthroughs[1] from the world of engineering.

The "ishoe"
Often when astronauts return from space, they **are not able to** balance.[2] MIT student Erez Lieberman invented the
10 "ishoe" to deal with this problem. The ishoe is a pad that goes inside a shoe and uses sensors[3] to send information about balance to a computer or cell phone. NASA scientists use this information to help the astronauts recover their balance. Lieberman **could** 15 see that his invention had other uses, for example, diagnosing[4] balance problems in elderly people.

The Autonomous Wheelchair
In the future, people **will be able to** tell their wheelchairs where they want to go. 20 The Autonomous Wheelchair **can** learn to recognize its environment by listening to its user's instructions. In addition, it uses Wi-Fi[5] to build a map of the person's home.

The Smart Pill
The doctor **can't** always be sure if some 25 people are taking their medication. Now a "smart" pill **can** tell a doctor when a patient last took his or her medication and report on the state of the person's health at the time.

[1]**breakthrough:** an important discovery or development that helps to solve a problem | [2]**balance:** have weight equally divided so something or someone can stay in one position | [3]**sensor:** a device that discovers and reacts to changes in things such as movement, heat, and light | [4]**diagnose:** recognize the exact disease or condition a person has | [5]**Wi-Fi:** a method of connecting to the Internet without using wires

The Rocket-Powered Arm

Another invention from space research 30
is the Rocket-Powered Arm. Until recently,
people with artificial arms **were not able to**
lift heavy objects. Now there is a new kind of
power for artificial arms – rocket fuel. With
rocket-powered arms, people **will be able** 35
to lift objects up to 20 pounds.

These are just some of the amazing
technological advances that will help
improve people's lives. Who knows what
other inventions they will come up with? 40

B *Comprehension Check* Match the technology with what it does.

1. The "ishoe" __b__
2. The Rocket-Powered Arm _____
3. The Autonomous Wheelchair _____
4. The Smart Pill _____

a. understands the human voice.
b. tells NASA scientists if you have problems
   with balance.
c. helps you pick things up.
d. gives doctors information about their
   patients' health.

C *Notice* Look at the verbs in **bold** in the article. Underline the verbs that are
about the past. Circle the verbs that are about the future.

2 | Ability with *Can* and *Could*

▶ Grammar Presentation

Can and *could* describe ability and possibility.	*Technology **can** often solve problems when doctors alone **can't** help.* *Lieberman **could** see that his invention had other uses.*

2.1 Statements

Subject	Modal Verb	Base Form of Verb
I You He / She / It We They	can can't cannot could couldn't could not	help people.

2.2 *Yes / No* Questions and Answers

Modal Verb	Subject	Base Form of Verb	Short Answers		
Can **Could**	I you he / she / it we they	help?	Yes, No,	I you he / she / it we they	can. can't. could. couldn't.

2.3 Information Questions

Wh- Word	Modal Verb	Subject	Base Form of Verb	
How **Where** **When**	can could can	we they you	solve	the problem?

Wh- Word	Modal Verb	Base Form of Verb
What **Who**	can could	help?

Modal Verbs and Modal-like Expressions: See page A7.

2.4 Using *Can* and *Could*

a. You can use *can / can't* to talk about general ability and what people know how to do.

*My grandfather **can** swim, but he **can't** walk very well.*

*Engineers **can** solve problems when doctors **can't**.*

b. You can use *can / can't* to talk about people's senses and mental abilities.

***Can** you **see** that tall building on the left?*

*Some patients **can't remember** if they took their medication.*

c. You can use *can / can't* to talk about what is or is not possible and about known facts.

*Elderly people **can** have serious health problems after a fall.*

*Technology **can't** solve every problem.*

d. Use *could / couldn't* for the past.

*Lieberman **could** see other uses for his product.*

*In the past, people with artificial arms **couldn't** lift heavy objects.*

▶ Grammar Application

Exercise 2.1 *Can* and *Can't*: Statements

Complete the article about how a computer is helping a man. Use *can* or *can't* and the verbs in the box.

breathe	~~move~~	move	move	send	speak	talk	use

Connecting with ⟩ ERICA

When he was younger, Steve Nichols was very fit. However, in 1994 he learned he had ALS, a disease that causes loss of muscle control. Now Nichols _can't move_ most of his body. For example, he _____ (2) his tongue. Because of this, he _____ (3). He also has trouble breathing. He _____ (4) without a machine.

However, Nichols _____ (5) his eyes. His computer, ERICA, has software that changes text to speech, so he _____ (6) to his wife and family. When Nichols looks at a letter on the keyboard on his computer screen, the computer types that letter. With ERICA, he _____ (7) e-mails. In addition, he _____ (8) the Internet. ERICA keeps Nichols connected to the rest of the world.

Exercise 2.2 *Can* and *Can't*: Questions and Answers

A Engineers in Japan have created nurse robots to help care for patients. Unscramble the words to write questions about these robots. Use *can*.

1. what / do / these robots / ?

   What can these robots do?

2. speak / they / ?

   _____

3. understand / how many languages / they / ?

   _____

4. they / patients / lift / ?

   _____

5. one robot / how much weight / lift / ?

_____

6. a robot / recognize / people / ?

_____

7. they / give medicine / to people / ?

_____

8. make / what kinds of decisions / they / ?

_____

B 🔊)) Listen to an expert answer the questions in A. Write the answers.
Write things the nurse robots *can* do.

1. _They can do a lot of things._   5. _____

2. _____   6. _____

3. _____   7. _____

4. _____   8. _____

C 🔊)) Listen again. Write three things nurse robots *can't* do.

1. _____

2. _____

3. _____

Exercise 2.3 *Can, Can't, Could,* or *Couldn't?*

A Complete the paragraphs with *can, can't, could,* or *couldn't.*

Do You Use This Technology?

The Cell Phone

    Before the invention of cell phones, you _couldn't_ easily contact people away from
their homes or offices. Now you _____ talk to friends and family at any time
and in any place. With text messaging, you _____ also communicate silently.
How fast _____ you type a message?

The Digital Music Player

    These days most people have a digital music player and _____ listen
to their favorite music anywhere. _____ you remember life before portable
music devices? Years ago you _____ only listen to your favorite music at
home, in your car, or in a record store.

The GPS Navigator

_____ you read maps? If you _____ read

(8)   (9)
a map very well, a GPS (global positioning system) can be very helpful.

You _____ just put an address into your GPS and follow the

(10)
instructions. Then you _____ go anywhere you want.

(11)

B *Group Work* Make your own list of four important inventions in everyday life.
Then compare your lists in a group and discuss the questions. Use inventions in
these areas or your own ideas.

Inventions in . . .
- medicine   • travel   • communication   • home appliances   • entertainment

1. Can you remember (or imagine) life without these inventions?
   What was it like?
2. What can people do now that they couldn't do before these inventions?
3. As a group, choose the three most important inventions. What are they?
   Why are they the most important?

3 | *Be Able To*

▶ Grammar Presentation

You can use *be able to* to talk about ability and possibility.	Some astronauts **are not able to** balance after a space flight. People **will be able to** talk to their wheelchairs.

3.1 Statements About the Present, Past, and Future

PRESENT AND PAST				
Subject	***Be***	***(Not) Able To***	**Base Form of Verb**	
I	am / 'm was			
You We They	are / 're were	(not) able to	use	a computer.
He / She / It	is / 's was			

3.1 Statements About the Present, Past, and Future *(continued)*

FUTURE				
Subject	*Will (Not)*	*Be Able To*	Base Form of Verb	
I You We They He / She / It	**will / 'll** **will not** **won't**	**be able to**	use	a computer.

3.2 *Yes / No* Questions and Short Answers About the Present and Past

Be	Subject	*Able To*	Base Form of Verb		Short Answers	
Are	you	**able to**	lift	heavy objects?	Yes, I **am**.	No, I**'m not**.
Were					Yes, I **was**.	No, I **wasn't**.

3.3 *Yes / No* Questions and Short Answers About the Future

Will	Subject	*Be + Able To*	Base Form of Verb		Short Answers	
Will	you	**be able to**	lift	heavy objects?	Yes, I **will**.	No, I **won't**.

3.4 Information Questions About the Present, Past, and Future

PRESENT AND PAST				
Wh- Word	*Be*	Subject	*Able To*	Base Form of Verb
When **How** **How often**	**are** **were**	you	**able to**	go?

Wh- Word	*Be*	*Able To*	Base Form of Verb
Who	**is / 's** **was**	**able to**	go?

FUTURE				
Wh- Word	*Will*	Subject	*Be + Able To*	Base Form of Verb
When **How** **How often**	**will**	you	**be able to**	go?

Wh- Word	*Will*	*Be + Able To*	Base Form of Verb
Who	**will / 'll**	**be able to**	go?

3.5 Using *Be Able To*

a. You can use *be able to* to talk and write about ability in the present, past, or future.

*Sometimes astronauts **are not able to** balance after a space flight.*

*In the past, artificial arms **weren't able to** lift heavy objects.*

*In the future, people **will be able to** tell their wheelchairs where to go.*

b. You can use *be able to* to talk and write about possibility.

*People **will be able to** talk to their wheelchairs in the future.*

c. In affirmative statements, you can use *was / were able to* for a specific event or a specific action that someone completed successfully in the past. Do not use *could*.

*Lieberman **was able to** design a special shoe a few years ago.*

Lieberman ~~could design~~ a special shoe a few years ago.

Both forms are correct in negative statements.

*In the past, they **weren't able to** lift heavy objects.*

*In the past, they **couldn't** lift heavy objects.*

d. You can use *be able to* after *going to, want to, would like to, need to,* and *have to*.

*In the future, people **are going to be able to** use these inventions.*

*Many people **would like to be able to** use these inventions now.*

Do not use *can (can't)* or *could (couldn't)* after these verbs.

*Scientists want to **be able to** invent new technologies.*

~~Scientists want to can invent new technologies.~~

 Can and *could* are more common than *be able to* in everyday conversation, especially in present time. Use *be able to* if you need to sound more formal.

***Can** your phone send e-mails?*

*The most advanced robots **are** now **able to** make facial expressions.*

Data from the Real World

People sometimes use *be unable to* instead of *be not able to*. This is more common in formal writing or speaking.

Formal: *When many astronauts return from space, they **are unable to** balance.*

Informal: *When many astronauts return from space, they **are not able to** balance.*

Be Unable To

in formal writing	
in formal speaking	
in conversation	

▶ Grammar Application

Exercise 3.1 Questions and Answers

A Complete the article from a magazine. Use a form of *be able to* and the verbs in parentheses. Then, on a separate piece of paper, write what numbers can use *could* instead of *was able to*.

Seeing Through You

Are brain scanners _able to see_ (see)
(1)   (1)
your thoughts? _____
                    (2)
they _____ (read) your mind?
          (2)
_____ they _____
        (3)   (3)
(see) your memories? Yes, according to some

scientists. At a conference in 2009, researchers

_____ (prove) this. One
            (4)
researcher watched a movie, and the brain scanning software

_____ (show) the basic pictures that he was looking at.
        (5)
    How _____ scientists _____ (use) this technology
                    (6)   (6)
in the future? Some scientists say they are already using brain scan technology.

They say that brain scans _____ (tell) if someone is lying.
                                            (7)
    Scientists are not the only ones who plan to use technology like this

in the future. Some companies think they _____
                                                        (8)
(use) brain scanners for advertising as well. Advertisers hope they

_____ (see) the way people respond to their products.
            (9)
    What do you think? How _____ we _____ (use)
                                    (10)   (10)
these technologies in the future?

B *Pair Work*   What do you think about the article? Are brain scanners a good thing or a bad thing? Discuss with a partner.

A *I think brain scanners are good because police will be able to tell if someone is lying.*
B *Perhaps the police will be able to catch more criminals with brain scanners.*

Exercise 3.2 *Be Able To* After Other Verbs

Data from the Real World 🌐

The simple past forms (*was / were able to*) are more frequent than the simple present forms (*am / is / are able to*). However, *be able to* is most common after modal verbs like *will* and *should* and after verbs like *going to* and *want to*.

Be Able To

am / is / are able to	
was / were able to	
modal verb / verb + be able to	

A *Over to You* Write five sentences about yourself. Write about work, school, technology, free time, or other ideas. For each sentence, choose one expression from Column A and one from Column B. Add *be able to*.

A	B
When I wake up in the morning,	would like to
When I am in class,	need to
Someday,	be going to
One day,	want to
Next year,	have to
In a few years,	will
When I finish school,	

Someday, I want to be able to buy a house.
When I finish school, I'm going to be able to get a better job.

B *Group Work* Compare your sentences. Give more information. Who has similar experiences and dreams?

4 Avoid Common Mistakes ⚠️

1. ***Cannot* is one word.**

   cannot
   This technology ~~can not~~ do everything, but it can help.

2. **Don't forget the *be* or *to* in *be able to*.**

   wasn't   to
   I ~~not~~ able ~~∧~~ understand the instructions for my new phone.

3. **In an affirmative sentence, use *was / were able to* for a specific action that someone completed successfully in the past. Do not use *could*.**

   was able to
   My grandmother fell yesterday, but she ~~could~~ get up.

Editing Task

Find and correct 11 more mistakes in this online review of an electronic translator. Some sentences have more than one mistake.

TECHNOLOGY TUESDAY REVIEW:
The Instant Interpreter

                  be

Will people really need to ∧ able to speak other languages in the future? That is a question language students ask after they hear about the Instant Interpreter. This little machine translates for you when you visit a foreign country. It listens to what you say and is able translate your speech into eight world languages. It is also easy to use. If you

5 are able use a smart phone, you will able to use this.

I tried the Instant Interpreter last week and I liked it. I able to order a cup of coffee in a restaurant. When the server asked me a question, the Interpreter gave me the translation, and I was able to answer. In the end, we were able to have a simple conversation. However, we not able understand everything we said to each other.

10   One problem with this machine is that it can not work quickly when your conversation becomes more complex. It needs time to able to learn your voice, too. I could solve the problem by talking to it a lot, so it learned my voice.

If you need to be able get around in a foreign city, this is a good buy. You can not find a better translating machine on the market today.

---

5 | Grammar for Writing ✎

Using *Can, Cannot,* and *Be Able To* in the Present and Future

Writers use *can, cannot,* and *am / is / are able to* to talk about what is possible now. They use *will be able to* to talk about abilities and possibilities in the future. Remember:

- **Use *can, cannot,* and *am / is / are able to* to talk about the present.**
  Today, we <u>are able to use</u> cell phones almost everywhere, but we often <u>cannot</u> use them in elevators or subway trains in some cities.

- **Use *will be able to* to talk about the future.**
  If companies build better cell phone networks, we <u>will be able to</u> make calls underground.

Pre-writing Task

1 Read the paragraphs below. How does the writer think people will be able to listen to music in the future?

Music Now and in the Future

Today people can listen to music everywhere they go. When you walk down the street, you can see old and young people using ear buds. Digital music players are essential devices for many people these days, and I think they will become even more convenient in the future.

5   When I was young, I had a portable CD player. I could take my CD player everywhere, but I had to carry disks and buy batteries. I did not care. I loved my CD player.

Now I have a digital music player. It is much better than my old CD player. I can take it everywhere, and I can download many different kinds of music. In the future, I think digital music players will continue to get better. They will be very thin, and they will stick

10 to the skin. People will be able to walk around and not worry about the devices. Also, we will not have to worry about batteries. The energy from our bodies will charge the batteries.

2 Read the paragraphs again. Underline *can* + verb. Circle *be able to* + verb. Which verbs talk about the present? Which talk about the future?

Writing Task

1 *Write* Use the paragraphs in the Pre-writing Task and the sentence starters below to help you write about something you would like to invent or a problem you would like to solve. How will this help people?

1. I am going to invent a _____ . It will be able to _____ .

2. People will be able to _____ with this invention.

3. Currently, we can _____ , but we still cannot _____ .

4. My invention will not be able to _____ , but it will be able
   to _____ .

2 *Self-Edit* Use the editing tips below to improve your paragraph. Make any necessary changes.

1. Did you use *can, cannot,* and *will be able to* to talk about abilities or possibilities?
2. Did you use *can, cannot,* and *am / is / are able to* to talk about the present?
3. Did you use *will be able to* to talk about the future?
4. Did you avoid the mistakes in the Avoid Common Mistakes chart on page 237?

Requests and Offers

Good Causes

1 Grammar in the Real World

A What kinds of volunteer work are common in your city or town? Read Lisa's e-mail about a volunteer project. What is she trying to do?

From: Lisa Chen
To: Bay City Community College Student Volunteer Group
Date: November 20
Subject: Volunteer Work Assignments for Thanksgiving

5 Hi Everyone!

Here are the volunteer work assignments for the Thanksgiving dinner at the Bay City Homeless Shelter. Please contact me if you have any questions.

Professor Rodriguez, **could** you please pick up the turkey on Wednesday evening? Then, **could** you take it to Ana's apartment?

10 Wei, **would** you make the pumpkin pies on Wednesday? That way, Ana can use the oven for the turkey.

Ana, **can** Eun give you a hand?[1]

Lara, **will** you do the vegetables? **Do you mind if** I help out? I make great sweet potatoes.

Marcus, you said you had plates and silverware. **Can** you please bring them? Let me 15 know if you cannot.

Mohammed has offered to take all the food in his van. Mohammed, **can** you go by Ana's around 11:00 on Thursday morning and pick everything up? **Can** I go with you? Then, Ana, **can** we go to the shelter together? **Do you mind if** we take your car?

I think that's everything. Let's all meet at the shelter
20 and start serving at 1:00 p.m. Oh, wait! We really need a few more people to help with serving. Professor Rodriguez, **may** I please contact your sister? Mohammed, **can** I get in touch with[2] your roommate?

Finally, would you like to get together at my apartment 25 on Friday for a "thank-you" pizza party?

See you soon, and thanks! Enjoy the attached photo!

Lisa

[1]**give you a hand:** help with doing something | [2]**get in touch with:** communicate with

B *Comprehension Check* Match the person with his / her work assignment.

1. Professor Rodriguez __d__   a. is going to bring plates.
2. Wei _____   b. will do the vegetables.
3. Lara _____   c. will pick up all the food.
4. Marcus _____   d. is going to pick up the turkey.
5. Mohammed _____   e. will make pumpkin pies.

C *Notice* Find the questions in the e-mail and complete them.

1. Professor Rodriguez, _____ please pick up the turkey on Wednesday evening?
2. Wei, _____ make the pumpkin pies on Wednesday?
3. Professor Rodriguez, _____ please contact your sister?
4. Mohammed, _____ get in touch with your roommate?

Which sentences ask permission to do something? Which sentences ask someone else to do something?

2 | Permission

▶ Grammar Presentation

You can use *can, could, may,* and *do you mind if* to ask permission to do something.	*"**Could** I go with you to Ana's?"* "Sure. No problem." *"**Do you mind if** we take your car?"* "No, not at all."

2.1 *Can, Could, May*: *Yes / No* Questions and Responses

Modal Verb	Subject	Base Form of Verb		Responses	
Can				Yes, you **can**.	No, you **can't**.
Could **May**	I	go	in your car?	Yes, (of course).	No, (I'm afraid not).

2.2 *Do You Mind If*: *Yes / No* Questions and Responses

Do you mind if	Subject	Verb	Responses	
Do you mind if	I	**drive**?	No, I don't. Not at all. Sure. No problem.	Well, actually, I prefer to drive.

2.3 Asking for Permission

a. Less formal	*can*	*Can* is very common in conversation and informal writing. Use *can* in most situations.	**Can** *I get in touch with your roommate?*
	could	*Could* is more formal and more polite than *can*.	**Could** *we ride to the shelter with you, please?*
More formal	*may*	*May* is very formal and polite.	**May** *I please contact your sister, Professor Rodriguez?*

b. Use the base form of the verb after modal verbs, including *can*, *could*, and *may*. Do not use other forms of the verb.	**Can** *I be part of your volunteer group?* *Can I ~~am~~ part of your volunteer group?* *Can I ~~being~~ part of your volunteer group?*
c. Use *Do you mind if* ... to be polite or when you think the request is inconvenient for the other person.	**Do you mind if** *we take your car?*
With *Do you mind if* ... ?, the verb agrees with the subject.	**Do you mind if Eun gives** *you a hand?*
You can also use *Do you mind?* alone.	*Can we go to the shelter together?* **Do you mind?**
d. You can say *please* with requests for permission, especially in formal situations. Use it at the end of the sentence or after the subject.	*Could I drive your car,* **please***?* *May I* **please** *drive your car?*

2.4 Answering Requests for Permission

a. Use *can* and *may* in short answers to requests for permission. Do not use *could*.	*"Can I come with you in your car?"* *"Yes, you* **can***."* *"Yes, you ~~could~~."*
	"Could I call you later?" *"Yes."* / *"Yes, you* **can***."* *"Yes, you ~~could~~."*
May is more formal.	*"May I sit here, please?"* *"Yes, you* **may***."*
b. In conversation, you can use other expressions such as *Sure, no problem.* / *Certainly.* / *Of course.*	*"Could I use your cell phone?"* **"Sure, no problem."**
Use *Certainly* and *Of course* in formal situations.	*"May I contact your sister?"* **"Of course."** / **"Certainly."**

c. You can soften negative responses with an apology and / or a reason.	*"Can I ride in your car?"* **"Sorry**, *I don't have room."*
	                                         "I'm afraid *I don't have room."*
	                                         "~~I don't have room~~."

2.4 **Answering Requests for Permission** *(continued)*

Be careful with negative responses. *No, you can't* and other direct negative responses often sound rude.

d. Say *No* or *No, not at all* to agree with requests with *Do you mind if*.	*"**Do you mind if** I borrow your cell phone?"* *"**No, not at all**. Here you are." / "**Sure, no problem**."* (*Yes* = Yes, I do mind. You can't use it.)
No means "No, I don't mind." You can also say *Sure* or *Sure, no problem*.	*"**Do you mind if** I call you this evening?"* *"**No, not at all.**"* (*No* = It's OK to call.)
Notice: *No* in response to *Do you mind if* means the opposite of *No* in response to *can, could,* and *may*.	*"**Can** I call you this evening?"* *"No, I'm afraid I'm busy."* (*No* = It's not OK to call.)

Data from the Real World

Research shows that most requests for permission use *I*, but it is possible to ask permission for other people.	***Can Eun*** *give you a hand?*

▶ Grammar Application

Exercise 2.1 Asking and Answering Requests for Permission

Lisa's volunteers reply to her e-mail, and their plans change. Correct the mistake in each request.

1. Dear Lisa: Yes, I can make the pies on Wednesday. Could I ~~to~~ borrow a pie pan from you? Thanks, Wei

2. Hi, Lisa: Do you mind if I picks up the turkey on Wednesday morning? Thank you, Professor Rodriguez

3. Dear Lara: Ana's oven is not working. Do you mind if she cook the turkey at your house? Thanks! Lisa

4. Hello, Lisa: Can my roommate calls you about volunteering? Do you mind if I give him your number? Mohammed

5. Dear Ana: May please I call you early on Wednesday morning to arrange a time? Professor Rodriguez

6. Dear Lisa: Yes, I can bring plates. Can you helping me carry them? Thanks! Marcus

7. Dear Professor Rodriguez: Yes, may you call on Wednesday morning. I'm available after 8:00 a.m. Ana

8. Hi, Ana: My car is not working. Could I please to ride to the shelter with you? Eun

Exercise 2.2 Formal Requests for Permission

A 🔊 Listen to a student asking a teacher for permission. Complete his requests in the chart below.

B 🔊 Listen again. Does the teacher agree to the student's requests? Check (✓) *Yes* or *No*.

	Yes	No
1. *Could I ask you* _____ a question, please?	☑	☐
2. _____ class early on Wednesday?	☐	☐
3. _____ the computer room?	☐	☐
4. _____ your CD player?	☐	☐
5. _____ our homework on Friday, not Thursday?	☐	☐

C *Pair Work* Now compare your answers with a partner.

Exercise 2.3 Asking for Permission

A Write two requests for permission to each person. Use the ideas in the box or your own ideas.

You want to:

ask a question about . . .	discuss an idea for . . .	get help with . . .	take a day off
borrow something	get a ride somewhere	sit down	talk after class about . . .

Your Teacher	A Friend	A Stranger in the Cafeteria	Your Boss
1. *Could I please talk to you after class about my paper?*	3.	5.	7.
2.	4.	6.	8.

B *Pair Work* Choose three of your requests. Read them to a partner. Do not identify the person you wrote the request to. Can your partner guess?

A *May I take a break now?*
B *Are you asking your boss?*

C *Pair Work* Take turns. Practice conversations. Use the situations from A. Make requests and respond.

(To a stranger in the cafeteria)
A *Do you mind if I sit down here?*
B *No, not at all.*

3 | Requests and Offers

▶ Grammar Presentation

You can use *can*, *could*, *will*, and *would* to ask people to do things. You can use *can*, *could*, *may*, and *will* to make offers.	"**Could** you give me a hand?" "Yes, of course." "I**'ll** help you with that." "Thank you."

3.1 Requests and Responses with *Can, Could, Will,* and *Would*

Modal Verb	Subject	Base Form of Verb	Responses	
Can **Could** **Will** **Would**	you	help?	Yes, I **can**. / Sure. No problem. Of course. / All right. / OK. Yes, I **will**. Yes, I'd be happy to. / I'd love to.	Sorry, I **can't**. I'm afraid I **can't**.

3.2 Asking People to Do Things with *Can, Could, Will,* and *Would*

a. Less formal More formal	*can / will* ↕ *could / would*	***Can*** *you stop by Ana's around noon?* ***Will*** *you help me make the vegetables?* ***Could*** *you take the turkey to Ana's apartment?* ***Would*** *you make the pies, please?*
	Could and *would* are more polite and less direct.	
b. You can say *please* to ask people to do things, especially in formal situations. Use it at the end of the sentence or after the subject.		*Would you help prepare the dinner,* **please**? *Can you* **please** *arrive at the shelter by noon?*
c. You can use *will* and *would* to ask if someone is willing to do something. *Would* is more polite than *will.* Use *would* in formal situations, and use *will* only with people you know well.		***Will*** *you buy the vegetables?* ***Would*** *you help us, Professor Rodriguez?*

3.3 Answering Requests to Do Things

a. Use *can* and *will* in short answers. Do not use *could* or *would.*	*"Could you drive me there?"* *"Yes, I* **can***."* *"Yes, I* ~~could~~*."* *"Would you help?"* *"Yes,* **I will***."* *"Yes, I* ~~would~~*."*
b. In conversation, you can use other expressions, such as *Sure, no problem. / Certainly. / Of course.*	*"Will you clean up after dinner, please?"* *"Sure, no problem."*
Certainly and *Of course* show emphasis. They can also sound more formal.	*"Would you please help me with this?"* *"Certainly."*
c. You can soften negative responses with an apology and / or a reason.	*"Can you help?"* *"***I'm sorry***, I don't have time this week."*
Be careful with negative responses. *No, I won't* and other direct negative responses often sound rude.	~~No, I won't,~~ *I don't have time this week.*

3.4 Making Offers with *Can, Could, May,* and *Will*

a. You can use questions with *can, could,* and *may* to make offers.		
Less formal More formal	*can* *could* *may*	***Can*** *I help you with dinner?* ***Could*** *I help you clean up after dinner?* ***May*** *I help you with that?*

3.4 Making Offers with *Can*, *Could*, *May*, and *Will* (continued)

b. You can also use statements with *I'll*, *We'll*, *I can*, and *We can* to make offers.

I'll cook the turkey this year.
We'll make dinner tonight.
I can drive you to the shelter.
We can prepare the vegetables.

3.5 Responding to Offers

a. You can say *Thank you* or *No, thank you* to respond to an offer. *Thanks* and *No, thanks* are less formal.

"I can give you a ride."
"Thank you." / *"Thanks."*

"Could I help you with that?"
"No, thank you."

You can also respond with *That would be great* or *OK*.

"I'll cook the turkey this year."
"That would be great." / *"OK, thank you."*

b. You can respond *Yes, please* or *That would be great* to an offer that is a question.

"Can I make the vegetables?"
"Yes, please."

▶ # Grammar Application

Exercise 3.1 *Can*, *Could*, *Will*, and *Would*: Requests and Answers

A You need your co-workers' help to plan a charity raffle (an event where everyone who donates to the charity has a chance to win a prize). Use the words to write requests with *please*.

1. could / buy snacks and drinks *Could you please buy snacks and drinks? /*
   Could you buy snacks and drinks, please?

2. would / set up tables _____

3. can / sell raffle tickets _____

_____

4. will / buy prizes for the raffle _____

_____

5. would / decorate the room _____

_____

6. could / serve snacks and drinks _____

_____

7. will / give a speech about the charity _____

_____

8. would / everyone / help clean up after the party _____

_____

B *Pair Work* Take turns asking and answering the requests in A.

    A *Could you please buy snacks and drinks?*

    B *Yes, of course. / I'm sorry. I don't have time to do that, but I can . . .*

Exercise 3.2 Formal and Informal Offers and Responses

A ◀)) It is the evening of the charity raffle. Listen. Complete the offers. Listen again. Complete the responses.

1. *A* Hi, Tony. *I'll drive* to the raffle tonight. OK?

    B Oh, that would be great. Thanks.

2. *A* Sarah, _____ carry those bags.

    B _____ . They're really heavy.

3. *A* _____ move those tables, Mr. Lee?

    B _____ . I just finished.

4. *A* _____ the snacks and drinks out now?

    B _____

5. *A* Jordy, _____ you take tickets.

    B _____

6. *A* Ms. Moncur, _____ with the decorations?

   B _____

7. *A* Oh, no!

   B _____

   A _____

8. *A* _____ that for you, Paula?

   B _____

B Which two conversations are the most formal?

_____   _____

Exercise 3.3 Requests and Offers

Data from the Real World

Research shows people also use *Do you want to* to make requests. These requests sound less direct.	*Do you want to help me with the dishes?* *Do you want to drive now?*

A *Pair Work* You and a partner are organizing a project for a good cause. Choose one of the projects below or use your own idea. Make a list of six to eight things you need to do.

- clean up a local park
- organize a party at a children's hospital
- organize a party at a senior center
- raise money for charity

Clean Up Green Park
1. *Put up fliers for volunteers:*
   Tina, Cho, and Luis
2. *Organize volunteer groups:*
   Victoria
3. *Plan jobs for each group:*
   Tomás and Sophie

B *Pair Work* Take turns. Offer to do jobs on your list from A. Write your name or your partner's name under the jobs you each offer to do.

C *Group Work* Work with another pair. Take turns making and responding to requests for help with your project. Ask questions with *can, could,* and *Do you want to . . . ?*

> A *Could you help me with a party at the children's hospital?*
> B *Yes, I can. What can I do?*
> A *Do you want to make a cake?*
> B *Oh, I'm not good at baking. Could I do something else?*

4 Avoid Common Mistakes ⚠

1. Use the base form of the verb after *can, could, may, will,* or *would*.

> Could Lin ~~to~~ ride with you tomorrow?

2. Use *please* in a request at the end of the sentence or after the subject.

>   *please*
> Can ~~please~~ I ride with you to the party?

> **or**

>   *party, please*
> Can ~~please~~ I ride with you to the ~~party~~?

3. Don't use *could* in short answers to requests for permission.

>   *can*
> "Could I use your phone, please?"   "Yes, you ~~could~~."

4. Don't use *could* or *would* to respond to requests to do things.

>   *will*
> "Would you carry this bag for me?"   "Yes, I ~~would~~."

Editing Task

Find and correct six more mistakes in the e-mail messages.

Hi, Luis. Do you mind if we change the time to meet at the park tomorrow? Could we ~~to~~ meet at noon?   Peg

Hi, Peg. Yes, we could. I will be there a few minutes before noon. Do you mind if Omar comes, too? He wants to help.   Luis

Hi, Luis. No, that's fine. Please would you ask him to call me?   Peg

Hi, Peg. Yes, I would. We'll ~~to~~ bring soda. OK?   Luis

Hi, Luis. That would be great. I can ~~to~~ make some snacks. Oh, could please you bring plates and napkins? Thanks!   Peg

5 | Grammar for Writing

Permission, Requests, and Offers in Writing

Writers use modals for permission, requests, and offers in e-mails and letters to plan events with other people.

These modals are common in e-mails, memos, and letters to friends and colleagues. Remember:

- **Use *may* and *could* to ask permission in more formal situations.**

  Mr. Smith, <u>could</u> we borrow your laptop for the meeting tomorrow?

- **Use *can, could, will,* and *would* to request things from other people. Use *Do you mind if . . .* for difficult or inconvenient requests.**

  Tom, <u>would</u> you take notes at the meeting? Also, <u>do you mind if</u> we change the time to 8:00 a.m.? Sorry it is so early.

- **Use *can, could,* and *will* to offer assistance.**

  I <u>can</u> bring coffee and breakfast food for the meeting.

Pre-writing Task

1 Read the e-mail about a volunteer project. What does Alicia offer to do? What does she need other people to do?

Dear Yan and Kobe,

We need to work on our group project tomorrow. Do you mind if I ask you both to help me with some things? Thanks. Here are the things we need to do.

5 • Could we all meet at 1:00 tomorrow to work on the project? The only problem is, my roommate is having a study group at the apartment at that time. Kobe, do you mind if we meet at your house instead of my apartment?

 • If we meet at Kobe's house, I could bring some sandwiches. Yan,
10 would you be able to bring some dessert? Kobe, could you provide soda or juice?

 • Yan, could you get the information on the soup kitchen before we meet?

 • Kobe, would you call the homeless shelter and set up an
15 appointment for us to talk to the director?

 • Kobe, could you let me know if you want me to bring my laptop?

See you both tomorrow!

Alicia

2 Read the e-mail again. Underline the requests and circle the offers.

Writing Task

1 *Write* Use the e-mail in the Pre-writing Task to help you write an e-mail requesting help to plan something. Use the words you underlined and circled in the paragraph to ask people to do things and to make offers. You can write about one of these events or your own idea.

• a car wash to raise money for charity

• a group cleanup of a neighborhood in need

• a yard sale to raise money for an organization

• a fund-raiser for an animal shelter

2 *Self-Edit* Use the editing tips below to improve your sentences. Make any necessary changes.

1. Did you use words like *can, could, may, will, would,* and *Do you mind if . . . ?* to plan an event?
2. Did you use *may* and *could* to ask for permission in more formal situations?
3. Did you use *Do you mind if . . . ?* for difficult or inconvenient requests?
4. Did you use *can, could,* or *will* to offer assistance?
5. Did you avoid the mistakes in the Avoid Common Mistakes chart on page 250?

21

Advice and Suggestions
The Right Job

1 | Grammar in the Real World

A What are some important things to think about when you plan your career or look for a job? Read the article on advice for people looking for jobs. Which suggestion do you think is the most useful?

The Right Job for You

What are some important considerations[1] when you look for a new job? According to experts, you **ought to** think about these things:

First, know yourself! You **should** ask yourself exactly
5 what you want from a job. Is it money, interesting work, nice co-workers, or something else? Different people want different things from a job. Assess[2] yourself. Where[3] are you now, and where do you want to be?

You also **might want to** think about your personal relationships. Consider which
10 relationships are going well, which ones are not, and, most importantly, why. This will help you understand how you relate to people you work with.

Make changes! If you had problems in another job (maybe you were always late, or you did not finish projects), then you **should** make changes *before* you take a new job. It is too late when you are in the job.

15 Decide what you *don't* want! If you just want a nine-to-five[4] job, you **had better not** work for a company that expects you to be on call 24-7.[5]

If you have an interview, prepare! You **should** find out about an employer's business before your interview. Study the company's website. You **could** also call the company. Ask to speak with someone about the job.

20 Of course, many of these ideas are common sense,[6] but a lot of people just don't think about them. As a result, they are very unhappy in their jobs.

[1]**consideration:** something to think about when making decisions | [2]**assess:** judge or decide about | [3]**where:** in what situation | [4]**nine-to-five:** 9:00 a.m. to 5:00 p.m., a typical workday | [5]**24-7:** twenty-four hours a day, seven days a week, all the time | [6]**common sense:** the ability to use good judgment in making decisions and to live in a safe way

B *Comprehension Check* Circle the correct words.

1. Everyone wants **the same things** / **different things** from a job.

2. Looking at your personal relationships **can** / **cannot** help you learn more about how you relate to co-workers.

3. It is **easy** / **difficult** to make changes after you have started a new job.

4. **Everyone** / **Not everyone** uses common sense when they look for a job.

C *Notice* Find the sentences in the article and complete them.

1. According to experts, you _____ think about these things.

2. You _____ ask yourself exactly what you want from a job.

3. You _____ also call the company.

In these sentences, do *ought to* and *should* show advice or show ability? Does *could* show ability or make a suggestion?

2 | Advice

▶ Grammar Presentation

Should, ought to, and *had better* are often used to give advice.	You **should** ask yourself exactly what you want from a job. You **had better** make changes before you take a new job.

2.1 Statements

Subject	Modal Verb / *Had Better (Not)*	Base Form of Verb	
I You He / She / It We They	**should** **shouldn't / should not** **ought to** **ought not to** **had better (not)** **'d better (not)**	make	changes.

2.2 *Yes / No* Questions and Responses

Should	Subject	Base Form of Verb		Responses	
Should	I you he / she / it we they	take	a different job?	Yes, you **should**. Yes, she **should**.	No, you **shouldn't**. No, she **shouldn't**.

2.3 Information Questions

Wh- Word	Should	Subject	Base Form of Verb		Wh- Word	Should	Base Form of Verb	
When **Who**	should	I you he / she / it we they	call?		**What** **Who**	should	come	next?

2.4 Using *Should, Ought to,* and *Had Better* for Advice

a. Use *should* and *ought to* for general advice.	You **should** assess yourself before you look for a job. She **ought to** look for a new job.
b. Use *had better (not)* only for very strong advice and warnings. *Had better (not)* is much stronger than *should* or *ought to*. It suggests that something negative will happen if you don't take the advice. We usually only use it in speaking.	You **had better** finish this project, or you might lose your job!
c. Use *should* in questions. *Ought to* and *had better* are not common in questions.	**Should** I ask about the salary at the interview?
d. Use *maybe, perhaps,* or *I think* to soften advice. These expressions usually go at the beginning of the sentence.	**Maybe** you should be more careful when you write your résumé. **I think** he ought to look for a different job.
e. You can also use *probably* to soften advice. It can go before or after *should*. It goes before *ought to*.	She **probably** should take the job. / She should **probably** take the job. She **probably** ought to take the job. She ~~ought to probably~~ take the job.

> *Should not* is much more common than *ought not to*.
> You can use *should not* in both speaking and writing.

Data from the Real World 🌐

Research shows that people often make advice stronger by adding *really*.

Really can go before or after *should/shouldn't*. When *really* goes before *should/shouldn't*, it is stronger.	You should **really** get advice from a career advisor. You **really** shouldn't quit your job before you've found another one.
Really goes before *ought to* and *had better*.	You **really** had better try to keep your current job. You **really** ought to update your résumé. You ~~ought to **really**~~ update your résumé.

▶ Grammar Application

Exercise 2.1 Statements

Unscramble the words and add *you* to write sentences that give advice. Sometimes more than one answer is possible.

1. decide what you want from a job / should / really / .

   You really should decide what you want from a job. / You should really decide what you want from a job.

2. had better / think about the hours you prefer / really / .

   _____

3. ought to / decide if you want to be on call 24-7 / perhaps / .

   _____

4. maybe / look for job advertisements online / should / .

   _____

5. tell your family about your plans / ought to / probably / .

   _____

6. really / shouldn't / get discouraged / .

   _____

7. should / ask for advice from a career counselor / I think / .

   _____

8. really / take a job you don't like / had better not / !

   _____

Exercise 2.2 Asking for and Giving Advice

A Complete the requests for job advice from an online forum. Add *should*. Sometimes you also need to add a *Wh-* word.

1. I've been offered my dream job. However, it is far from my family and friends. _Should_ I take the job?

   – Arthur, New York, NY

2. I need help to make plans for my career.

   _____ I talk to?

   – Ari, Toledo, OH

3. I've been looking for a job for several months. I finally have an offer, but it's not the perfect job for me. However, I really need money.

   _____ I take the job?

   – Camilla, San Francisco, CA

4. I absolutely hate my job! I want to look for another one, but I have lots of student loans. _____ I do?

   – Samuel, Miami, FL

5. I would like to change careers, but I don't have experience in the career I like. My friend told me to do volunteer work to get experience.

   _____ I do this?

   – Eleni, Austin, TX

6. I'm almost finished with school and I don't know what kind of job I want.

   _____ I do?

   – Katya, Denver, CO

7. My parents think money is the most important thing in a job. I want to look for a job that makes me happy. _____ I listen to my parents?

   – Helen, Seattle, WA

B *Pair Work* Discuss the situations in A with a partner. What do you think each person should do? Compare your answers.

> *A I think Arthur ought to talk to his family about his decision.*
> *B I think he should just take the job. It's his dream job.*

C Listen to a career counselor give advice for each situation. Write the advice you hear.

1. Arthur *had better not take* the job and move.

2. Ari _____ to a career counselor.

3. _____ Camilla _____ the job.

4. _____ Samuel _____ for another job.

5. Yes, Eleni _____ some volunteer work.

6. Katya _____ talking to people.

7. _____ Terry _____ looking for

   another job. It doesn't sound good, but he _____

   to his boss, too.

8. Helen _____ what makes her happy.

Exercise 2.3 More Asking for and Giving Advice

A Write two to four questions asking for advice about jobs / work or school.

B *Pair Work* Exchange your questions from A with a partner. Write responses to your partner's requests for advice. Then read and compare the advice. Do you agree with the advice? Why or why not?

> *A I need to find a part-time job. Where should I look?*
> *B I think you should ask at the school cafeteria. They often need help there.*

3 | Suggestions

▶ Grammar Presentation

Might (want to), *could*, *why don't / doesn't*, and *why not* are often used to make suggestions. Suggestions are not as strong as advice.	You **might want to** schedule your interview in the afternoon. **Why don't** you prepare questions for the interview?

3.1 Suggestions with *Might Want To* and *Could*

Subject	Modal Verb	Base Form of Verb	
I You He / She / It We They	**might want to** **might not want to** **could**	call	the company.

3.2 Suggestions with *Why Don't / Doesn't . . . ?*

Why Don't / Doesn't	Subject	Base Form of Verb
Why don't	I you we they	ask?
Why doesn't	he / she / it	

3.3 Suggestions with *Why Not . . . ?*

Why Not	Base Form of Verb	
Why not	buy	a new suit for the interview?

3.4 Making Suggestions

a. Use *might (want to)* and *could* to make suggestions. They often express a choice of possible actions.	You **might** *schedule your interview in the morning, or you* **could** *wait until the afternoon.*
Might is often used with *want to*.	You **might want to** *think about volunteer work.* You **might not want to** *ask that question in an interview.*
Do not use *could not* in negative suggestions. Use *might not want to*.	You ~~could not~~ *ask that question in an interview.*
b. *Why not* and *Why don't / doesn't* are both question forms and end with a question mark.	**Why don't you** *prepare questions for your interview?* **Why not** *prepare questions for your interview?*
Why don't / doesn't and *Why not* are very common in conversation. Do not use them in academic writing.	Say: "**Why don't** *you practice for your interview?*" Write: *Interviewees* **might want to** *practice for their interviews.*

▶ Grammar Application

Exercise 3.1 Making Suggestions

Complete the conversations. Circle the correct words.

1. *A* I sent my résumé in for a job a few weeks ago, but I haven't had any response.

   B **You could** / **Why don't you** call the company.

2. *A* I have an interview next week, and I'm worried about getting there on time. Traffic is so bad.

   B **You might** / **Why not** schedule the interview for the middle of the day, when traffic isn't as bad?

3. *A* I can't find a job in my field. I really need some work, any work!

   B You **why not** / **might want to** look for temporary work. That's often easier to find.

4. *A* I have an interview tomorrow, but I don't know a lot about the company.

   B **You might want to** / **Why don't you** do some research online. I'll help you.

5. *A* I'm nervous about my interview on Monday. I don't know what they'll ask me.

   B Well, **we could** / **why not** practice together. I can ask you questions.

6. *A* I'm going to dress casually for my interview tomorrow. It's a very informal company.

   B You **could not** / **might not want to** dress too casually. It's still a job interview.

7. *A* I have to drive to my interview tomorrow, and I always get lost when I drive.

   B **You might want to** / **Why don't you** print out directions or use a GPS.

8. *A* I just had a good interview, and I'm really interested in the job.

   B **Why don't** / **Why not** you follow up with a thank-you note? It's always a good idea.

Exercise 3.2 More Suggestions

A *Pair Work* Read about Alex. He has a job interview in a few days. Write three more suggestions for him. Then compare answers with a partner.

I always stay up late and wake up late in the morning.

My suit is pretty old.

I don't know what questions they'll ask me at the interview.

I don't have directions to the interview location.

I haven't had a haircut in a long time.

I talk too much when I'm nervous.

1. *You could go to bed early.* _____

2. _____

3. _____

4. _____

B *Pair Work* Tell a partner what you worry about in job interviews. Give each other suggestions.

   A I worry about the questions they might ask.

   B You might want to research the job and the company. Maybe that will help you.

4 Avoid Common Mistakes ⚠

1. Do not forget *had* or *'d* when you write *had better*.

      had
   You ⱯBetter start looking for another job.

2. Use *had better (not)* only for very strong advice and warnings.

           should
   At an interview, you ~~had better~~ speak clearly and look interested in the questions.

3. Do not use *could not* in negative suggestions. Use *might not want to*.

    might not want to
   You ~~could not~~ wear jeans for the interview.

4. Do not use an *-ing* form or a *to-* infinitive after *Why not*.

      go
   Why not ~~going~~ to a career advisor?

   Why not ~~to~~ leave at 6:00 a.m.?

Editing Task

Find and correct five more mistakes in the conversation.

Jordan There are a lot of changes happening at my company.

I'm worried I might lose my job.

Isabela Well, you better probably start looking for something else.

                had (inserted above "you")

Jordan I guess so.

5 **Isabela** At the same time, you better try to keep your current job. They say

it's a lot harder to find a new job when you're unemployed.

Jordan Is there anything I can do?

Isabela Yes, there's a lot you can do. First, why not to talk to your boss? You get along

well, right? Why not asking for feedback on your work? Then, you probably ought

10   to tell your boss you're working on those things. You might want to keep in touch

with her by e-mail.

Jordan OK. What else?

Isabela Well, do extra work. You ought to take on extra tasks whenever you can. And you

could not complain about anything.

15 **Jordan** That makes sense. Thanks, Isabela. I'd better ask you for advice more often!

5 | Grammar for Writing ✎

Giving Advice and Suggestions

Writers use *should, ought to, had better,* and *might (want to)* to describe ways to solve problems, offer solutions, and say why the solutions are good.

These modals are common in magazine articles, advice columns, personal e-mails, and other texts that give people advice.

Remember:

- **Use *had better* only to give strong advice or warnings.**
  You <u>had better</u> apologize to the boss. If you do not, you will probably lose your job.

- **You can make advice stronger with *really* before or after *should*. When *really* goes before *should*, it is even stronger.**
  They <u>really</u> should leave soon. You should <u>really</u> check the traffic report.

- **You can soften advice with *maybe, perhaps,* and *I think* at the beginning of sentences.**
  <u>Perhaps</u> he shouldn't wear those pants to the interview.

Pre-writing Task

1 Read the advice column below. What is the question about? Which suggestion in the reply do you think is best?

Problems? Ask Aunt Advice!

Dear Aunt Advice,

I have my first job interview next week. I am nervous. Please help.

– Nervous in New York

Dear Nervous,

5   Here is some general job-interview advice. Good interviewers ask you questions, but they also want you to ask questions. You should come to the interview with interesting questions. This will help you to feel well prepared. Also, you should be ready to write down some questions during the interview, so you should bring a small notebook. This shows that you are very interested in what the interviewer is saying. You
10 might want to ask the interviewer if it is all right to take notes first, though. Interviewers often ask about your weaknesses. You really should make a list of them in advance. I think you should be honest about your weaknesses, but only the weaknesses that will not cause problems on the job. Also, you had better be ready to talk about your plans to

overcome these weaknesses. This shows that you want to learn and grow in your job. In
15 addition, you really ought to practice an interview in advance. Perhaps you could ask a
friend to help you. However, you had better do that a few days in advance so you have
time to fix any problems.

   If you follow this advice, you show the interviewer that you are serious about the
job and the company, and that helps you feel less nervous.
20 Good luck,
   Aunt Advice

2 Read the text again. Underline the sentences that give advice. Which sentences
offer strong advice? What words make the advice strong?

Writing Task

1 *Write*   Use the advice column in the Pre-writing Task to help you write a letter
about a problem and a reply letter that gives advice. You can ask for advice about:

- asking a boss for more money or time off
- getting along with a difficult co-worker
- finding a job
- your own idea

2 *Self-Edit*   Use the editing tips below to improve your paragraph. Make any
necessary changes.

1. Did you use *should*, *ought to*, *had better*, and *might (want to)* to describe ways
   to solve a problem?
2. Did you use *had better* for strong advice or warnings?
3. Did you use *really* to make advice stronger?
4. Did you avoid the mistakes in the Avoid Common Mistakes chart on page 262?

Necessity, Prohibition, and Preference

How to Sell It

1 | Grammar in the Real World

A What are three different kinds of advertising you see every day? Read the article about advertising companies. What are two difficulties for advertisers?

The Challenges[1] of Advertising[2]

Advertising is not a new idea. Long ago, sellers called out to people on the street. They tried to persuade[3] people to buy their products. Now advertising is everywhere. It is on the street, on the Web, in magazines, and on phones.

Although there are now many ways to advertise, it is not an easy business. There are
5 many challenges. Companies **need to** appeal[4] to consumers so they buy their products. This can be quite difficult because people have so many choices these days. Each advertiser **must** make its choice seem better than all the others.

Advertising is also very expensive. Companies **would rather** not spend a lot of money on it. They **would prefer** to save their money. However, to sell their products, companies
10 often **need to** spend large amounts of money on ads. Consumers see or hear up to 3,000 advertising messages each day. Each one **has to** be clever.[5] This means companies **have to** pay to show the ads on TV, online, or in other places, and they also **need to** pay creative people to make them.

There is another challenge for companies when they advertise. Today, there are
15 numerous rules they **must** follow. For example, they **must not** lie. Companies also **need to** be careful when they try to sell products to children.

Advertisers **must** do a number of different things at once. This is not easy, but it is also a big business with big rewards. Just one good advertisement can convince millions of people to buy a product.

---

[1]**challenge:** something that needs great mental or physical effort to be done well | [2]**advertising:** making something known generally in public, especially in order to sell it | [3]**persuade:** cause someone to do or believe something, especially by explaining why they should | [4]**appeal (to):** be attractive or interesting | [5]**clever:** showing quick intelligence in doing something

B *Comprehension Check* Answer the questions.

1. How did people advertise in the past?
2. Why is it difficult for advertisers to appeal to consumers?
3. How many advertisements do people see or hear each day?
4. What must advertisers not do?

C *Notice* Find the sentences in the article and complete them.

1. Companies _____ appeal to consumers so they buy their products.

2. Companies _____ not spend a lot of money on it.

3. They _____ to save their money.

4. Each one _____ be clever.

Which of these sentences talk about something that is necessary? Which talk about something that is preferred?

2 | Necessity and Prohibition

▶ Grammar Presentation

Have to, have got to, need to, and *must (not)* are used to say what is necessary, not necessary, or prohibited.	*An ad* **has to** *appeal to consumers.* (necessary) *They* **do not need to** *advertise abroad.* (not necessary) *Companies* **must** *follow rules when they create ads.* (necessary) *They* **must not** *lie in their advertising.* (prohibited)

2.1 *Have To, Have Got To,* and *Need To*: Statements

Subject	Have To / Have Got To / Need To	Base Form of Verb	
I You We They	**have to / do not have to** **have got to** **need to / do not need to**	be buy	clever. advertising.
He / She / It	**has to / doesn't have to** **has got to** **needs to / doesn't need to**		

2.2 *Must*: Statements

Subject	Modal Verb	Base Form of Verb	
I You He / She / It We They	**must** **must not / mustn't**	be buy	clever. advertising.

2.3 *Have To* and *Need To*: Yes / No Questions

Do / Does	Subject	Have To / Need To	Base Form of Verb
Do	you	**have to**	advertise?
Does	he / she / it	**need to**	

2.4 *Have To* and *Need To*: Information Questions

Wh- Word	Do / Does	Subject	Have To / Need To	Base Form of Verb
When **Why**	do	you	**have to**	advertise?
Where	does	he / she / it	**need to**	

Wh- Word	Have To / Need To	Base Form of Verb
Who	**has to** **needs to**	advertise?

2.5 Expressing Necessity and Prohibition

a. Use *have to* and *need to* to say something is necessary.	*Advertisers **have to** think about consumers.*
Have to is twice as common as *need to*.	*The company **needs to** be more creative.*
b. You can also use *have got to* in affirmative statements. It is usually less formal. The contraction for *has* is *'s*.	*The ad **has got to** appeal to a lot of people. It**'s got to** be interesting.*
Have got to is not usually used in negative sentences.	*The ad **hasn't got to** appeal to children.*
c. *Must* is very strong and sounds formal or official. It is often used in writing to state rules or laws and is rare in speaking.	*Advertising companies **must** follow these rules.* *He **must** report this immediately.*
d. You can use *don't have to* and *don't need to* to say something is not necessary.	*She **doesn't need to** finish that.*
However, use *must not / mustn't* to express strong prohibition or to forbid something.	*Companies **must not** lie in their advertising.*
Be careful: *have to* and *must* have a similar meaning in the affirmative, but they are very different in negative sentences.	*You **must / have to** use a pen.* (A pen is necessary.) *You **don't have to** use a pen.* (A pen is not necessary. You have a choice.) *You **must not** use a pen.* (A pen is prohibited. You have no choice.)

2.5 Expressing Necessity and Prohibition *(continued)*

e. Use *have to* and *need to* to ask about necessity. Use a form of *do* in the question and answer.	*"**Do** we **have to** follow this rule?"* *"Yes, we **do**."* *"**Does** this ad **need to** appeal to kids?"* *"No, it **doesn't**."*
We often use *can't* instead of *must not* to express prohibition, especially in spoken English.	Say: *"You **can't** do that. It's against the rules."* Write: *Drivers **must not** exceed the speed limit.*

🔊 Pronunciation Focus: *Have To, Has To, Have Got To*

In informal conversation:	*have to* is often pronounced "hafta." *has to* is often pronounced "hasta." *got to* is often pronounced "gotta."

▶ Grammar Application

Exercise 2.1 Statements

A 🔊 Listen to an advertising manager discuss plans with his employees. Complete the sentences with the verbs you hear.

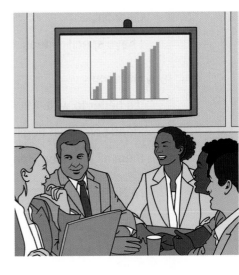

1. We *'ve got to* do this quickly, so we really *have to* work together.

2. Each team _____ choose a leader.

3. The leader _____ organize the team.

4. Then, you'll all _____ work together to make a plan for the project.

5. I absolutely _____ have all plans by the end of the week.

6. You really _____ e-mail a report of your progress to me at the end of each week.

7. The report _____ be long, but it _____ explain your progress clearly.

8. You _____ forget this because I _____ report to the president every week.

9. We _____ create some really interesting ads.

10. But remember, we _____ be honest in all of the ads.

B Which sentence says that something is not necessary? Which sentence says that something is prohibited?

Exercise 2.2 Questions and Answers

Complete the e-mail messages with the correct form of the verbs in parentheses.

Hi team,   October 21, 10:00 a.m.

Remember, we are meeting tomorrow to discuss our plan. I _need to_ (need to)
get your ideas on it. I _____ (have to) hand the plan in on Friday. Let
me know if you have questions.   – Nick

Nick,   October 21, 10:15 a.m.

_____ we _____ (have to) bring specific ideas for ads
to the meeting?   – Blanca

Hi Blanca,   October 21, 10:30 a.m.

No, you _____ (not need to) have specific ideas. But, we
_____ (must) start brainstorming soon. I _____ (have to)
give Mr. Gomez an update on our ideas next week.   – Nick

Dear Nick,   October 21, 10:45 a.m.

I have specific ideas. Is it OK if I start to work on them?   – Jason

Hi Jason,   October 21, 11:00 a.m.

It's better to wait. Mr. Gomez _____ (have to) approve our
ideas before we begin work on them. He _____ (need to) put
them all together. Bring them tomorrow, and we can discuss them.   – Nick

Hi Nick,   October 21, 11:15 a.m.

When _____ Mr. Gomez _____ (need to) have the
ideas? I will be on vacation for a few days next week. _____ I
_____ (have to) finish them before I leave?   – Claire

Dear Claire,   October 21, 11:30 a.m.

Yes, I'm afraid so. We _____ (have got to) do them quickly. He
_____ (need to) have them sometime next week.   – Nick

Exercise 2.3 More Questions and Answers

A *Over to You* Write answers to the questions.

1. What is one thing you have to do every day?

   _____

2. What is something you need to do but haven't done yet?

   _____

3. What is something you do at work or school that you don't have to do?

   _____

4. What is something that you must do at work or school?

   _____

5. What is something that you must not do at work or school?

   _____

B *Pair Work* Ask and answer the questions in A with a partner. Try to add extra information.

   A What is one thing you have to do every day?
   B I have to take my children to school every day. Their school starts at 7:30, so I have to get up at 6:15.

C *Group Work* Tell the class about your partner.

   Raul has to take his children to school every day. Their school starts at 7:30, so he has to get up at 6:15.

3 | Preference

▶ Grammar Presentation

Would rather, would like to, and *would prefer* are used to express preferences.	I **would rather not watch** those commercials. They **would like to see** some new and interesting ads. I**'d prefer to turn** the TV off.

3.1 *Would Rather*: Statements

Subject	*Would Rather (Not)*	Base Form of Verb
I You He / She / It We They	**would rather (not)**	advertise.

3.2 *Would Like* and *Would Prefer*: Statements

Subject	Would (Not) Like / Would Prefer (Not)	Infinitive
I You He / She / It We They	**would (not) like** **would prefer (not)**	to advertise.

3.3 *Yes / No* Questions

Would	Subject		Infinitive		Would	Subject		Base Form of Verb
Would	you	**like** **prefer**	to advertise?		**Would**	you	**rather**	advertise?

3.4 Information Questions

Wh- Word	Would	Subject		Infinitive		Wh- Word	Would		Infinitive
What	would	you	**like** **prefer**	to advertise?		**Who**	would	**like** **prefer**	to buy this product?

Wh- Word	Would	Subject	Base Form of Verb		Wh- Word	Would		Base Form of Verb
What	would	you	rather advertise?		**Who**	would	rather	buy this product?

3.5 Expressing Preferences

a. You can use *would rather, would like,* and *would prefer* to express preference. *Would prefer* is more formal.	I **would rather** spend a little money on advertising. I **would prefer** to listen to the radio.
Use *would rather* with a base form of the verb. Use *would like* and *would prefer* with an infinitive. The contraction of *would* is *'d.*	I **would rather** see more interesting advertising. I **would like / would prefer** to see more interesting advertising. I**'d like** to see more interesting advertising.
b. In negative sentences, *not* goes between *would* and *like.* It goes after *would prefer* and *would rather.*	He **wouldn't like** to work at that advertising company. He **would prefer not** to work at that advertising company. We**'d rather not** watch all the commercials.

3.5 Expressing Preferences (continued)

c. You can use the verb *prefer* without *would*. When used without *would*, *prefer* takes *-s* with *he / she / it*.	She **would prefer to** watch shorter commercials. She **prefers** to watch shorter commercials. She ~~prefer~~ to watch shorter commercials.
d. *Would prefer* and *prefer* can be followed by a noun, an infinitive, or a verb + *-ing*.	He prefers / would prefer **a TV channel** without ads. He prefers / would prefer **to watch** TV without commercials. He prefers / would prefer **watching** TV without commercials.
e. Use *or* in questions about preference to offer a choice. The verb after *or* is usually in the base form.	Would you like to go out **or** (to) stay home? Would you rather go out **or** stay home?
f. You can use *I'd rather not* to respond to suggestions or requests.	A We could go out tonight. B **I'd rather not.** I'm tired.
g. You can make a comparison with *would rather* and *than*. If there is a verb after *than*, it is also in the base form.	**I'd rather see** one long ad **than** a few short ones. **I'd rather see** ads on the Internet **than watch** them on TV.

▶ # Grammar Application

Exercise 3.1 Questions and Answers

Complete the conversation between two colleagues at an advertising agency. Use the correct form and the correct order of the words in parentheses. Add words if necessary.

A Let's discuss the ad for the new music player. What do you think? What

*would* consumers _*like to see*_ (would like / see)?
(1)   (1)

B Well, we need to give some detail about the size, weight, memory – things like that.

Not too much, though. People _____ (not / would rather / get)
(2)

all the details in an ad. I think a consumer usually _____ (prefer / get)
(3)

a general idea and then research it more if they're interested.

A OK, good point. _____ they _____ (would rather / see)
(4)   (4)

an ad that's more informative or one that's more fun?

B Well, I _____ (not / would like / see) an ad that's just informative.
(5)

I _____ (would rather / see) one that's really fun than one that's
(6)

really informative. That seems a little boring.

A OK, but I think we need to do both – entertain and inform.

B True. Now, what do you think? _____
(7)
people _____ (would prefer / see)
(7)
a man or a woman in the ad?

A Let's include both.

B I _____ (not / would rather). It
(8)
costs a lot to hire two actors.

A Both men and women buy music players.

I _____ (would prefer / hire) both. I think it's worth the cost.
(9)

B Let's think about that. This is a good start. We can discuss all of this tomorrow.

Exercise 3.2 More Questions and Answers

Unscramble the words to make questions.

1. see a lot of ads on TV / would / rather / not / you / ?

   Would you rather not see a lot of ads on TV?

2. prefer / e-mail ads / you / advertising by mail / do / or / ?

   _____

3. a lot of ads before you buy things / to see / like / would / you / ?

   _____

4. you / to watch TV / prefer / without commercials / would / ?

   _____

5. not / have advertising / would / you / online / rather / ?

   _____

6. ads on the radio / you / ads on TV / do / prefer / or / ?

   _____

7. more informative ads or more funny ads / you / like / to see / would / ?

   _____

8. not / rather / would / any advertising at all / you / have / ?

   _____

4 Avoid Common Mistakes ⚠

1. **Use *don't have to* or *don't need to* to say something is not necessary, not *must not*.**

   don't need to
   You ~~must not~~ take notes. I'll give you a copy at the end of the meeting.

2. **Do not use an infinitive with *would rather*. Use an infinitive with *would like* and (*would*) *prefer*.**

   We would rather ~~to~~ use this idea for the ad.

3. **Use *would* before *rather*.**

   would
   I ∧ rather not start work at 7 o'clock.

Editing Task

Find and correct seven more mistakes in the e-mail messages.

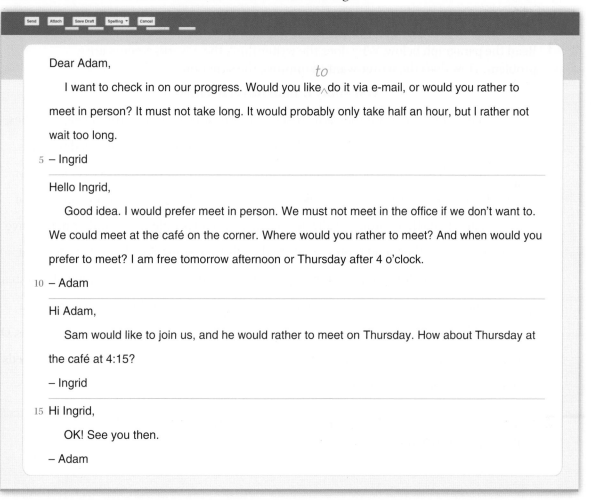

Dear Adam,

    I want to check in on our progress. Would you like ∧*to* do it via e-mail, or would you rather to meet in person? It must not take long. It would probably only take half an hour, but I rather not wait too long.

5 – Ingrid

Hello Ingrid,

    Good idea. I would prefer meet in person. We must not meet in the office if we don't want to. We could meet at the café on the corner. Where would you rather to meet? And when would you prefer to meet? I am free tomorrow afternoon or Thursday after 4 o'clock.

10 – Adam

Hi Adam,

    Sam would like to join us, and he would rather to meet on Thursday. How about Thursday at the café at 4:15?

    – Ingrid

15 Hi Ingrid,

    OK! See you then.

    – Adam

5 | Grammar for Writing

Writing About Necessities and Expressing Preferences

Writers use *have to*, *need to*, *must*, *would rather*, *would like*, and *would prefer* to talk about problems or situations that they want to change or improve.

Have to, *need to*, *must*, *would rather*, *would like*, and *would prefer* are common in articles, newspaper editorials, and other texts that give personal opinions. Remember:

- **Have to and need to describe things that are necessary. Must is very strong.**
  The government <u>must</u> do something about ads on highways. People <u>need to</u> pay attention when they are driving, not look at ads.

- **Use would rather, would like, would prefer, or prefer to talk about preferences.**
  I <u>would like</u> to know about good deals near me, but I <u>would rather not</u> receive advertisements for them on my phone.

Pre-writing Task

1 Read the paragraph below. Why does the writer think the advertisements are a problem? How does the writer want to improve the situation?

Too Many E-mail Advertisements

There are too many e-mail advertisements. These e-mails advertise cheap watches, medicine, diet pills, online classes, and other things. Most people do not need to buy these things. They would prefer not to see ads for them. They often have to delete 20 or 30 of these e-mails every day. This takes too much time. Many people would like to use

5 an e-mail service that automatically deletes them. Some people would rather not receive these e-mails, so they send reply e-mails to the ads to unsubscribe them. This does not usually help. In addition, many of these e-mails are from criminals who would like to steal from you. For example, the e-mail offers a great price on jewelry, but you need to enter your credit card number. The thieves use your credit card to buy things for themselves. Of

10 course, the law says they must not do this, but it is very common. The government needs to do more to stop these criminals.

2 Read the paragraph again. Underline the sentences with necessities and requirements. Circle the sentences with preferences.

Writing Task

1 *Write* Use the paragraph in the Pre-writing Task to help you write a paragraph complaining about something and insisting on some changes. You can write about:

- ads on TV
- ads on the radio
- ads in text messages
- ads on roads
- ads on websites
- your own idea

2 *Self-Edit* Use the editing tips below to improve your paragraph. Make any necessary changes.

1. Did you use *have to*, *need to*, *must*, *would rather*, *would like*, and *would prefer* to talk about something you want to change or improve?
2. Did you use *have to* and *need to* when something is necessary? Did you use *must* only for very strong meanings?
3. Did you use *would rather*, *would like*, *would prefer*, or *prefer* to express preferences?
4. Did you avoid the mistakes in the Avoid Common Mistakes chart on page 275?

Present and Future Probability
Life Today, Life Tomorrow

1 | Grammar in the Real World

A What is one way you think society will be different in the future? Read the article about trends in the United States. What is happening in the United States now? What might happen in the future?

The United States of Tomorrow

Now

30 years from now

    Which current trends¹ are likely to affect us most? Which trends **might** be important for society in the future? One trend that **could** be important in the United States is a decline² in the yearly birthrate.³ The birthrate has been going down for several years. Why is this happening? According to experts, there **may** be more
5 than one reason for this change. Women **might** be choosing to have fewer children because more women now have careers. The economy **might** also affect birthrates. Today, it costs more than $300,000 to raise a child from birth to age 17. Even small changes in the economy **could** increase this cost. As a result, couples **may** worry about having children during unsure economic times.
10   How **could** a lower birthrate today affect U.S. society in the future? This is not completely clear. Some effects **could** be positive. For example, cities **could** become less crowded, and there **may** be less pollution. However, other effects **could** be negative. There **might** be fewer people in the workforce. This **could** cause economic

¹**trend:** direction of changes or developments | ²**decline:** a decrease in amount or quality | ³**yearly birthrate:** a measure of how many children are born each year

difficulties. In addition, as people age, there **could** be fewer doctors and other
15 health professionals to care for them. This **could** cause a decline in the general
health of the population.

No one can predict[4] exactly what society will be like in the future. However,
when experts study trends like the yearly birthrate, they can learn important facts
to help us plan for a better tomorrow.

[4]**predict:** say that an event will happen in the future

B *Comprehension Check* Answer the questions.

1. What are two possible reasons for the decline in the yearly birthrate?
2. How much does it cost to raise a child in the United States?
3. What is one possible positive result of the change in the birthrate?
4. What is one possible negative result of this change?

C *Notice* Find the sentences in the article and complete them.

1. The economy _____ also affect birthrates.

2. Even small changes in the economy _____ increase this cost.

3. For example, cities _____ become less crowded.

4. There _____ be fewer people in the workforce.

Do these sentences describe something that is certain or uncertain? Are *could* and
might used to talk about the present, the future, or both?

2 Present Probability

▶ Grammar Presentation

The modals *can't, cannot, could (not), may (not),
might (not), must (not),* and *should (not)* talk about
probability in the present. These modals express
how certain you are that something is true.

This **could** be because more women now
have careers.

The economy **might** also affect birthrates.

2.1 Affirmative Statements

Subject	Modal Verb	Base Form of Verb	
I	**must**		
You	**should**		
He / She / It	**may**	be	important.
We	**might**		
They	**could**		

2.2 Negative Statements

Subject	Modal Verb		Base Form of Verb	
I You He / She / It We They	**must not / mustn't could not / couldn't cannot / can't should not / shouldn't may not might not**	be		important.

2.3 Expressing Present Probability

Certain	**a.** When you are **certain** that something is true in the present, you do not need a modal. Use a present form.	*The birthrate this year **is** not the same as last year.* *The birthrate **is declining**.*
Almost Certain	**b.** Use *must (not)* to draw a conclusion about the present, often because you have evidence. You are **almost certain** about your conclusion.	*She **must not live** nearby. She never walks to work.*
	Do not use the contraction *mustn't* in this case.	*She ~~mustn't~~ live nearby. She never walks to work.*
	c. Use *could not, couldn't, cannot,* or *can't* when you are **almost certain** that something is impossible. These modals usually express strong disbelief or surprise. We usually use *can't* or *couldn't*.	*The birthrate statistics **can't be** right. They look completely wrong.* *They **couldn't be** at home. They left for vacation yesterday.*
Fairly Certain	**d.** Use *should, should not,* or *shouldn't* when you are **fairly certain** that something is true, often because you have evidence. We often use *shouldn't*.	*They **should be** at work. They usually are at this time of the day.* *They **shouldn't be** at work. It's Saturday.*
Not Certain	**e.** Use *may (not), might (not),* or *could* when you are **not certain** that something is true. You are uncertain, but you are making an "educated guess."	*The economy **may (not) be** the reason for the declining birthrate. Experts are not sure.*
	Do not use *mightn't*. It is very rare.	*The economy **might not be** the reason for the declining birthrate.* *The economy ~~mightn't~~ be the reason for the declining birthrate. Experts are not sure.*
	f. *Can* is not usually used for present probability. Use *may, might,* or *could*.	*They ~~can be~~ related. They look similar.* *They **might be** related. They look similar.*

2.4 Answers to Questions About the Present

a. You can use modals of present probability to answer questions about the present. Use them when you are not 100 percent sure about your answer.	*"Where are they?"* *"They **might be** at home."* *"What does this information mean?"* *"It **could mean** society is changing."*
b. In short answers to *Yes / No* questions, you can use the modal alone.	*"Do they know about this?"* *"They **must**."*
c. If *be* is the main verb in *Yes / No* questions, use the modal + *be* in short answers.	*"Are they correct?"* *"They **must be**."*

▶ # Grammar Application

Exercise 2.1 Present Probability

A ◀)) Listen to the conversation about a trend for young adults. Complete the sentences you hear.

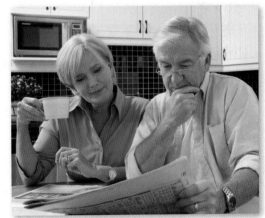

1. The economy _must_ be part of the reason.

2. It _____ be easy if you have a lot of debt and college loans.

3. And it _____ be hard for young people to find a good job these days.

4. Yes, but there _____ be other reasons, too.

5. They _____ be able to afford an apartment.

6. It _____ be better financially for them to live at home.

7. It _____ always be easy for them.

8. Maybe, but it _____ be nice, too.

9. Some parents _____ like to have their children around as they get older.

10. I guess it _____ depend on the family.

11. Of course. It _____ .

B 🔊 Listen again. How certain are the speakers about each statement? Check (✓) the correct box.

	Not Certain	Almost Certain
1. The economy is part of the reason young adults move back home.	☐	☑
2. It isn't easy if you have a lot of debt and college loans.	☐	☐
3. It is hard for young people to find a good job these days.	☐	☐
4. There are other reasons students move home.	☐	☐
5. Students can't afford apartments.	☐	☐
6. It is better financially for them to live at home.	☐	☐
7. It isn't always easy for parents.	☐	☐
8. It is nice when children return home, too.	☐	☐
9. Some parents like to have their children around as they get older.	☐	☐
10. It depends on the family. (female speaker)	☐	☐
11. It depends on the family. (male speaker)	☐	☐

Exercise 2.2 Questions and Answers About Present Probability

Circle the correct words. Add *be* where necessary.

1. *A* Is this information correct?

   B It (**must**)/ **could** ___*be*___ . We checked it very carefully.

2. *A* Is the birthrate changing?

   B It **must not** / **may** _____ . We'll know when we have all the statistics.

3. *A* Does he have children?

   B He **shouldn't** / **must** _____ . I see him walking with a little boy every morning.

4. *A* Does she know him?

   B She **should** / **can't** _____ . They work in the same office.

5. *A* Do they know about this?

   B They **couldn't** / **might not** _____ . I'm not sure if anyone has discussed it.

6. *A* Is she away on vacation?

   B She **might not** / **can't** _____ . I just saw her a few minutes ago.

7. *A* Does he live far away?

   B He **might** / **can't** _____ . He's sometimes late for work.

8. *A* Does the birthrate affect society?

   B It **may** / **must** _____ . It's hard to know.

Exercise 2.3 Using Modals of Present Probability

A *Over to You* Write possible reasons for these trends. Use modals of present probability.

1. More people are going to college. *This might be because there are fewer jobs.*

2. More young adults live with their parents. _____

3. People have more credit card debt. _____

4. Fewer people have phones at home. _____

5. People are getting married later. _____

6. Couples are having children later. _____

B *Pair Work* Compare your reasons with a partner. Are they similar or different?

3 | Modals of Future Probability

▶ Grammar Presentation

Cannot, could (not), may (not), might (not), and *should (not)* talk about future probability.	Society **might change** a lot in the future. It **shouldn't be** difficult to see how things change.

3.1 Affirmative Statements

Subject	Modal Verb	Base Form of Verb	
I You He / She / It We They	**will** **should** **may** **might** **could**	be	different in the future.

3.2 Negative Statements

Subject	Modal Verb		Base Form of Verb	
I You He / She / It We They	will not / won't could not / couldn't cannot / can't should not / shouldn't may not might not	be		different in the future.

3.3 Expressing Future Probability

Certain	**a.** Use a future form (*will* or *be going to*) when you are **certain** about the future.	More people **will live** in cities in the future. A lot of cities **are going to be** bigger in the future.	
Almost Certain	**b.** Use *cannot* or *can't* when you are **almost certain** that something is impossible in the future. They usually express strong disbelief or surprise. We usually use *can't*.	The economy **can't** get any worse!	
Fairly Certain	**c.** Use *should (not)* or *shouldn't* when you are **fairly certain** about the future, often because you have evidence. In the negative, we usually use *shouldn't*.	The changes in society **should be** clear. It **shouldn't be** difficult to see the changes.	
Not Certain	**d.** Use *may (not)*, *might (not)*, or *could* when you are **not certain** about the future. You are uncertain, but you are making an "educated guess."	More people **may live** with their families in the future. It **could be** more difficult to find affordable housing.	
	Do not contract **may not**. **Mayn't** is rare.	There **may not** be any changes in the statistics next year. There ~~mayn't~~ be any changes in the statistics next year.	
	e. *Must*, *can*, and *couldn't* are not usually used for future probability.	They ~~must~~ be tired tomorrow. They ~~can~~ be tired tomorrow. They ~~couldn't~~ be tired tomorrow.	

3.4 Questions and Answers About Future Probability

a. *Should*, *may*, *might*, and *could* are not usually used to ask questions about the future. Use a future form instead. You can use modals of future probability to answer questions about the future.	"**Are** you **going to** go to the lecture?" "Yes, but I **might be** late." "When **is** the lecture **going to** start?" "It **should start** in a few minutes." "How long **will** the economy have problems?" "It **could be** a long time."

3.4 Questions and Answers About Future Probability *(continued)*

b. In short answers to *Yes / No* questions, you can use the modal alone.	*"Will society change?"* *"It **should**."*
c. If *be* is the main verb in *Yes / No* questions, you can use the modal + *be* in short answers.	*"Is the economy going to be different?"* *"It **should be**.*

▶ Grammar Application

Exercise 3.1 Future Probability

A ◀)) Listen to an interview about what schools and education might be like in the future. Complete the sentences with the words you hear.

1. Schools and education __*will*__ be quite different.

2. There _____ be small changes.

3. There _____ be larger ones.

4. Technology _____ be the most important thing.

5. It _____ be necessary to have physical schools in the future.

6. For example, parents and schools _____ organize social activities in new places.

7. In some ways, we _____ need libraries.

8. There _____ always be some people who want to read real books.

B ◀)) Listen again. How certain is Professor Li about each idea? Check (✓) the correct box.

	Not Certain	Certain
1. Schools and education will be quite different.	☐	☑
2. There will be small changes.	☐	☐
3. There will be larger changes.	☐	☐
4. Technology will be the most important thing.	☐	☐
5. There will not be physical schools in the future.	☐	☐
6. There will be new places to learn social skills.	☐	☐
7. There will not be libraries in the future.	☐	☐
8. Some people will want books in the future.	☐	☐

Exercise 3.2 Practicing Future Probability

Complete the online postings about future family trends. Circle the correct words.

Family Life in the Future: What Do You Think It Might Be Like?

Family life in the future will be more like it was in the past. Grandparents will live with their children and grandchildren. This **may** / **must** be for economic reasons, or it
(1)
may not / **might** just be easier. Grandparents could help raise the grandchildren. Also, it
(2)
might / **should not** be nice for grandparents to have young people in the same house.
(3)
– Miriam H.

Couples are having children later, when they are older. This **can't** / **may** cause problems.
(4)
Older parents **could** / **might not** find it difficult to deal with children, especially during their
(5)
children's teenage years.

– Jake P.

Technology **couldn't** / **might** affect families in the future. We're all busy texting,
(6)
talking on cell phones, or using computers. We don't have time to just talk anymore.
It shouldn't surprise us if families communicate less in the future. This **could** / **can't**
(7)
change family life a lot.

– Pete N.

Young adults are going to live at home longer. It **could** / **should not** be more difficult for
(8)
them to find jobs in the future, so they **should** / **may** need to live with their parents. This is
(9)
not necessarily a bad thing. It **may** / **may not** make families stronger over time.
(10)
– Darla B.

Exercise 3.3 Using Modals of Future Probability

A *Over to You* Write three predictions about the future. Use these topics or your own ideas.

- family life
- jobs and the workplace
- technology
- transportation
- living situations
- schools

I think family life could change a lot. More people may live in one house together.
We might have better public transportation in the future.

1. _____

2. _____

3. _____

B *Group Work*   Compare your predictions as a class or group. How similar or different are your ideas?

4 Avoid Common Mistakes ⚠

1. Do not use *can* for present or future probability.

It's after 5 o'clock, but they ~~can~~ *could* still be at work.

2. Do not confuse *maybe* with *may be*.

The situation ~~maybe~~ *may be* different in the future. ~~May be~~ *Maybe* things will change.

3. Do not use *couldn't* when you aren't certain. Use *may not*, *might not*, or *shouldn't*.

She ~~couldn't~~ *may not* be in a meeting right now. I'll check and see.

4. Do not use *must* or *must not* to talk about probability in the future.

The situation ~~must~~ *will* be different next year. It always changes.

5. Use the modal alone in short answers to *Yes / No* questions. Use the modal + *be* in short answers when *be* is the main verb in a *Yes / No* question.

"Do they work together?"   "They might ~~work~~."

"Is the meeting starting at 11:00 a.m.?"   "It may ∧ *be*."

Editing Task

Find and correct 11 more mistakes in the discussion about a class presentation.

   Jim   OK. The trend we're going to discuss in our presentation is the increase in

            the number of people going to college. Let's start by discussing reasons.

   Lucy   Well, it ~~can~~ *might* be because a lot of people are unemployed. They can be getting

            a degree because they don't have work. They stay busy at school.

5 *Alex*   Yes, I think that maybe the most important reason.

   Jim   But is that the only reason?

   Lucy   No, it can't.

   Alex   May be students are also preparing for a better job.

   Lucy   Yes, that can be another reason.

10 *Jim*   OK, good. May be we'll add more reasons later. What about the future

            effects of this trend, though? Will they be good or bad?

Alex There must be a lot of good effects in the future, I'm sure. It must be good to have more educated people in the workplace in the future.

15

Lucy Yes, but there can be some problems in the future, too. People could have a lot of debt when they finish school.

Jim Hmm. Good point. I think it couldn't be difficult to think of several more effects. We're doing very well so far. Let's summarize our ideas and see if we need any more information. We couldn't have enough, or we might have just what we need.

20

5 | Grammar for Writing ✎

Writing About Probability in the Present and Future

Writers often use modals like *cannot, could (not), may (not), might (not), must (not)*, and *should (not)* to talk about changes in the present that will affect things in the future.

These modals are common in newspaper reports, magazine articles, and academic writing about trends and future predictions.

Remember:

- **People do not usually use *must (not), can*, or *couldn't* to talk about future probability. Instead, use *cannot, should (not), may (not), might (not)*, or *could.***
  We do not know for sure, but we think more people <u>may</u> take courses online in the future.

- **Use *should (not)* when you are fairly certain because you have evidence.**
  More children are studying Chinese today, so there <u>should</u> be more fluent Chinese speakers in the future.

Pre-writing Task

1 Read the paragraph below. What trend is the writer writing about?

A New Trend in Education

More students are going to community colleges these days. Many of these students are planning to transfer to universities after two years. This trend could be because universities are getting more expensive. They are also becoming more competitive. This could be because more young people want to go to college than

5 before. This must be making the universities harder to get into. It should also make

community colleges more competitive in the future. In addition, class sizes might get

bigger. Students may not be able to register for the classes they want. It could take

longer than two years for a full-time student to finish. The average age of university

juniors and seniors could start to rise. However, community colleges are also getting

10 more tuition money. As a result, they should be able to avoid these problems by hiring

more teachers in the future.

2 Read the paragraph again. Underline the modal verbs. Which express present
probability? Which express future probability? When is the writer certain about
the future because he or she has evidence?

Writing Task

1 *Write* Use the paragraph in the Pre-writing Task to help you write a paragraph
about a current trend. Why do you think this trend is happening? How will it
affect the future? You can write about:

- the cost of housing
- popular subjects to study
- the use of plastic bags
- the availability of jobs
- clothing changes
- your own idea

2 *Self-Edit* Use the editing tips below to improve your paragraph. Make any
necessary changes.

1. Did you use modals like *cannot, could (not), may (not), might (not), must (not),*
   and *should (not)* to write about changes in the present that will affect things
   in the future?
2. Did you use the correct modals to express future probability?
3. Did you use *should (not)* to express future probability when you have evidence?
4. Did you avoid the mistakes in the Avoid Common Mistakes chart on page 287?

Transitive and Intransitive Verbs;
Verbs and Prepositions

Getting Along at Work

1 | Grammar in the Real World

A How often do you read advice columns? Where do you read them: in newspapers, in magazines, or online? Read the advice column about problems in the workplace. What do you think is the best advice for getting along at work?

Ask the Expert

Welcome to our advice column, where you can **ask an expert for** advice on all your workplace problems. Here are this week's questions and our expert's answers.

5 *Dear Expert: A new employee **arrived** yesterday. She **wears too much perfume**, and it **distracts**¹ **the other employees**. I'm her boss. What should I do? – Rosa M.*

Dear Rosa: You should **discuss this with** your employee. You can tell her that most
10 offices ask employees not to **use perfume** because some people are allergic² to it.

*Dear Expert: Something terrible **happened** last week! I **told a joke** at work, and now a co-worker from China is angry with me. I think I **offended him**. – Jorge P.*

Dear Jorge: **Apologize for** your behavior. Humor is very different in different cultures, so you probably shouldn't **tell jokes** to people you don't know well. It's
15 also not a good idea to **talk about** politics, religion, or how much money a person has.

*Dear Expert: I have a very difficult boss. She constantly **makes outrageous**³ **demands**. For example, she asked me to **get her suit** from the dry cleaners the other day. This is a personal task, not a work-related task, and she shouldn't ask me to do this. How can I handle this? – Mei Lee W.*

20 Dear Mei Lee: This is a difficult situation to **deal with**. It might help to **make a list** of things you are working on for your boss. When she asks you to run an errand,⁴ **show the list** to her. Then she will know how busy you already are.

¹**distract:** take someone's attention away from what the person is doing | ²**allergic:** having an illness from eating, touching, or breathing something specific | ³**outrageous:** shocking and unacceptable | ⁴**run an errand:** make a short trip to do something, such as buy groceries

B *Comprehension Check* Answer the questions.

1. According to the advice column, why is it a bad idea to wear perfume in the workplace?
2. Why does Jorge think his co-worker is angry?
3. According to the advice column, why should people avoid telling jokes to people they don't know well?
4. Why does Mei Lee have a problem with her boss?

C *Notice* Find the sentences in the advice column and complete them.

1. A new employee _____ yesterday.

2. Something terrible _____ last week!

3. I _____ a joke at work.

4. I think I _____ him.

Which verbs are followed by a noun or pronoun?

2 Transitive and Intransitive Verbs

▶ Grammar Presentation

A transitive verb needs an object. The object completes the meaning of the verb. An intransitive verb does not need an object.	VERB OBJECT The new employee **wears perfume**. (transitive) VERB The new employee **arrived**. (intransitive)

2.1 Transitive Verbs

Subject	Verb	Object
I You We They	wear	perfume.
He / She / It	wears	

2.2 Intransitive Verbs

Subject	Verb
I You We They	arrived.
He / She / It	arrived.

2.3 Using Transitive and Intransitive Verbs

a. The object after a transitive verb is often a noun or an object pronoun.	*She wears **perfume**.* *My boss doesn't like **me**.*
b. An intransitive verb does not have an object. However, it is often followed by an expression of time, place, or manner.	*The flight arrived **at 5:30 p.m.*** *How many people work **at your office**?* *She resigned **unexpectedly**.*
c. Some verbs can be transitive or intransitive. Sometimes the meaning of the verb is the same.	TRANSITIVE *He **drives a truck**.* INTRANSITIVE *He **drives** badly.*
Sometimes the meaning of the verb is different.	TRANSITIVE *She **runs a company** in Phoenix.* (manages) INTRANSITIVE *She can **run** fast.*

Data from the Real World

Most English verbs are transitive. The most common intransitive verbs in speaking and writing are *come, die, fall, go, happen, live, remain, rise, stay,* and *work.*	*He **died** in 1998.* *Gas prices **are rising**.*
The most common verbs that can be transitive or intransitive are *begin, call, change, leave, move, open, run, start, stop,* and *study.*	OBJECT *Could you **move** your car, please?* (transitive) *We all sat very still. No one **moved**.* (intransitive)

▶ Grammar Application

Exercise 2.1 Transitive or Intransitive?

Read the e-mail. Label each underlined verb *T* (transitive) or *I* (intransitive) according to how it is used in the e-mail. Circle each object.

Hi Emily,

Our new assistant started work yesterday. He seems great, except for one thing. He chews gum all the time. It distracts me and the other employees. We hear it all day long. Maybe I should explain my feelings, but I don't want to offend him. He works hard and everyone likes him. I discussed the problem with my co-worker, Kyle, but he didn't care. He just laughed. When I arrived at work this morning, my manager and I spoke. She understood the problem. She's going to say something to the new assistant. Maybe that will help.

I hope your workday is going better than mine!

Yvette

Exercise 2.2 Questions and Answers

A Underline all of the transitive verbs in the questions. Circle all of the intransitive verbs.

1. What distracts you most when you are studying?
2. How often do you stay late at work (or school)?
3. What time do you usually leave for work (or school)?
4. What has changed in your work (or school) life recently?
5. What time do you usually begin your workday (or school day)?
6. What time does your workday (or school day) usually end?

B *Pair Work*   Ask and answer the questions in A with a partner. Are your answers similar or different?

> A *What distracts you most when you are studying?*
> B *Nice weather really distracts me. I always want to go outdoors.*

3 | Verb + Object + Preposition Combinations

▶ Grammar Presentation

<table>
<tr>
<td>Some verbs are followed by an object and a prepositional phrase.</td>
<td>

VERB   OBJECT   PREPOSITION
*She **discussed** **company policies** **with** the new employees.*

VERB   OBJECT   PREPOSITION
*He **borrowed** **a laptop** **from** his co-worker.*

</td>
</tr>
</table>

3.1 Some Verb + Object + Preposition Combinations

a. Verb + object + *about* *remind . . . about*	We **reminded** them **about** the meeting at 3 o'clock.

b. Verb + object + *for*
   ask . . . for
   thank . . . for
	He **asked** me **for** advice.
	I **thanked** him **for** his help.

c. Verb + object + *from*
   borrow . . . from
   get . . . from
   learn . . . from
   take . . . from
	She **borrowed** the book **from** me.
	We **got** some good feedback **from** our manager.
	Have you **learned** a lot **from** her?
	They **took** the information **from** the new employees.

d. Verb + object + *to* *explain . . . to*	She **explained** the problem **to** her boss.

e. Verb + object + *with*
   discuss . . . with
   help . . . with
   spend . . . with
	I **discussed** the project **with** my manager.
	He **helps** her **with** the mail.
	Does she **spend** a lot of time **with** him?

▶ Grammar Application

Exercise 3.1 Verb + Object + Preposition Combinations

🔊 Listen to the conversation about a woman's day at work. Complete the sentences with the verbs and prepositions you hear.

1. I _explained_ company policies _to_ them.

2. I _____ some time _____ them after the meeting.

3. I _____ everything _____ them one more time.

4. I couldn't fix them, so I _____ a laptop _____ the technology department.

5. I _____ Robert _____ some information.

6. I had to wait and _____ it _____ Carrie.

7. Carrie _____ me _____ a department meeting at 11:30.

8. Robert and Carrie both had time to _____ me _____ it then.

9. I _____ Carrie and Robert _____ their help.

Exercise 3.2 More Verb + Object + Preposition Combinations

A *Over to You* Write three sentences about things you have to do or have recently done at work or school. Choose from these topics.

- discuss something with someone
- explain something to someone
- get something from someone
- remind someone about something
- borrow something from someone
- help someone with something

  I had to discuss a problem at work with my boss yesterday.

  _____

  _____

  _____

B *Pair Work* Read a partner's sentences. Tell the class about your partner.

Nuria borrowed some books from her teacher, and then she lost them. She doesn't know what to do about this.

4 | Verb + Preposition Combinations

▶ Grammar Presentation

Some verbs are often followed by specific prepositions.	I always **listen to** my co-workers during meetings. Don't **worry about** the project. I'll help you.

4.1 Some Verb + Preposition Combinations

a. Verb + *about*

ask about	The new employees **asked about** company policies.
talk about	We **talked about** the problem at our meeting.
think about	I **thought about** it, and I don't think it's a good idea.
worry about	Do you **worry about** work problems?

b. Verb + *at*

laugh at	She is **laughing at** us.
look at	Could you **look at** this report and tell me what you think?

c. Verb + *for*

apologize for	I **apologize for** my behavior.
ask for	Did she **ask for** a raise?
look for	I'm **looking for** my boss. I have a question for him.
wait for	We've been **waiting for** you.

d. Verb + *on*

count on	You can **count on** me in a crisis.
depend on	A company's success **depends on** every employee's hard work.
rely on	He **relies on** me for help.

e. Verb + *to*

belong to	Does this **belong to** you?
happen to	What **happened to** Tom's boss? I haven't seen her lately.
listen to	We **listened to** the discussion.
talk to	Our boss **talked to** all the employees on Monday.

f. Verb + *with*

agree with	No one **agrees with** him.
argue with	It's not a good idea to **argue with** your co-workers.
deal with	I can't **deal with** her.

▸▸ Verb and Preposition Combinations: See page A5.

4.2 Using Verb + Preposition Combinations

a. Verb + preposition combinations often include verbs for communication and verbs for thinking and feeling.	*You should **ask about** the new job.* (communication) *Don't **worry about** it.* (thinking and feeling)
b. The preposition can come at the end of an information question.	*"What did you talk **about**?"* *"We talked about work."* *"Who does this bag belong **to**?"* *"It belongs to me."*
c. Some verbs can combine with more than one preposition. The meaning may be different.	*I **talked to** him yesterday.* (had a conversation with) *We **talked about** our new project.* (discussed)

▶ Grammar Application

Exercise 4.1 Verb + Preposition Combination in Statements

Complete the text about company policies with the correct form
of the verbs in parentheses and the correct preposition from the box.

about	about	for	~~to~~	to	with
about	at	to	to	with	

Yesterday, our boss _talked to_ (talk) the new
(1)
employees on their first day. She _____

(2)
(talk) company policies. The employees

_____ (listen) her attentively. She said
(3)
everyone should _____ (think) the policies.
(4)
She told them to _____ (ask) anything that
(5)
was unclear.

One employee asked if it was acceptable to speak

his first language at work. The boss said, "We prefer everyone to speak English, but we think

it's important to _____ (look) each situation. Sometimes it's acceptable to use
(6)
your first language, for example, if you're _____ (talk) a customer who speaks
(7)
your language."

At the end of the meeting, she said, "We all _____ (belong) the
(8)
same organization and have the same goals. If you need help, please don't hesitate to

_____ (ask) it." It seemed like everyone _____ (agree) the
(9) (10)
boss's views. Nobody _____ (argue) her.
(11)

Exercise 4.2 Verb + Preposition Combinations in Questions

A Use the words to write questions. Add the correct preposition.

1. Who / you / talk / most at work (or school) / ?   *Who do you talk to most at work?*

2. What / you / usually talk / at work (or school) / ? _____
   _____

3. What / you / worry / at work (or school) / ? _____
   _____

4. Who / you / depend / for help / ? _____

5. Whose advice / you / listen / most / ? _____
   _____

6. Who / you / sometimes argue / ? _____

7. Who / you / usually agree / ? _____

8. What / clubs or professional organizations / you / belong / ? _____
   _____

B *Pair Work* Ask and answer the questions in A with a partner.

A Who do you talk to most at work?

B I talk to my co-worker, Sandra.

5 | Avoid Common Mistakes ⚠

1. A transitive verb needs an object. Don't forget the object.

   it
I went to see the movie, but I didn't like∧.

2. Some verbs need a preposition. Don't forget the preposition.

   to
My co-workers often don't listen∧me.

3. Use the correct preposition with verbs that need them.

   about
Don't worry ~~on~~ the presentation. I'll help you finish it.

4. Don't use a preposition with verbs that don't need them.

Let's discuss ~~about~~ the problem.

Editing Task

Find and correct eight more mistakes in this magazine article.

))))))) Not Appreciated at Work?))))))

Do these problems sound familiar to you? If so, you are not alone. These are the common problems our readers sent to us in our recent survey. Try our solutions! They could help you change your work life forever!

> Problem: Some people do not appreciate me, or even like.
                                                       me

5   Solution: Maybe you should talk your boss about the problem.

> Problem: My co-workers often argue me. I don't like it.

   Solution: You could talk with the problem with your co-workers.

> Problem: Nobody listens me when I have a new idea.

   Solution: Maybe you need to explain your ideas more clearly to them.

10 > Problem: I always thank my co-workers for their help, but they never thank.

   Solution: You could discuss about the problem with them, but this may not change.

> Problem: My co-worker always asks me help. I don't mind helping him, but then I don't finish my own work.

   Solution: Discuss this him. Tell him you want to help, but you must also do

15   your work. I think he'll understand.

6 | Grammar for Writing ✎

Using Transitive and Intransitive Verbs

Writers often use transitive and intransitive verbs to show how people interact with each other.

Remember:

- **Transitive verbs need an object to complete the sentence.**

  John <u>received his boss's e-mail</u> yesterday.

- **You can use verb + preposition combinations to talk about communicating, thinking, and feeling.**

  A good boss <u>listens to</u> her employees.   *She is <u>thinking about</u> her employees.*

Pre-writing Task

1 Read the paragraph from a magazine article. What are two suggestions in the article?

Getting a Raise

If you are like most people, you work hard at your job and you believe you are good at it. You also probably believe that you deserve more money. The problem is, how do you ask your boss for a raise? Here are a few suggestions. First, choose the right time to ask your boss. Some managers believe their
5 employees should not ask for them. Other bosses are happy to discuss salary with their employees, but only when they are in a good mood and are not too busy. Second, before you ask your boss, be prepared. Think about things you do to help the company. What do people depend on you for? Do you look for ways to save money? Make a list of these things so you can remind
10 your boss about them. Finally, when you ask your boss, be confident. Don't apologize for your desire to make more money. At the same time, you should also be polite. Explain your opinion to your boss gently, with a smile. Also, don't forget to thank your boss for his or her time.

2 Read the paragraph again. Underline the verb + object + preposition combinations and circle the verb + preposition combinations.

Writing Task

1 *Write* Use the paragraph in the Pre-writing Task to help you write some suggestions for improving things at work or at school. Use verb + preposition and verb + object + preposition combinations from the unit. You can write about:

- getting a raise
- getting along with a difficult co-worker
- finding a new job
- asking a teacher for extra help
- looking more professional at work or school
- your own idea

2 *Self-Edit* Use the editing tips below to improve your paragraph. Make any necessary changes.

1. Did you use verbs with the correct prepositions to show how people interact with each other?
2. Did you use objects after transitive verbs to complete the meaning of the sentence?
3. Did you use verb + preposition combinations to describe communicating, thinking, and feeling?
4. Did you avoid the mistakes in the Avoid Common Mistakes chart on page 298?

Phrasal Verbs
Money, Money, Money

1 | Grammar in the Real World 🌐

A What are some good habits for managing money? What are some bad habits? Read the article about managing money. What two steps does the author's plan include?

Money Matters

Does your money usually **run out** before the end of the month? Do you spend more money than you earn? Are you starting to **build up** credit card debt? Have you **taken out** a loan and can't **pay** it **off**? If this describes you, you might want to **sort out**[1] your finances now, before bad habits **set in**.[2]
5 Do not **put** it **off** until tomorrow. Here is a plan to help you get control of your money.

Step 1: **Figure out** your income and your spending habits. **Sit down** with a notebook and **write down** how much you make every month. Then **find out** where your money goes. Over the next month, **write down** all your
10 monthly expenses and **add** them **up**. Include everything you buy or spend money on. The purpose of this exercise is to get a clear picture of your usual spending habits. Do you **eat out** too much? What do you need to **give up**?

Step 2: **Set up** a budget. Use your notebook to **work out** what you can
15 spend. Then, prioritize[3] your expenses. Rent, food, electricity, and gas are the most important. These are high-priority[4] expenses. Movies and dinners out are not. You can allow yourself some treats, but remember to **put** money **away** for unexpected expenses, such as repairs when your car **breaks down**.

Once you are in control of your finances, you can set a goal like **paying**
20 **off** your credit card or saving for a large purchase. You can also relax, enjoy life more, and worry less.

[1]**sort out:** organize something or solve a problem | [2]**set in:** begin and continue for a long time |
[3]**prioritize:** put things in order of importance | [4]**high-priority:** important

B *Comprehension Check* Answer the questions.

1. Why should you write down your expenses?
2. According to the article, which expenses are the most important ones?
3. According to the article, what are some expenses that are not important?
4. What are two financial goals that the article mentions?

C *Notice* Find the sentences in the article and complete them with the missing verbs.

1. If this describes you, you might want to _____ your finances now,

   before bad habits _____ .

2. _____ with a notebook.

3. Over the next month, _____ all your monthly expenses.

How many words are there in each blank, one or two? Which words are followed by an object (transitive)? Which words are not followed by an object (intransitive)?

2 | Intransitive Phrasal Verbs

▶ Grammar Presentation

<table>
<tr><td>Phrasal verbs are two-word verbs. They include a verb and a particle. A particle is a small word like up, down, back, out, on, off, or in.</td><td>VERB PARTICLE
Does your money usually run out before the end of the month?
VERB PARTICLE
Sit down with a notebook.</td></tr>
</table>

2.1 Intransitive Phrasal Verbs

Subject	Verb	Particle
I You We They	**sit** **sat**	**down.**
He / She / It	**sits** **sat**	

2.2 Using Intransitive Phrasal Verbs

a. Intransitive phrasal verbs do not need an object to complete their meaning.	*Sit down* with a notebook. Do you **eat out** too much?
b. The particle comes after the verb. Note: Do not put a word or phrase between the verb and the particle of an intransitive phrasal verb.	They **came back** from vacation today. They came ~~from vacation~~ back today.
c. The meaning of some phrasal verbs is easy to understand.	I **go out** every night. Can you **stand up** for a moment? She **went away** for a month and then **came back**.
d. Some intransitive phrasal verbs have more than one meaning. The meaning of some phrasal verbs is not easy to understand.	She walked into the room and then **ran out**. (left) Does your money **run out**? (be completely used) Her plane **takes off** at 12:00. (leaves) Debt counseling has **taken off**. (grown; been successful) My car **broke down** last week. (stopped working) He **broke down** in tears. (started to cry) We **work out** at a gym. (exercise) My job **didn't work out**. (didn't go as planned)
e. Many everyday spoken commands use intransitive phrasal verbs.	Hold on. / Hang on. (Wait.) Go ahead! (Do it!) Come on. (Hurry. Let's go.) Go on. (Continue.) Look out! / Watch out! (Be careful!) Sit down. (Sit.)

2.3 Some Intransitive Phrasal Verbs

break down (1. stop working 2. lose control)

come back (return)

come on (1. hurry 2. start)

eat out (eat in a restaurant)

get along (have a good relationship)

give up (stop)

go ahead (start or continue)

go away (leave; go to another place)

go on (continue)

go out (not stay home)

go up (rise; go higher)

grow up (become an adult)

hang on (1. wait 2. keep going)

hold on (1. wait 2. persist)

look out (be careful)

move in (1. take your things to a new home 2. begin living somewhere)

run out (1. leave 2. be completely used)

set in (begin and continue for a long time)

sit down (sit; take a seat)

stand up (stand; rise)

take off (1. leave on an airplane 2. grow; be successful)

watch out (be careful)

work out (1. exercise 2. go as planned)

▸▸| Phrasal Verbs: Transitive and Intransitive: See page A10.

In general, phrasal verbs are less common in academic writing, but writers often use these verbs: *grow up, go on, go back, turn out, break down, come up, work out.*	Talks between the two countries have **broken down**. One question **came up** in the discussion.

▶ Grammar Application

Exercise 2.1 Intransitive Phrasal Verbs

Underline the phrasal verbs in the conversations. Circle the particles.

1. *A* Come ⟨on⟩! We're going to be late.

   B Hold on. I'm coming.

2. *A* It's Friday night. Let's eat out somewhere.

   B I can't. My money's already run out, and I don't get paid until next week.

3. *A* I have some new neighbors. They moved in last week.

   B Are they nice? Do you think you'll get along?

4. *A* I want to go out now. Do you want to come?

   B No, go ahead. I'm tired. I'm going to stay home.

Exercise 2.2 Using Phrasal Verbs

A Complete the story. Use the particles from the boxes.

along	away	back	in	~~up~~

Peter and Carlos grew _up_ in the same neighborhood.
(1)
They were good friends and got _____ really well.
(2)
Carlos went _____ to college when he was 18, but they
(3)
kept in touch. When Carlos came _____ , they decided
(4)
to share an apartment. Peter found an apartment, and they
moved _____ .
(5)

on	out	out	out	up

It all worked _____ well for a while. They shared the bills. They went _____ for
(6)   (7)
pizza or to see a movie after work. Then Carlos got a great job in a bank and wanted to eat

_____ more often and in more expensive restaurants.
(8)
Peter couldn't afford it, but he used his credit card and tried

not to worry. Life went _____ as normal, but Peter's
(9)
spending was going _____ every day.
(10)

down	down	on

One morning Peter sat _____ to have coffee and pay some bills online while
(11)
Carlos was at work. He saw his high credit card bill and broke _____ . "I can't go
(12)
_____ like this," he said. He called Carlos's voice mail and left a message. He said . . .
(13)

B *Pair Work* Study the story for two minutes. Tell it to your partner using the phrasal verbs.

Two boys grew up together. They were good friends and . . .

C *Group Work* What do you think Peter said in his voice mail to Carlos? What do you think Carlos said to Peter in his response? Discuss in a group.

I think Peter said, "Hi Carlos, it's Peter calling. I read my credit card bill this morning. It's very high. I can't go on like this. . . ."

Exercise 2.3 Questions and Answers

A Complete the questions with the correct particle. Use Chart 2.3 on page 304 to help you.

1. Do you go _out_ on weekends very often?

2. Do you eat _____ for lunch, or do you bring your own lunch?

3. Do you exercise at home or work _____ at a gym?

4. Has your computer or car broken _____ lately and needed expensive repairs?

5. Have prices for anything been going _____ lately? If so, what has been getting more expensive?

6. After this course, would you like to go _____ and study more? If so, what would you study?

7. Do you make a budget? If so, does it usually work _____ ?

B *Pair Work* Ask and answer the questions with a partner. How similar or different are your answers?

3 | Transitive Phrasal Verbs

▶ Grammar Presentation

Transitive phrasal verbs need an object.	VERB PARTICLE OBJECT *Have you* **taken out** *a* **loan**? VERB OBJECT PARTICLE *Can you* **pay it back**?

3.1 Transitive Phrasal Verbs

Subject	Verb	Particle	Object (Noun)
I You We They	**figure** **figured**	**out**	the budget.
He / She / It	**figures** **figured**		

Subject	Verb	Object (Noun or Pronoun)	Particle
I You We They	**figure** **figured**	the budget it	**out**.
He / She / It	**figures** **figured**		

3.2 Using Transitive Phrasal Verbs

a. Some phrasal verbs are transitive. They need an object to complete their meaning.	*He paid back **the money he owed**.* *She added up **her expenses**.*
b. Most transitive phrasal verbs are "separable." This means that noun objects can come **before** or **after** the particle.	VERB PARTICLE OBJECT ***Write down** your expenses.* VERB OBJECT PARTICLE ***Write** your expenses **down**.*
Object pronouns come **before** the particle.	***Write them down**.*
Do not put an object pronoun after the particle.	***Write down** ~~them~~.*

3.2 Using Transitive Phrasal Verbs *(continued)*

c. Indefinite pronoun objects (e.g., *something, nothing, someone, no one, everyone*) can come before or after the particle.	*She **throws away** everything.* *She **throws** everything **away**.*
d. Longer objects usually go after the particle.	*Is he **setting up** a new financial management company?* *Is he **setting** ~~a new financial management company~~ up?*
e. Some transitive phrasal verbs have more than one meaning.	*They are **bringing up** three children.* (raising a child) *I'd like to **bring up** the subject of money.* (introduce a topic) *Please **turn down** the radio. It's too loud.* (lower the volume) *I **turned down** the invitation to the party because I had to work.* (rejected)
f. Some phrasal verbs have one meaning when they are transitive. They have a different meaning when they are intransitive.	*I **worked out** a budget.* (transitive; solved or calculated something) *I **work out** at a gym every day.* (intransitive; exercise)

3.3 Some Transitive Phrasal Verbs

add up (add together; combine)
bring up (1. raise a child 2. introduce a topic)
build up (accumulate)
figure out (find an answer; understand)
find out (discover information; learn)
give up (quit)
pay back (repay money)
pay off (repay completely)
put away (1. save for the future
       2. put in the correct place)

put off (delay, postpone)
set up (1. arrange 2. plan 3. build)
sort out (1. organize 2. solve)
take out (1. remove
       2. obtain something officially)
throw away (get rid of something; discard)
turn down (1. lower the volume 2. reject)
work out (solve; calculate)
write down (write on paper)

▸▸ Phrasal Verbs: Transitive and Intransitive: See page A10.

Data from the Real World

Research shows that the following transitive phrasal verbs are common in academic writing:

break off	*cut off*	*point out*	*sum up*
carry out	*find out*	*set up*	

▶ Grammar Application

Exercise 3.1 Transitive and Intransitive Phrasal Verbs

Label the phrasal verbs *T* (transitive) or *I* (intransitive) according to their use in the sentences. Circle the objects.

1. Experts say you should work on your money problems now. Don't **put** (them) **off**. ___*T*___

2. Most experts say it's a good idea to **write down** all your expenses. _____

3. For example, Mariah S., from Chicago, **adds up** everything she's spent at the end of the month. _____

4. After Mariah **worked out** a budget, she changed some of her spending habits. _____

5. She used to pay for an expensive gym membership, but now she **works out** at home. _____

6. She also decided to **give up** expensive dinners in order to save money. _____

7. Mariah didn't **give up** and eventually saved enough money to start a business. _____

8. She also **paid back** some money her family had loaned her. _____

Exercise 3.2 Transitive Phrasal Verbs

🔊 Listen to the expert give advice about money. Complete the list of advice. Use phrasal verbs.

Dana's Money Advice

1. _Put away_ a little money each month.

2. Even a small amount will _____ over time.

3. You need to _____ a budget.

4. _____ your expenses.

5. Don't _____ receipts.

6. Don't _____ a lot of debt.

7. _____ your credit card every month.

8. You need to _____ the topic _____ and discuss it.

9. Don't _____ money matters.

Exercise 3.3 More Transitive Phrasal Verbs

A Complete the conversations. Unscramble the words in A's questions. Use the verb given and an object pronoun in B's answers.

1. *A* Do you usually _write your expenses down / write down your expenses_ (your expenses / write down)?

   B No, I don't. I _don't add them up_ (not add up) every month, either.

2. *A* Do you _____ (your receipts / throw away), or do you keep them?

   B I usually _____ (throw away).

3. *A* Do you ever _____ (things / put off), like doing your finances?

   B I do. I know I should _____ (sort out).

4. *A* Do you think it's a good idea to _____ (a loan / take out)?

   B Yes, but only if you can _____ (pay off) quickly.

5. *A* Do you think it's difficult to _____ (a budget / work out)?

   B I don't think so. You just need to _____ (figure out).

B *Pair Work* Ask and answer the questions in A with a partner. Answer with your own opinion or information.

A Do you usually write down your expenses?

B Yes, I do. I write everything down. Then I add it up at the end of the month.

4 Avoid Common Mistakes ⚠

1. **Don't forget a particle when you need one. Be especially careful with these verbs:** *pick up, break down,* **and** *point out.*

   He's picked˄bad spending habits, like eating out every night.
   (up inserted above ˄)

2. **Don't use a particle when you don't need one. Be especially careful with these verbs:** *fall, rise, go, find.*

   Gas prices fell ~~down~~, then rose ~~up~~.

   Things are going ~~on~~ well for me.

3. **Don't confuse** *grow up* **and** *grow. Grow up* **means to grow from a child to an adult.** *Grow* **means get bigger.**

   Before the children grew˄, we didn't have any savings.
   (up inserted above ˄)

   Now our savings have grown ~~up~~.

4. **Do not put object pronouns after particles. They go before particles.**

   She summed ~~up it~~.
   (it up inserted above)

Editing Task

Find and correct eight more mistakes on this website.

Debt Help Website

It is easy to get into debt. Prices are going˄all the
(up inserted above ˄)
time. Maybe you have to change jobs and your income
decreases. Maybe you've picked bad habits, like ordering
a pizza instead of cooking. You are using your credit

5 card more and more. Soon your debt has grown up, and
it is more than you can afford. Or maybe you have a loan
and you cannot pay back it. If you do not watch, you may
find that you have thousands of dollars of debt. It is hard
to know what to do with debt that has risen up. We can

10 help! Our website is full of financial advice. It points the
things you must and must not do when you get into debt.

Do you have difficulty
with your budget? Read
our **Budget Guide**. It will
help you figure out it.

Do you want to get
married? First, find how
your partner feels about
money. Read our **Money
and Relationships Guide**.

5 | Grammar for Writing

Using Transitive and Intransitive Phrasal Verbs

Writers often use transitive and intransitive phrasal verbs to give instructions.

Phrasal verbs appear in almost every kind of text and are very common in informal texts that give advice or instructions.

Remember:

- **The meaning of verbs often changes when they are paired with particles.**

  Work out a plan for your retirement early. Then you know how long you will have to work.

- **The object can appear before or after the particle in most transitive phrasal verbs.**

  They added up their expenses.   They added their expenses up.

Pre-writing Task

1 Read the paragraph from a magazine article about money. What is the writer's suggestion for teaching teens about money?

Teens and Money

Teenagers have a lot of problems with money. They can easily spend money, but they often do not know how to save it. Teaching teenagers about money is important. One way to do this is to loan your teen money. Imagine your teenage son wants a new cell phone, but he
5 does not have enough money. You can loan him the money and then, each month, your teen can pay you back a percentage of the loan. Do not forget to write the loan agreement down on a piece of paper or in a notebook. In addition, make sure your teen pays back all the money and does not give up. This is a good way for your teen to find out the value of
10 money and possessions. This is a lesson that will last a lifetime.

2 Read the paragraph again. Underline the phrasal verbs. Which are intransitive? Which are transitive? What are the objects of the transitive phrasal verbs?

Writing Task

1 *Write*   Use the paragraph in the Pre-writing Task to help you write a paragraph that gives people instructions on managing money. What tips do you know for managing money? How can they help people?

2 *Self-Edit*   Use the editing tips below to improve your paragraph. Make any necessary changes.

1. Did you use phrasal verbs to give instructions?
2. Did you choose the correct particle to express the correct meaning of the verb?
3. Did you use an object with the transitive phrasal verbs?
4. Did you avoid the mistakes in the Avoid Common Mistakes chart on page 311?

1 Grammar in the Real World

A Think of a family you know with more than one child. How similar or different are the children's personalities? Read the web article about birth order and personality. Do you agree with the results of the research it describes?

Does Birth Order[1] Affect Personality?

Some researchers believe that birth order affects people's personalities. According to Dr. Frank Sulloway, professor of psychology, birth order differences are **as strong as** gender differences.[2]

First-born children, he says, are often **more responsible** and **more conservative**.
5 They are also **more likely** to be successful, and many first-born children are presidents and CEOs. Because first-born children are usually **bigger** and **stronger** than their **younger** siblings,[3] they can try to dominate[4] them.

As a result, says Sulloway, **younger** children can be rebellious and **less likely** to obey rules. Younger children are often **more adventurous** and **more creative**
10 **than older** children. They are also **more independent**. They may **try harder** to get attention from their parents, and parents often do not discipline **younger** children **as strictly as** their **older** siblings.

Not all researchers agree with these ideas, but most do agree that middle children can have a very difficult time. They are **more likely** to have to repeat a
15 grade in school. Middle children often worry that they are **not** loved **as much as** their siblings. However, middle children are often the peacemakers in the family and are **more easygoing** as a result.

Parents are often **less strict** with the "baby,"
20 or last-born child of the family. Last-born children are **more often** spoiled. Parents are usually **more relaxed** with them, and they often seem to have an easy time. However, if you are from a large family, that may be
25 something you already know!

[1]**birth order:** order in which children were born | [2]**gender difference:** difference between men and women | [3]**sibling:** brother or sister | [4]**dominate:** control

B *Comprehension Check* Match the child with the description.

1. The first-born child _____   a. can be good at resolving conflicts.
2. The younger child _____   b. often has an easy time.
3. The middle child _____   c. often wants to be a leader.
4. The last-born child _____   d. can often be creative and break rules.

C *Notice* Find the sentences in the article and complete them.

1. Because first-born children are usually _____ and

   _____ _____ their younger siblings,

   they can try to dominate them.

2. Younger children are often _____ _____ and

   _____ _____ _____ older children.

Look at the adjectives and other words you wrote. The sentences show two ways
to make comparisons. How are the two ways similar? How are they different?

2 | Comparative Adjectives and Adverbs

▶ ## Grammar Presentation

Comparative adjectives and adverbs show how two things or ideas are different.	COMPARATIVE ADJECTIVE *First-born children are usually **bigger than** their siblings.* COMPARATIVE ADVERB *Younger children try **harder** to get their parents' attention.*

2.1 Comparative Adjectives

Subject	Verb	Comparative Adjective	*Than*	
First-born children	are	**stronger** **more responsible** **less easygoing**	**than**	their siblings.

2.2 Comparative Adverbs

Subject	Verb (+ Object)	Comparative Adverb	*Than*	
First-born children	do things obey rules get spoiled	**better** and **more easily** **more often** **less often**	**than**	their siblings.

2.3 The Spelling of Comparative Adjectives and Adverbs

a. Add -er to one-syllable adjectives and adverbs.	fast → fast**er** hard → hard**er** strong → strong**er**
For one-syllable adjectives that end in a vowel + consonant, double the consonant. Do not double the consonant w.	big → big**ger** hot → hot**ter** low → low**er**
b. Remove the -y and add -ier to two-syllable adjectives ending in -y.	early → earl**ier** funny → funn**ier** heavy → heav**ier**
c. Use more with most adjectives and adverbs that have two or more syllables.	hardworking → **more** hardworking intelligent → **more** intelligent quickly → **more** quickly often → **more** often

d. Some comparative adjectives and adverbs are irregular.	**Adjectives** good → better bad → worse	**Adverbs** well → better badly → worse

▶▮ Adjectives and Adverbs: Comparative and Superlative Forms. See page A12.

2.4 Using Comparative Adjectives and Adverbs

a. You can use comparative adjectives to describe how two nouns are different.	NOUN ADJECTIVE NOUN *First-born children are sometimes **taller than** their siblings.*
You can use comparative adverbs to compare the way two people do the same action.	VERB ADVERB VERB *My son **works harder** in school **than** my daughter works.*
b. Less is the opposite of more.	Julia is **more independent than** her brother Lucas. Lucas is **less independent than** Julia. He plays **more quietly than** his sister does. His sister plays **less quietly**.
Less is not usually used with one-syllable adjectives or adverbs, except clear, safe, and sure.	My daughter is **younger than** my son. My daughter is ~~less old~~ than my son.
c. You can use a pronoun after than instead of repeating the noun. In academic writing, use a subject pronoun + verb.	*Tim's sister is more creative than **he is**.*

2.4 Using Comparative Adjectives and Adverbs *(continued)*

When both verbs are the same, you do not need to repeat the verb after *than*.	*She works harder than* **Tim**.
You can also use an auxiliary verb.	*Tim's sister works harder than* **he does**. *She did better in college than* **he did**. *She's gone further in her career than* **he has**.
d. You do not need *than* plus the second part of the comparison when the meaning is clear.	*Older children* **are** *often* **more conservative**. *(than younger children)*
e. You can also use a comparative adjective without *than* before a noun when the comparison is clear.	*Parents are strict with* **older** *children*. *(older than other children)*
f. In speaking, you can use an object pronoun after *than*. In formal speaking or academic writing, use a noun or subject pronoun and a verb or auxiliary verb.	*Say: "Tim's sister works harder than* **him**.*"* *Write: Tim's sister works harder than* **Tim / he does**.

Data from the Real World

Some two-syllable adjectives have two comparative forms. However, one form is usually more frequent, especially in writing.	
Use *-er* to form these comparative adjectives: *easier, narrower, quieter, simpler*	*Mateo is* **quieter** *than his sister.*
Use *more* to form these comparative adjectives: *more likely, more friendly*	*Do you think she is* **more friendly** *than her brother?*

▶ Grammar Application

Exercise 2.1 Comparative Forms

◀⅔) Listen to the news report about birth order and intelligence. Fill in the blanks with the words you hear.

A Norwegian study says that there may be differences in intelligence between brothers. The study showed that older siblings are <u>*more intelligent than*</u> their younger

(1)
siblings. The researchers gave intelligence tests to 60,000 pairs of brothers. They found

that the older siblings did _____ their brothers on the tests. The

(2)

_____ boys' scores were definitely _____ ,

(3)   (4)

although not by very much.

Researchers say one reason for this may be that older siblings have

_____ language skills. Their language may develop
                (5)

_____ because they have been in an adult environment
                (6)

_____ . It is possible that younger siblings are
              (7)

_____ in other ways, for example, in emotional intelligence.
              (8)

The Norwegian study did not look at age differences. However,

_____ research suggests that when the age difference
              (9)

between two brothers is _____ , the difference in
                                      (10)

intelligence is _____ .
                          (11)

Exercise 2.2 More Comparative Forms

A Complete the sentences with the correct comparative forms. Use the information in the chart.

	Tom Mason	Dave Mason
Age	32	28
Height	6 feet, 3 inches tall	5 feet, 11 inches tall
Weight	200 pounds	152 pounds
Work style	hardworking	doesn't work hard
Personality	very conservative, serious, not very friendly	a little conservative, easygoing, funny, friendly
Hobbies and skills	good at sports, especially tennis; not good at guitar	plays tennis but not very athletic; plays guitar well

1. Dave is _younger than_ (young) Tom.

2. Tom is Dave's _____ (old) brother.

3. Tom is _____ (tall) Dave.

4. Tom is _____ (heavy) Dave.

5. Dave is _____ (hardworking) Tom.

6. Tom works _____ (hard).

7. Tom is a _____ (conservative) person.

8. Tom is _____ (athletic) Dave.

9. Tom is _____ (friendly) Dave.

10. Dave plays the guitar _____ (good) Tom.

B Write three more sentences about Tom and Dave. Use comparatives.

Dave is shorter than Tom.
Tom is better at sports than Dave.

_____

_____

_____

Exercise 2.3 Comparatives with *Be* and *Do*

A Rewrite the sentences about Sarah and Louisa, two sisters who go to the same college. Use comparatives with the correct form of *be* or *do*.

1. In Biology 101, Sarah works really hard, but Louisa doesn't.
   Sarah works harder than Louisa does.

2. Louisa is very creative. Sarah isn't.

   _____

3. Sarah lives very far from school. Louisa doesn't.

   _____

4. Louisa is good at writing. Sarah isn't.

   _____

5. Sarah learns quickly. Louisa doesn't.

   _____

6. Louisa is very quiet. Sarah isn't.

   _____

B What happens when you cross out *be* or *do*? Is the meaning still clear?

C *Pair Work*   Rewrite the sentences in A so they are true for you and your partner. Give reasons. Tell the class about your partner.

Virginia works harder than I do. She has three jobs!

Exercise 2.4 More Comparative Practice

A How have you changed? Answer the questions. Use comparatives and try to give extra information.

1. Are you more or less shy than you used to be?

   I'm less shy than I used to be. Now I enjoy parties because I'm more

   confident.

2. Do you work or study harder than you did when you were younger?

   _____

   _____

3. What can you do more easily now than last year?

   _____

   _____

4. What do you do on weekends more often than you used to?

   _____

   _____

5. What has been more difficult about studying English than you thought? What has been easier?

   _____

   _____

B *Group Work* Discuss your answers in a group. Have you changed in similar or in different ways?

I am less shy than I used to be, but Leona is more shy. She doesn't like speaking in front of the class. We've changed in different ways.

3 | Comparisons with *As . . . As*

▶ Grammar Presentation

You can use *as . . . as* to say that two ideas are the same or similar. *Not as . . . as* means "less."	*Birth order differences are **as strong as** gender differences.* *Older children are sometimes **not as creative as** younger children.* (= Older children are less creative.)

3.1 *As . . . As* with Adjectives

Subject	Verb	*As*	Adjective	*As*	
Younger children	are are not aren't	**as**	**smart** **creative** **good**	**as**	older children.

3.2 *As . . . As* with Adverbs

Subject	Verb	*As*	Adverb	*As*	
The younger boys	learned didn't learn	**as**	**easily** **quickly** **well**	**as**	their older brothers.

3.3 Using (*Not*) *As . . . As*

a. You can use *as* + adjective + *as* to show that two nouns are similar or the same.	*Max is **as intelligent as** his brother.*
You can use *as* + adverb + *as* to show that the way two people do things is the same or the way that two events happen is the same.	*Max **works as hard as** his brother.* *(How Max works = how his brother works.)*
b. *Not as . . . as* shows that two ideas are not similar. It means "less than."	*Andreas is **not as ambitious as** his brother.* *(= Andreas is less ambitious than his brother.)*
Use *not as . . . as* instead of *less* with short adjectives and adverbs, such as *bad, easy, high, great,* and *big.*	*My brother's test score **was not as high as** my score.* *(= My brother's score was lower than my score.)*
c. *As . . . as* can be followed by a noun or a subject pronoun + a verb or auxiliary verb.	*Kate's brother is as intelligent as **Kate / she is**.* *Kate's brother did as well in college as **she did**.* *He works as hard as **she does**.* *He's gone as far in his career as **she has**.*
d. You do not need to use *as* + the second part of the comparison when the meaning is clear.	*Middle children feel their parents **don't love them as much** (as the other children).*
e. In speaking informally, you can use an object pronoun after *as . . . as.*	*Say: "Kate's brother isn't as creative as **her**."*
In formal speaking or academic writing, use a noun or subject pronoun and a verb or auxiliary verb.	*Write: "Kate's brother is not as creative as **Kate / she is**."*

Research shows that these are some of the most common adjectives and adverbs with (*not*) *as . . . as* in speaking and writing:

adjectives: *bad, big, easy, good, great, hard, high, important, popular, simple, strong*
adverbs: *easily, fast, hard, much, often, quickly, well*

▶ Grammar Application

Exercise 3.1 Forming (*Not*) As . . . As Sentences

A Rewrite the sentences in the article with (*not*) *as . . . as*. Keep the same meaning.

How Much Gender Difference Is There?

The following statements are common beliefs about gender differences:

1. Boys are better than girls at math.	Girls *are not as good as* boys at math.
2. Women are better than men at communication.	Men _____ women at communication.
3. Teenage boys are more confident than teenage girls.	Teenage girls _____ teenage boys.
4. Men solve problems more easily than women.	Women _____ men.

A study by psychologist Janet Shibley Hyde (2007) showed that these beliefs may not all be true. According to her study:

5. People think the differences between boys and girls are big, but they aren't.	The differences _____ people think.
6. Young girls and boys do equally well in math.	Young girls _____ boys in math.
7. Communication is equally hard for men and women.	Communication for women _____ _____ it is for men.
8. Girls and boys are equally likely to have low confidence.	Boys _____ girls to have low confidence.

Hyde found that in 78 percent of tests, men and women were about the same. She did find some differences.

9. Boys are more aggressive than girls.	Girls _____ _____ .
10. Men get angry more quickly than women.	Women _____ _____ .
11. Men can throw objects further than women.	Women _____ _____ .

Hyde's study shows that most differences are in our beliefs, and not really in our gender. She hopes these beliefs will change.

B *Pair Work* Discuss the information with a partner. What did you know? What surprised you?

A *I didn't know that girls do as well as boys in math.*

B *I know. That surprised me, too.*

Exercise 3.2 Using As . . . As

A *Pair Work* Answer the questions. Then ask and answer the questions with a partner.

What is something . . .

1. you do as often as possible? Why?

   I play soccer as often as I can because it is my favorite sport.

   _____

2. you can't do as often as you'd like? Why?

   _____

3. you do as quickly as you can each day? Why?

   _____

Who is . . .

4. as creative as you? Why do you think so?

   _____

5. as adventurous as you? Why do you think so?

   _____

B *Group Work* Tell the class about your partner.

A *Agnes plays soccer as often as possible. It's her favorite sport.*

B *Boris visits his parents as often as he can because he misses them.*

Exercise 3.3 Using (*Not*) As . . . As

A *Over to You* Think of a person you know who fits each description below. Write a sentence about each person using (*not*) *as . . . as* + a subject pronoun + verb.

1. works as hard as you   *My sister works as hard as I do.*

2. doesn't talk as much as you   _____

3. did as well as you in school   _____

4. isn't as old as you   _____

5. hasn't lived here as long as you _____

6. can speak English as well as you _____

7. doesn't drive as carefully as you _____

8. has studied as much as you   _____

B *Pair Work* Discuss the people you know with a partner. Are your friends, relatives, and teachers similar or different?

A *My sister works as hard as I do.*
B *What does she do?*
A *She's a nurse. We're both nurses.*

4 Avoid Common Mistakes ⚠

1. Do not use a comparative when you are not comparing two ideas.

I have two very ~~younger~~ *young* sons.

2. Use *than*, not *that*, after a comparative.

I am more patient now ~~that~~ *than* I was.

3. Do not use *more* and -*er* together.

My work is ~~more~~ better than it used to be.

I work ~~more~~ harder now than I used to.

4. Do not forget the second *as* in *as . . . as* comparisons.

I do not see my family now as much ∧*as* I did last year.

Editing Task

Find and correct 12 more mistakes in this student's personal essay.

How I Have Changed

I think I have changed in three important ways since high school. First,
I have a ~~more~~ kinder personality now. I used to be less patient that I am
now, especially with my grandparents. I have spent a lot of time with my
grandparents in the last three years, and I have learned to be more patient
5 with them and to understand them more better. I can see that getting old can
be more difficult, so I try to help my grandparents as often I can.

Second, I did not use to be as serious I am now about my education. I
now realize that I need to study as much possible so I can get a diploma in
engineering. Five years ago, I was very younger and did not study a lot. Now
10 I'm studying more harder than I did then, and I do not skip classes as much I
did in high school.

Finally, I worry less that I did because I have goals now. I know what I
want and where I am going. In general, I have grown up and become more
clearer about who I am and what I want out of life. I believe I am a better
15 person that I used to be.

5 | Grammar for Writing ✏

Using Comparatives with Adjectives and Adverbs

Writers often use adjectives and adverbs to compare people when writing about family or friends.

Comparatives are common in reviews, academic writing, and personal essays that compare products, things, ideas, and people.

Remember:

- **Use adjectives to compare people's appearance and their personalities.**

  Younger siblings often aren't <u>as serious as</u> their older siblings, but I am much <u>funnier</u> than my younger siblings.

- **Use adverbs to compare the way people do things.**

  My mother speaks English <u>more fluently</u> than my father, but <u>not as well as</u> my sister.

Pre-writing Task

1 Read the paragraph about types of parents. How are the writer's parents different from other parents?

Different Ways to Be a Parent

Everyone has strong ideas about the right and wrong ways to take care of children. Some parents watch their children more closely than others – some are stricter, while others are more lenient. My parents always gave my brother and me a lot of freedom. They were not as strict as our friends' parents. They wanted us to learn to make
5 our own decisions about things. Most of my friends' parents were stricter with their children, and the parents made the decisions for them. Our friends were not allowed to stay out as late as we were, for example. Also, when our friends' grades were not as good as they could be, they were punished. When our grades were not good, our parents talked to us about how to do better in school. In my opinion, this was more effective. I
10 think my brother and I matured faster than some of our friends. I also think some of our friends are less confident about themselves and their decisions than we are. There are many different ways to take care of children, and I feel lucky that my parents raised us the way they did.

2 Read the paragraph again. Underline the comparative adjectives and circle the comparative adverbs. What verbs are the adverbs comparing? What nouns are the adjectives comparing?

Writing Task

1 *Write* Use the paragraph in the Pre-writing Task to help you write a paragraph comparing families or family members. Use adjective and adverb comparisons from the unit. You can write about:

- parents
- siblings
- grandparents
- aunts and/or uncles
- cousins
- your own idea

2 *Self-Edit* Use the editing tips below to improve your paragraph. Make any necessary changes.

1. Did you use adjectives and adverbs to compare family members?
2. Did you use comparative adjectives to compare people's appearance or personalities?
3. Did you use comparative adverbs to compare the way people do things?
4. Did you avoid the mistakes in the Avoid Common Mistakes chart on page 324?

Superlative Adjectives and Adverbs
The Best and the Worst

1 | Grammar in the Real World

A What are some ways we can help people during disasters? Read the web article about technology and disaster relief. What is one way people use technology for disaster relief?

The Technology of Relief

Natural disasters[1] can strike at any time and with no warning. However, **today's newest** technologies can help disaster victims in new and amazing ways. Here are a few examples.

5   When Hurricane Katrina hit the southern United States in 2005, it was a terrible disaster. The city of New Orleans was hit **the hardest**. TV, newspapers, and radio all covered the storm, but **one of the best** sources of news about the disaster was Craigslist, an online network

10 for free advertising. Soon after the storm hit, Craigslist dedicated part of its site to disaster relief.[2] People used it to post[3] reports of missing persons and to share news and stories. This seemed to be **the quickest** and **the most efficient** way to give and get information. The news on the

15 radio and TV was often not **the most current**.[4]

    Social networking sites have also become important during disasters. **One of their most important** roles is to help raise money.[5] Soon after the major earthquake in Haiti in 2010, the Red Cross and other organizations that help people in disasters were very popular topics on social networking sites. The Red Cross raised more than $8 million in fewer than 48 hours

20 through these sites. This was **the fastest** worldwide money-raising event in history.

    Unfortunately, disasters will continue to happen. Hopefully, however, new technologies will continue to develop as well. They can help people to get and to give disaster relief in **the best** ways possible.

[1]**natural disaster:** a natural event (e.g., hurricane) that causes great damage | [2]**relief:** help | [3]**post:** announce; put something on the Internet | [4]**current:** up-to-date, present | [5]**raise money:** convince people to give money, usually for a charity

B *Comprehension Check* Answer the questions.

1. When did Hurricane Katrina happen?
2. Which city was hit hardest by the hurricane?
3. What is Craigslist?
4. What is one way people used Craigslist after the hurricane?
5. How did the Red Cross use social networking sites after the 2010 earthquake in Haiti?

C *Notice* Read the sentences from the article and answer the questions.

1. "The city of New Orleans was hit the hardest."
   Was another city hit harder?

   _____

2. "This (Craigslist) seemed to be the quickest and the most efficient way to give and get information."
   Did there seem to be a quicker and more efficient way to get and give information?

   _____

3. "This was the fastest worldwide money-raising event in history."
   Was there a faster worldwide money-raising event?

   _____

2 | Superlative Adjectives and Adverbs

▶ Grammar Presentation

Superlative adjectives and adverbs compare one idea to other ideas. They mean "more / less than all of the others."	SUPERLATIVE ADJECTIVE *Social networking sites are **the newest** way to communicate after a disaster.* SUPERLATIVE ADVERB *The city of New Orleans was hit **the hardest**.*

2.1 Superlative Adjectives

Subject	Verb	The	Superlative Adjective	
The hurricane	was is	the	**biggest** **most expensive** **least damaging**	storm of the season.

2.2 Superlative Adverbs

Subject	Verb	(*The*)	Superlative Adverb	
Rescuers	worked	(**the**)	**hardest** **most quickly** **least efficiently**	right after the disaster.

2.3 Forming Superlative Adjectives and Adverbs

a. Add *the* and *-est* to one-syllable adjectives and adverbs.	*fast* → **the** fast**est** *hard* → **the** hard**est** *strong* → **the** strong**est**
b. For adjectives that end in a vowel + consonant, double the consonant.	**big** → the bi**gg**est **hot** → the ho**tt**est
c. Remove the *-y* and add *-iest* to two-syllable adjectives ending in *-y*.	*busy* → the bus**iest** *early* → the earl**iest** *heavy* → the heav**iest**
d. Use *the most* with almost all adjectives that have two or more syllables and with adverbs ending in *-ly*.	*expensive* → **the most** expensive *frequently* → **the most** frequently
e. Some superlative adjectives and adverbs are irregular.	**Adjectives** *good* → the best *bad* → the worst **Adverbs** *well* → the best *badly* → the worst

▸◂ Adjectives and Adverbs: Comparative and Superlative Forms: See page A12.

2.4 Using Superlatives

a. Superlative adjectives show that a noun has the most or least of a certain quality. They compare one noun to the other nouns in a group.	*It was **the biggest** forest fire in the state.* (Compares one forest fire to all others in the state.)
b. Superlative adverbs show that a verb happens in the most or least of a certain way. They compare one action or situation to others in a group.	*That group worked **most effectively** after the disaster.* (Compares the way that group worked to the way all other groups worked.)
c. *The least* + adjective or adverb is the opposite of *the most* + adjective or adverb.	*This storm was **the least dangerous** one of the season. There wasn't much damage from it.*
The least is not usually used with one-syllable adjectives or adverbs.	*My daughter is **the youngest** of my children.* *My daughter is the ~~least old~~ of my children.*
d. You do not need to repeat words after the superlative when the meaning is clear.	*That disaster was **the biggest** (disaster).* *Of all the technologies we use, this is **the easiest** (technology).*

2.4 Using Superlatives *(continued)*

e. You can identify the group being compared with:
- a prepositional phrase (*in* and *of* are the most common prepositions).

*It was **the worst** storm **in** years.*

- a possessive form, like a possessive pronoun or noun. You do not need *the* before the superlative when you use possessives.

***Today's newest** technologies help us during disasters.*
***Our biggest** problem was raising relief money.*

f. You can use *one of the* or *some of the* before a superlative adjective.

*It is **one of the** best ways to communicate quickly.*

Use a plural noun or a noncount noun with these expressions.

*These are **some of the** most interesting new technologies.*

Data from the Real World

The five most common superlative adjectives with *-est* in writing are *best, biggest, greatest, highest,* and *largest*.	*They are **the best** workers to have during a disaster.* *The disaster struck **the largest** city in the country.*
The five most common superlative adjectives with *most* in writing are *most common, most effective, most famous, most important,* and *most popular*.	*It's **the most popular** site for social networking.* *What is **the most common** problem after a disaster?*
Research shows that *the* is rarely used before superlative adverbs, except in formal speaking and writing.	*Rescue workers worked **fastest** in the first days after the event.*

▶ Grammar Application

Exercise 2.1 Superlative Forms

Complete the sentences with the superlative form of the adjectives or adverbs in parentheses. Use *most* or *-est* with ↑. Use *least* with ↓. Some forms are irregular.

1. The flood was _the largest_ (↑ large) disaster of the past 10 years.

2. Rescue workers worked _____ (↑ hard) during the first few days.

3. It was one of _____ (↑ big) earthquakes in history.

4. This is _____ (↓ useful) way to help during a disaster.

5. This disaster was the state's _____ (↑ bad) storm.

6. People donated money _____ (↑ quickly) using websites.

7. It was the area's _____ (↓ damaging) hurricane of the year.

8. Medical staff worked _____ (↓ effectively) during the night.

Exercise 2.2 More Superlative Forms

A 🔊 Write the superlative form of each of the words below. Then listen to the lecture about the eruption of Mount Vesuvius and the Great Chicago Fire. Listen for the superlative forms of the words in the chart, and check (✔) which event they describe.

		Eruption of Mount Vesuvius	Great Chicago Fire
1. bad	*the worst*	☐	☐
2. big		☐	☐
3. famous		☑	☐
4. fast		☐	☐
5. good		☐	☐
6. helpful		☐	☐
7. important		☐	☐
8. interesting		☐	☐
9. popular		☐	☐

B 🔊 Listen again. Complete the sentences with the words you hear.

1. The eruption of Mount Vesuvius is _____

   _____ natural disasters in history.

2. It is also probably _____
   disaster in history.

3. However, it has also been _____
   events in history for archeologists.

4. It was _____ fire and

   _____ disaster in the history
   of the city.

5. _____ story is that a cow kicked
   over a lantern in a barn and started the fire.

6. The way people worked together after the fire was

   _____ result.

7. I think that has to be _____
   building projects in history.

8. This also shows how people often work together

   _____ when they are helping
   one another.

Mount Vesuvius

The Great Chicago Fire

Exercise 2.3 More Superlative Practice

A Look at the information in the chart about three forest fires. Write eight more sentences about the information. Use superlative adjectives and adverbs from the box. Use some words more than once.

big   damaging   expensive   long   quickly   short   small

Highside Fire

Westland Fire

Lakeview Fire

	Westland Fire	Highside Fire	Lakeview Fire
1. Size of fire	100 acres	25 acres	50 acres
2. How long the fire lasted	10 days	3½ days	4 days
3. Damage from the fire (+ = 20 cabins destroyed)	++++	++	+++
4. Cost of fighting the fire	$$$$$	$$	$$$
5. How quickly the firefighters arrived to fight the fire	5 minutes	7 minutes	8 minutes

The Westland fire was the biggest fire. The Highside fire was the smallest.

1. _____
2. _____
3. _____
4. _____
5. _____
6. _____
7. _____
8. _____

B *Pair Work* Check your partner's sentences. Are they similar or different from yours?

Exercise 2.4 Using Superlatives

A *Over to You* Write three superlative sentences about yourself or people you know. In each sentence, use one word or expression from each column.

Expressions	Adjectives	Nouns
one of the	good	job
some of the	bad	family
my friend's / brother's / family's . . .	interesting	story
my / our / your	exciting	classes
	difficult	hometown
	useful	technology
	funny	life
	enjoyable	pet
	unusual	hobby

This has been one of the least exciting years of my life.

My brother's most unusual pet was a spider.

B *Over to You* Write three more superlative sentences about yourself or people you know. In each sentence, use one word or expression from each column.

Verbs	Adverbs	Expressions
study	well	I know
work	badly	of anyone I know
play	carefully	of my life
learn	quickly	of the year
walk	slowly	in my life
run	easily	in my family
speak English	fast	in the world
cook	quietly	
drive	creatively	

My friend Lisa cooks the best of anyone I know.

In my family, my mother drives the most carefully.

C *Pair Work* Compare your sentences with a partner.

D *Group Work* Tell the class something interesting about your partner and the people he or she knows.

This has been the most exciting year of Natalia's life. First, she came to the United States and started studying English. Then she met her fiancé.

3 | Avoid Common Mistakes ⚠

1. Use *the most* with long adjectives. Do not use -*est*.

most helpful
They were the ~~helpfulest~~ workers after the hurricane.

2. *Good* and *bad* have irregular superlative adjective and adverb forms.

worst   *best*
It was the ~~baddest~~ fire of the year.   Everyone worked ~~wellest~~ early in the morning.

3. Use a possessive pronoun before a superlative. Do not use an object pronoun.

his
Cleaning up after the storm was ~~him~~ biggest problem.

4. Do not put a superlative adverb between the verb and the object.

the fastest
They helped ~~the fastest~~ those people ∧ after the storm.

Editing Task

Find and correct nine more mistakes in the e-mail.

Hi Miko,

                                                       worst
    We had a terrible storm last week. It was the ~~baddest~~ storm of the decade. It was probably the terrifyingest experience of my life. The children were home with me. All three of them were scared, but Alexis behaved the wellest. She was the helpfulest. She kept the

5 other children calm. The dog was probably the difficultest! He barked and barked.

    After the storm, we went outside. The damage to our house is the baddest. Me biggest problem is getting someone to help us fix it. There were some people injured, so rescue workers helped the fastest those people. After that, they started cleaning up the most quickly our neighborhood. A tree fell on our garage and is still there, so that's us biggest

10 problem right now. We hope someone will move it tomorrow.

Pat

4 | Grammar for Writing ✏

Using Superlative Adjectives and Adverbs

Writers often use superlative adjectives and adverbs when writing about disasters and other extreme events.

Superlatives are common in news articles, academic writing, and other texts about important events in the news or in history.

Remember:

- **Use superlative adjectives and adverbs to focus on only one thing or situation and to show how it is the best, worst, least, or most of all the others.**

  The latest oil leak disaster was in the Gulf.

  One of the scariest days of my life was during Hurricane Andrew.

- **Put *the* in front of superlatives unless the superlative immediately follows a possessive.**

  The fire burned down many houses in the richest part of town. It was one of this year's worst fires.

Pre-writing Task

1 Read the paragraph below. What extreme event did the writer write about, and why was it so extreme?

The Worst Wildfire

There have been a lot of wildfires since we moved to California, but last year's fire was the worst because it was the biggest and it came the closest to our neighborhood. It was very hard to put out, and it lasted the longest of all the fires in the last few years. We watched the fire begin in the hills behind our neighborhood. At first, it was

5 very small, but it spread quickly. A lot of ash fell on us for days. The thickest ash fell during the first few days of the fire. It looked like thick, white snow. The air was also the smokiest on those days because the winds were blowing the hardest then. Those were my family's scariest days and nights. Many people think that lightning is the most common cause of wildfires, but this is not true. People are the biggest cause of wildfires.

10 In fact, the fire behind our neighborhood was caused by people camping in the woods.

2 Read the paragraph again. Underline the superlative adjectives and circle the superlative adverbs. <u>Double underline</u> the possessive + superlative combination.

Writing Task

1 *Write* Use the paragraph in the Pre-writing Task to help you write about an extreme event that you or someone you know experienced. Use superlative adjectives and adverbs to describe the event. You can write about events such as:

- a hurricane or very heavy rainstorm
- snow, hail, or a thunderstorm
- a very hot or very cold period
- a flood
- a tornado
- your own idea

2 *Self-Edit* Use the editing tips below to improve your paragraph. Make any necessary changes.

1. Did you use superlative adjectives and adverbs to write about an extreme event?
2. Did you use superlatives to focus on a single thing that was the worst or most compared to all the others?
3. Did you use *the* with superlatives unless you used a possessive?
4. Did you avoid the mistakes in the Avoid Common Mistakes chart on page 335?

28
Gerunds and Infinitives (1)
Managing Time

1 Grammar in the Real World

A Think of a time when someone made you wait. How did you feel? Read the web article about how different cultures think about time. What are some different ways that people see time?

Views of Time

Joe is a new manager at his company. He is leading his first team meeting today, and he is feeling frustrated. He **remembered to e-mail** everyone about the meeting, but one person is missing. Did she **forget to come**? Also, Joe **needs to leave** soon, but the group has not discussed everything on the agenda.¹ He **remembers arranging** a
5 two-hour meeting, and he has **tried to keep** the discussion moving forward. However, he has not succeeded. What is the problem? Many of Joe's team members are from different cultures, and different cultures see time very differently.

For people in some cultures, like Joe's, time is linear.² Events happen one after the other, along a time line, and each one has a beginning and an end point. People in
10 these cultures **like to control** their time. For example, Joe **enjoys keeping** a schedule, and he **likes being** punctual.³

However, people from other cultures, like some of Joe's team members, see time
15 as a cycle.⁴ In this view, events do not have specific beginning and end points – they occur and then reoccur. People from these cultures do not **expect to control** time, so they often do not **like to make** schedules.
20 Instead, they **prefer to be** flexible.

¹**agenda:** list of points to discuss | ²**linear:** following a straight line; continuing in a clear way from one part to the next | ³**punctual:** on time | ⁴**cycle:** a process that repeats

How can Joe **avoid experiencing** problems with multicultural meetings? Here are some tips: Get other people on the team to help plan the meeting. If they help create the agenda, it will be more realistic for them. Also, **try to be** flexible. Understand the reasons behind different ideas about time. **Try following** these tips, and you will
25 have more productive meetings.

B *Comprehension Check* Answer the questions.

1. Why does Joe feel frustrated?
2. If people like to control time, which view do they have?
3. If people don't expect to control time, which view do they have?
4. What are two tips for avoiding time problems with multicultural groups?

C *Notice* Underline the first verb (main verb) in the sentences below. Circle the second verb.

1. Joe needs to leave soon.

2. People from these cultures do not expect to control time.

3. Joe enjoys keeping a schedule.

4. How can Joe avoid experiencing problems with multicultural meetings?

Look at the second verb in the sentences. How are the second verbs in sentences 1 and 2 different from the ones in sentences 3 and 4?

2 | Verbs Followed by Gerunds or Infinitives

▶ Grammar Presentation

A gerund is the *-ing* form of a verb, used as a noun.	VERB GERUND I **kept looking** at the clock during the meeting.
An infinitive is *to* + the base form of a verb.	VERB INFINITIVE We **expected to finish** by 4:00 p.m.

2.1 Using Verbs with Gerunds and Infinitives

a. Some verbs can be followed by a gerund, but not by an infinitive.	I **kept looking** at the clock during the meeting. I kept ~~to look~~ at the clock during the meeting.
b. Some verbs can be followed by an infinitive, but not by a gerund.	We **expected to finish** by 4:00 p.m. We expected ~~finishing~~ by 4:00 p.m.

2.1 Using Verbs with Gerunds and Infinitives *(continued)*

c. Some verbs can be followed by an infinitive or by an object + an infinitive. These verbs include *expect*, *need*, and *want*.	VERB INFINITIVE *Roberto* *expects* *to go* *soon.* VERB OBJECT INFINITIVE *Roberto* *expects* **us** *to go* *soon.*
d. When a verb is followed by an infinitive or gerund, use *not* before the infinitive or gerund to form a negative statement.	*Jim suggested **not leaving** early today.* *We agreed **not to work** after 5 o'clock.*
e. You can use *and* or *or* to connect two infinitives or two gerunds. When you connect infinitives, you don't usually repeat *to*, especially when the sentence is short.	*We **suggested waiting and going** another day.* *I **need to stop and think** about this for a minute.*

▸◂ Spelling Rules for Verbs Ending in *-ing*: See page A4.

2.2 Verbs Followed by a Gerund Only

avoid	involve
consider	keep (continue)
deny	mind (object to)
enjoy	recall (remember)
finish	suggest

▸◂ Verbs + Gerunds and Infinitives: See page A5.

2.3 Verbs Followed by an Infinitive Only

agree	plan
decide	refuse
expect	seem
hope	tend (be likely)
need	want

Data from the Real World

Research shows that these are the most common verbs followed by a gerund in speaking and writing:			These are the most common verbs followed by an infinitive in speaking and writing:		
avoid	finish	miss	agree	hope	seem
consider	involve	practice	decide	need	tend
deny	keep	risk	expect	plan	want
enjoy	mind	suggest	fail	refuse	

▶ Grammar Application

Exercise 2.1 Listening for Gerunds and Infinitives

🔊 Listen to a podcast about how people think about time. Complete the sentences with the gerund or infinitive you hear.

Most people feel that time speeds up as they get older. At the end of each day, adults often ask themselves: Why haven't I done the things that I planned _to do_ (do) today?
(1)

When you are a child, time seems

_____ (go) very slowly. As you get
(2)

older, time tends _____ (pass) more quickly. Why do adults and children
(3)

see time differently?

According to psychologists, one theory is that children tend

_____ (look) forward. On a car trip, for example, children always
(4)

want _____ (arrive). They ask, "Are we there yet?" Children
(5)

look forward, so time seems _____ (last) longer. Adults, on the
(6)

other hand, enjoy _____ (look) back and _____ (think)
(7)   (8)

about their memories.

In addition, adults tend _____ (be) busy, so time
(9)

often passes more quickly for them. Also, most adults will keep

_____ (look) at their watch throughout the day, and as a
(10)

result, be more aware of time.

Finally, children have a lot of new experiences to process, but as people get

older, they do not tend _____ (have) so many new experiences.
(11)

This also speeds time up. Maybe experiencing new adventures as we get older

can help us feel as if we can regain a little bit of that childhood sense of time.

Exercise 2.2 Gerund or Infinitive?

Complete the e-mail about problems with time in multicultural business settings.
Circle the correct answer.

| Send | Attach | Save Draft | Spelling ▾ | Cancel |

To: Production Team
From: jj@cambridge.org
Date: Wednesday, July 13
Subject: Time Management Issues

B *I* <u>U</u> ≡▾ ≔ ⇥

Dear Team,

As you all know, yesterday morning we had an important meeting. I hoped
(**to finish**)/ **finishing** at noon. However, the meeting did not end until 1:30 p.m. In
   (1)
addition, we did not finish **to discuss / discussing** everything on the agenda. I do
                              (2)
not mind **to end / ending** late. However, we need **to cover / covering** everything on
           (3)   (4)
the agenda.

At the end of the meeting, some of you suggested **to continue / continuing**
                                                          (5)
our discussions over lunch. I usually avoid **to combine / combining** work with
                                                  (6)
meals, so I suggested **not to do / not doing** that. We also considered
                          (7)
to stop / stopping and **to continue / continuing** another day. In the end, we decided
    (8)   (9)
to arrange / arranging another meeting for next week.
    (10)
I want **to feel / you to feel** good about coming to meetings when I ask you to
          (11)
come. For this reason, I need **to help / the team to help** me plan meetings from now
                                  (12)
on. Can we agree **to write / writing** the agenda for next week's meeting together?
                      (13)
Can I expect **to participate / everyone to participate** with me in this?
                  (14)
Good time management involves **to agree / agreeing** on an agenda and then
                                      (15)
follow / following it. I hope you all agree.
    (16)
Sincerely,

Joe

Exercise 2.3 Using Gerunds and Infinitives

A What can you tell the people in these situations? Give advice with gerunds or infinitives.

Situation	Advice
1. My friends always come late to my parties.	Your friends need _to call you and tell you that they are going to be late_ .
2. Heather is always late for class.	She should plan _____ _____ .
3. Roberto always turns his homework in late.	He should avoid _____ _____ .
4. Time goes so slowly for me at work. I look at the clock again and again, but it never changes!	You shouldn't keep _____ _____ .
5. Wei doesn't leave me a message when he's going to be late.	He should agree _____ _____ .
6. Lisa refuses to wear a watch.	She needs _____ _____ .

B *Pair Work* Compare answers in A with a partner. Is your advice similar or different?

A *I think Heather should plan to get to class on time.*
B *I said Heather should plan to have a friend call her one hour before class starts.*

3 | Verbs Followed by Gerunds and Infinitives

▶ Grammar Presentation

Some verbs can be followed by both a gerund and an infinitive. Sometimes the meaning is the same. Sometimes it is different.	*I **stopped e-mailing** the agendas.* (For a while, I e-mailed the agendas. Then I stopped doing that.) *I **stopped to e-mail** the agendas.* (different meaning) (First I stopped what I was doing. Then I e-mailed the agendas.)

3.1 Using Verbs Followed by Gerunds and Infinitives

a. Some verbs can be followed by an infinitive or a gerund without a change in meaning. These verbs include *begin*, *continue*, *hate*, *like*, *love*, *prefer*, and *start*.	*Everyone **began to speak / speaking** at the same time.* *Wei **loves to get up / getting up** early.*
b. Some verbs can be followed by an infinitive or a gerund, but the meaning changes. These verbs include *forget*, *remember*, *stop*, and *try*.	*Luis **will** never **forget meeting** the president.* (Luis met the president, and he will never forget that he did this.) *Luis **must** not **forget to enclose** his résumé with his application.* (Luis has not enclosed his résumé with his application yet, and he must not forget to do this.)
c. In sentences with *forget*, *remember*, or *stop* + a gerund, the gerund tells what happens first.	SECOND EVENT FIRST EVENT *Jim **remembered making** an appointment.* (First Jim made the appointment. Later, he remembered this.)
In sentences with *forget*, *remember*, or *stop* + an infinitive, the infinitive tells what happens second, after the action of the main verb.	FIRST EVENT SECOND EVENT *Jim **remembered to make** an appointment.* (First Jim remembered that he needed to make an appointment. Then he made it.)
d. In sentences with *try* + gerund, the action of the gerund generally happens.	*Marta **tried setting** her alarm for 6:00 a.m., but she was still late.* (She set the alarm.)
In sentences with *try* + infinitive, the action of the infinitive often does not happen or is not successful.	*Marta **tried to set** her alarm for 6:00 a.m., but the clock wasn't working.* (She didn't set the alarm.)
e. You can use *and* or *or* to connect two infinitives or two gerunds. With infinitives, you don't usually repeat *to*, especially when the sentence is short.	*He **loves planning and attending** meetings.* *He **loves to plan and attend** meetings.* *I **like walking or riding** a bike to work.*
With verbs that can be followed by either a gerund or an infinitive, use the same form for both after the verb.	*I **like walking and riding** a bike to work.* *I like walking and ~~to ride~~ my bike to work.*

▶ # Grammar Application

Exercise 3.1 Same or Different Meaning?

A Rewrite the sentences. Change the gerunds in **bold** to infinitives and the infinitives in **bold** to gerunds. If the meaning of the sentence stays the same, write *S* next to the sentence. If the meaning is different, write *D*.

1. I remembered **making** an appointment with the doctor.

I remembered to make an appointment with the doctor.   *D*

2. My co-workers and I like **to learn** about how different cultures view time.

_____   _____

3. We began **discussing** our plans for next year.

_____   _____

4. To manage her time, our colleague Kelly tried **to buy** a calendar.

_____   _____

5. Our boss started **to accept** that different cultures see time differently.

_____   _____

6. Kelly and I love **having** a very long lunch break.

_____   _____

7. Our colleague Bill hates **mixing** work and social activities.

_____   _____

8. Our co-workers didn't stop **eating** lunch until 4:00 p.m.

_____   _____

9. We continued **to discuss** our problems until very late at night.

_____   _____

10. Jill forgot **to contact** Janet last week.

_____   _____

11. Bo remembered **writing** and **sending** the memo.

_____   _____

B *Pair Work* In which sentences in A does the meaning change? Explain the difference in meaning to a partner.

The meaning is different in number 1. In the first sentence, he made the appointment and later remembered that. In the second sentence, he first remembered that he needed to make an appointment. Then he made it.

Exercise 3.2 *Forget, Remember, Stop,* and *Try*

Read the class discussion. Circle the correct answer.

Ms. Vargas Class, tell me how you did research for this assignment. Did most of you use the web?

Laura Well, yes. I tried **reading**/ **to read** a long article on the web. The conclusion
(1)
was good, but I didn't learn much from the rest of the article. I found another article on a website about linear time, but I stopped **reading** / **to read** it
(2)
because it wasn't very academic.

Wendy I tried **getting / to get** on to a website about

(3)
time and psychology, but I couldn't make it
work. It kept shutting down.

Ms. Vargas Did anyone else have trouble?

Ahmet No. Not really. I remember **reading / to read**

(4)
one article that wasn't very good. I found
another really good website, though, and I
luckily remembered **bookmarking / to bookmark**

(5)
it before I closed it.

Wendy That was a good idea! I found one good site, but I forgot
bookmarking / to bookmark it. I was reading an article, but then

(6)
I stopped **reading / to read** and answered the phone. When I got

(7)
back, my computer was off. That was weird because I don't remember
shutting / to shut it down!

(8)

Diego I didn't use the web. In fact, I read a book. I prefer books. I read for a
while and take notes, then I stop **thinking / to think** for a few minutes

(9)
about my own ideas. Then I add my ideas to the notes.

Exercise 3.3 Using Verbs Followed by Gerunds and Infinitives

A *Over to You* Answer the questions about time. Write complete sentences.

1. Where do you like to go when you have free time?

   I like to go/going to the beach when I have free time.

2. What do you prefer to do after work or school?

   _____

3. What do you try doing when you feel bored?

   _____

4. How do you remember not to miss appointments?

   _____

B *Pair Work* Ask and answer the questions in A with a partner. Are your answers
similar or different?

4 Avoid Common Mistakes ⚠

1. Do not use gerunds after verbs that require infinitives.

to discuss
They did not expect ~~discussing~~ work during lunch.

2. Do not use infinitives after verbs that require gerunds.

writing
We finished ~~to write~~ our report at 5:00 p.m.

3. Remember: Infinitives include *to*.

to
I want∧learn about other cultures.

Editing Task

Find and correct eight more mistakes in this paragraph from a web article about time and boredom.

Fighting Boredom

looking
Do you keep ~~to look~~ at the clock when you are bored? Does time seem going slowly for you? If you expect having a boring life, you will have a boring life. It is time to make a change! Here are things you can do to avoid to feel bored. First, try look at the

5 clock less often. Time will go more quickly. Next, use your time differently. Start thinking about things that interest you. Try do things that you know will be interesting. If you enjoy to do an activity, time will pass more quickly. In addition, do things that involve changing your daily habits. For example, try wearing your

10 watch on the other wrist or to brush your teeth with the other hand. If your mind is active, time will seem passing more quickly.

5 | Grammar for Writing ✏

Using Gerunds and Infinitives

Writers often use verb + gerund or verb + infinitive combinations to describe people's behavior or habits.

Verb + gerund and verb + infinitive combinations are common in personal stories, letters or e-mails, advice columns, and other texts about people's behavior or habits. Remember:

- **Some verbs take only gerunds after them, while others take only infinitives. It's a good idea to check when you aren't sure.**

  I don't <u>mind waiting</u> for people.   He always <u>seems to be</u> late for things.

- **Some verbs take both gerunds and infinitives, but the meaning can change.**

  She <u>stopped to talk</u> to her friend and was late to class. (She talked to her friend.)

  She <u>stopped talking</u> to her friend after she was late again. (She no longer talked to her friend.)

Pre-writing Task

1 Read the paragraph below. What is one good way to stay organized?

Getting Organized

The expression "There are never enough hours in a day" **seems to be** true more and more these days. Our lives are filled with lots of tasks. To use your time well, **try organizing** yourself. **Learning to do** this **involves organizing** both your space and your mind. Organizing your space **involves creating** a way to organize the piles of

5 papers and mail you receive at home, school, and work. **Try dividing** this paper into separate files, for example, have one each for home, work, and school. If you work in an office, you will probably **need to organize** your papers into several categories. Ones that work very well are "in" and "out" boxes and a "work in progress" box. Next, **start to organize** your mind. Remembering everything you have to do is impossible,

10 so **try creating** a "to do" list. The next step is prioritizing the tasks on the list. Which ones are the most important to finish? When do you **expect to finish** them? After answering these questions, write the tasks on a calendar. Once you are organized, it is important to stay organized. For example, if you **decided to finish** your homework in the mornings and go grocery shopping after class, stick to this plan.

15 Also, **focus on finishing** the most important tasks on the calendar. After a week, check how well this new organization is going and make any changes. You will soon find that by managing your time and space, you have saved a lot of time.

2 Read the paragraph again. Look at the words in **bold**. Underline the verb + gerund combinations and circle the verb + infinitive combinations. Which verbs can take gerunds or infinitives? Does the meaning change for these verbs?

Writing Task

1 *Write*   Use the paragraph in the Pre-writing Task to help you write suggestions for organizing your schedule. Use verb + gerund and verb + infinitive combinations from the unit.

2 *Self-Edit*   Use the editing tips below to improve your paragraph. Make any necessary changes.

1. Did you use verbs + gerunds and verbs + infinitives to describe people's behavior or habits?
2. Did you use the correct form (gerund or infinitive) after each verb?
3. Did you use any verbs that can take both gerunds or infinitives? If so, did you use the correct form to express the meaning you wanted?
4. Did you avoid the mistakes in the Avoid Common Mistakes chart on page 347?

29

Gerunds and Infinitives (2)

Civil Rights

1 Grammar in the Real World

A Are all people treated fairly in the United States today? Read the article about the civil rights movement. What types of discrimination have become illegal since the 1960s?

The 1960s and Civil Rights

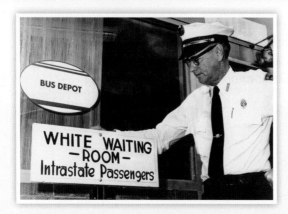

BUS DEPOT

WHITE WAITING
—ROOM—
Intrastate Passengers

In the 1960s, a 35-year-old American woman applied for a job as a flight attendant. The airline **was not interested in hiring** her. They told her she was too old.

5 **Discriminating**[1] against people because of their age or for other reasons was common in the United States in the past. However, certain laws make it less common today. The struggle to pass many of these laws began during the
10 civil rights movement.[2]

In the 1960s, laws in many states segregated[3] African Americans. For example,

in some states, African Americans and whites went to separate schools. In addition, African Americans couldn't buy houses in many 15 "white" neighborhoods. Civil rights workers opposed this segregation and worked hard **to call** attention to unfair laws. **Changing** the laws wasn't easy. However, in 1964, the U.S. Congress passed the Civil Rights Act. Now, 20 because of this law, **it is illegal to segregate** people.

After the Civil Rights Act of 1964, other groups became **interested in fighting** for civil rights. These groups included women and 25 people with disabilities.[4] This led to many new laws. Today, for example, **it is against the law to build** a school without access[5] for people in wheelchairs. Not **hiring** people because of their age is also illegal. 30

Discrimination is still a problem in the United States today. Hopefully, however, people will **keep on working** for equal rights for all groups. **By working** hard, we can **succeed in passing** even more new laws to stop the 35 spread of discrimination.

---

[1]**discriminate:** treat people differently, in an unfair way | [2]**the civil rights movement:** the struggle for equal rights for African Americans | [3]**segregate:** keep one group of people separate because of race, religion, etc. | [4]**disability:** a physical or mental challenge, such as difficulty walking or seeing | [5]**access:** easy ways to enter

B *Comprehension Check*   Answer the questions.

1. What kinds of discrimination were there in the United States in the past?
2. What are two examples of segregation?
3. What did civil rights workers want to change?
4. What other groups fought for civil rights after Congress passed the Civil Rights Act of 1964?

C *Notice*   Find the sentences in the reading and complete them.

1. _____ the laws wasn't easy.
2. _____ against people because of their age or for other reasons was common in the United States in the past.
3. Now, because of this law, it is illegal _____ people.
4. Civil rights workers opposed this segregation and worked hard _____ attention to unfair laws.

Look at sentences 1 and 2. You learned that gerunds can come after certain verbs. Where else can gerunds occur in a sentence? Look at sentences 3 and 4. One infinitive shows a purpose or reason for the action. Which one?

2 More About Gerunds

▶ Grammar Presentation

Gerunds can be the subjects of sentences and the objects of prepositions. They can also come after *be*.	SUBJECT GERUND ***Changing** the laws wasn't easy.* OBJECT OF A PREPOSITION *We can change the law **by working** hard.* BE + GERUND *His job **is trying** to help people fight for their rights.*

2.1 Using Gerunds as Subjects, After Prepositions, and After *Be*

a. Gerunds can be the subjects of sentences. A gerund subject is singular. It takes third-person singular verb forms.	***Discriminating** against people because of age is illegal.*
b. Gerunds can be used after prepositions.	*We can succeed **in passing** more laws against discrimination.*
Note: An infinitive cannot be the object of a preposition.	*They weren't interested **in ~~to hire~~** her.*
c. Use *by* + gerund to express how something is done.	*You can change laws **by voting**.*

2.1 Using Gerunds as Subjects, After Prepositions, and After *Be* (continued)

d. Certain verb + preposition + gerund combinations are very common.	VERB PREP. GERUND We **believe in fighting** for our rights.
Certain adjective + preposition + gerund combinations are also very common, especially after the verb *be*.	ADJECTIVE PREP. GERUND They weren't **interested in hiring** her.
e. Gerunds can also come after *be*.	VERB GERUND The worst part of her job **was talking** to angry customers.

Data from the Real World

Research shows that these are very common verb + preposition + gerund combinations:

believe in	*forget about*	*succeed in*	*think about*	*worry about*
disagree with	*keep on* (continue)	*talk about*	*think of*	

Research shows that these are very common adjective + preposition + gerund combinations:

afraid of	*good at*	*important in*	*involved in*	*tired of*
aware of	*important for*	*interested in*	*sorry about*	*worried about*

▸▸ Verb + Gerunds and Infinitives: See page A5.
▸▸ Verb and Preposition Combinations: See page A5.

▶ Grammar Application

Exercise 2.1 Gerunds as Subjects, After Prepositions, and After *Be*

A Complete the essay on Rosa Parks with the gerund form of the verbs in parentheses.

Rosa Parks is a hero in the American civil rights movement. Her work was important in
ending (end) segregation in Montgomery,
(1)
Alabama. Parks's major contribution to civil rights was one very simple act. That act was

_____ (refuse) to stand up and
(2)
move to another seat on a bus.

In Montgomery, Alabama, in the 1950s, African Americans had to stand if a white person wanted a seat on a city bus. This was a law. Rosa Parks did not agree with this law. She worked very long hours every day, and she often had to stand up and give her seat to a white person, even though she was exhausted and her feet hurt. Parks was tired of _____ (do) this. She did not believe
(3)
in _____ (give) her bus seat to a white person for no reason. In
(4)
addition, she was not afraid of _____ (try) to stop something that
(5)
was wrong. Therefore, one day, Parks refused to stand up and move when the bus driver asked her to.

The police arrested Parks. Her arrest angered many African Americans in Alabama. In fact, many people across the entire United States did not believe in _____ (treat) African Americans this way. They were
(6)
interested in _____ (support) civil rights. These people helped by
(7)
_____ (send) money to the civil rights organizers in Alabama. This
(8)
support succeeded in _____ (pressure) the state of Alabama. As a
(9)
result, Alabama changed its laws.

Rosa Parks was involved in _____ (get) an important civil right
(10)
for African Americans. Her one simple act also inspired other people around the country to keep on _____ (work) to end discrimination.
(11)

B *Pair Work* Ask and answer questions with a partner about Rosa Parks. Use a form of the words in the box and a gerund, or your own ideas.

be afraid of	be involved in	disagree with
be important in	believe in	keep on
be interested in	be tired of	succeed in

A *What was Rosa Parks tired of doing?*
B *She was tired of giving up her seat on the bus.*

Exercise 2.2 More Gerunds as Subjects, After Prepositions, and After *Be*

A Complete the sentences in the civil rights time line with the words in parentheses. Use the gerund form, and add prepositions where needed. Note: All main verbs are in the present tense.

Civil Rights Time Line – The Early Days

1948 – _Discriminating_ (discriminate) against people in the military because of race,
(1)
religion, or national origin becomes illegal.

1954 – After much debate and discussion, the U.S. Supreme Court _agrees to ending_
(2)
(agree / end) segregation in public schools.

1955 – Martin Luther King Jr. _____ (be involved / start) the
(3)
Montgomery bus boycott.

1957 – Martin Luther King Jr. starts a civil rights organization, the Southern Christian
Leadership Conference. King and his organization have many ideas about
_____ (fight) for civil rights peacefully.
(4)

1960 – Four African-American students fight segregation by _____ (sit)
(5)
at a lunch counter. No one serves them, but they _____ (keep / sit)
(6)
at the counter. By _____ (do) this, they start the idea of "sit-ins" –
(7)
peaceful demonstrations in the civil rights movement.

1962 – James Meredith _____ (succeed / become) the first
(8)
African-American student to enroll at the University of Mississippi.

1963 – 200,000 people _____
(9)
(be involved / march) in Washington, D.C. They
do this to show their support for civil rights.

1967 – _____ (not allow)
(10)
interracial marriage becomes illegal. African
Americans and whites can now marry each other.

1968 – More and more Americans _____
(11)
(be involved / work) for civil rights.

B *Group Work*   Discuss civil rights in a group. Answer the questions.

1. Are there civil rights issues you are interested in supporting? If so, which ones?
2. Have you ever been involved in marching or protesting to support a civil right? If so, where and when?

3 | More About Infinitives

▶ Grammar Presentation

Infinitives can come after *be*. They are also often used with *in order* to show a purpose.	One idea was **to organize** farm workers. African-American children had to walk **(in order) to get** to school.
It + infinitive sentences are also very common.	**It** was difficult **to be** an African American in the 1960s.

3.1 Using Infinitives After *Be*, to Show Purpose, and in *It* + Infinitive Sentences

a. Like gerunds, infinitives can follow *be*.	Her job is **to help** other people. The purpose of the demonstration is **to get** people's attention.
b. *In order* + infinitive expresses a purpose. It answers a "*Why?*" question. You can use the infinitive alone when the meaning is clear.	People are fighting **in order to change unfair laws**. People are fighting **to change** unfair laws. Why are people fighting? **To change** unfair laws.
When *and* connects two infinitives of purpose, *(in order) to* is usually not repeated.	They were working **(in order) to change laws and help** people.
c. *It* + infinitive sentences are very common. *It* + infinitive sentences often include the verbs *be, cost, seem,* and *take*.	**It** is important **to fight** against discrimination. **It** costs a lot of money **to run** for office. **It** seems difficult **to revise** immigration laws. **It** takes time **to change** people's minds.
An *It* + infinitive sentence usually has the same meaning as a sentence with a gerund subject. The gerund subject is more formal.	**It** was her dream **to have equal rights for everyone**. **Having equal rights for everyone** was her dream.

► Grammar Application

Exercise 3.1 Infinitives After *Be*, to Show Purpose, and with *It*

🔊 Listen to a podcast on an early hero in the women's rights movement. Complete the sentences with the words you hear.

It was difficult _to be_ a woman in the United
    (1)
States in the early part of the twentieth century.

Women did not have many rights. For example, they

were not able to vote.

In 1917, Alice Paul organized a group of

women _____ for the right to vote in
         (2)
national elections. The group demonstrated in front

of the White House in order _____
                             (3)
the president's attention. This angered many people. The police arrested many women

_____ the demonstrations. However, this didn't work, so they arrested Paul
    (4)
and gave her a seven-month jail sentence in order _____ the other women.
                                                   (5)
This was unfair, but Alice Paul was strong. She stopped eating. She went on a hunger strike

_____ attention to the issue of women's rights.
    (6)
Paul suffered in order _____ the right to vote, but in the end, this and
                        (7)
other demonstrations worked. Congress finally gave women the vote in 1920.

Exercise 3.2 More Infinitives

A Complete the textbook passage about César Chávez. Use the correct form of the verbs in the boxes.

focus	get	help	improve

César Chávez was a Mexican-American farm worker.

He was also a civil rights worker. He fought _to get_ equal
                                              (1)
rights for Mexican Americans and _____ the
                                  (2)
lives of farm workers.

Chávez was interested in workers' rights at an early age. He was born in Arizona in 1927. When he was growing up, he experienced discrimination. **For example, it was against school rules to speak Spanish.** If children spoke Spanish, the teacher punished them.

In the 1950s, Chávez joined a civil rights group _____ Mexican (3) Americans register and vote in elections. He gave speeches _____ (4) people's attention on workers' rights. Later, he started the National Farm Workers Association.

| be | help | pay | stop | use |

It was difficult _____ a farm worker in the 1950s. For (5) **example, it was common _____ farm workers very low wages.** (6) **It was also common _____ dangerous pesticides (toxic chemicals)** (7) **on farm crops.**

It was Chávez's dream _____ these things. In the 1960s, he (8) organized a strike _____ farm workers. (9)

| convince | get | help | show |

The purpose of the strike was _____ higher pay for the workers. (10) The strike succeeded, and finally, farm workers got higher wages. In the 1980s, Chávez used another strike _____ growers to stop the use of (11) pesticides on grapes.

César Chávez worked all his life _____ Mexican Americans and (12) farm workers. Today, his birthday is a state holiday in California and in seven other states. The purpose of César Chávez Day is _____ respect for (13) his important work.

B Rewrite each **boldfaced** sentence from the reading. Use a gerund subject.

For example, it was against the rules to speak Spanish.

1. _For example, speaking Spanish was against the rules._

2. _____

3. _____

4. _____

5. _____

C *Pair Work* Ask and answer the questions about César Chávez with a partner. Use infinitives.

1. What did César Chávez work for all his life?

   He worked to improve the lives of Mexican Americans and farm workers.

2. Why did Chávez join a civil rights group in the 1950s?

3. Why did Chávez give speeches in the 1950s?

4. Why was it difficult to be a farm worker?

5. Why did Chávez organize a strike in the 1960s? in the 1980s?

6. What is the purpose of César Chávez Day?

D *Over to You* Think about civil rights today. Are there still problems? What do we still need to work on? Complete the following sentences on a separate piece of paper. Then share your sentences with the class.

Today, it is still difficult to help women get the same pay as men.

It still seems hard for [group] to . . .

People are still fighting to . . .

We are still working to . . .

It is my dream to . . .

4 Avoid Common Mistakes ⚠

1. Gerund subjects take singular verbs.

　　　　　　　　is
　Changing laws ~~are~~ a slow process.

2. Use the correct preposition in verb + preposition and adjective + preposition combinations.

　　　　　　　　in
　They succeeded ~~on~~ getting more rights.

　　　　　　　　of
　Do not be afraid ~~for~~ standing up for your rights.

3. Do not use an infinitive after a preposition.

　　　　　　　　hiring
　They weren't interested in ~~to hire~~ her.

4. Do not use *for* in infinitives of purpose.

　He worked hard ~~for~~ to help workers with disabilities.

5. Don't forget *It* or *to* in *It* sentences.

　It is　　　　*to*
　~~Is~~ important ∧ attend the march this weekend.

Editing Task

Find and correct ten more mistakes in this paragraph.

　　　　　　　　　　　　　to
　　　It was more difficult ∧ be disabled in the United States in the
past. It was hard do things like enter buildings or cross the street if
you were in a wheelchair. In many places, it was impossible bring a
guide dog into a restaurant. Many people were interested in to help
5　the disabled. They worked hard for to help people with disabilities.
They finally succeeded on passing an important law. It was the
Americans with Disabilities Act of 1990. Today, sight-impaired
people are not afraid for bringing their dogs into any building.
Making streets accessible to people with physical disabilities are
10　another result of the 1990 law. For example, adding gentle slopes
to the edges of sidewalks help the disabled. Now a person in a
wheelchair doesn't worry about to get from one side of the street
to the other. Making changes like these are a slow process, but an
important one.

5 | Grammar for Writing ✏️

Using Gerunds and Infinitives

Writers often use gerunds as subjects and after prepositions to focus on the importance of an action. They use infinitives to show a purpose when describing people's goals and reasons for doing something.

Gerunds and infinitives with prepositions appear in almost every kind of text and are common in interviews, personal profiles, and other articles that describe people's goals and motivations.

Remember:

- **Focus attention on an action by making it a gerund subject. The gerund is singular.**

  Fighting for your rights is an important thing to do.

- **Gerunds often follow certain verbs + prepositions or adjectives + prepositions.**

  Many people are not interested in making the effort to fight for their rights.

- **You can use infinitives with or without *in order* when talking about the purpose of an action.**

  I e-mailed my senator (in order) to ask her to help us.

Pre-writing Task

1 Read the paragraph below. What group of people is the paragraph about? What was the problem and what was the solution?

Taking Care of Families

Being a full-time employee and a mother of small children is not easy. What happens when your child gets sick? In the past, you could lose your job for taking time off to take care of a sick child or give birth to a baby. Many people struggled to change this situation, and in 1993, the passing of the Family and Medical Leave Act improved things for pregnant women and for families in general in the United States. This law stopped employers from firing new mothers. Now, employers have to give employees up to 12 weeks off from work in order to take care of their new babies. In addition, after 12 weeks, employers have to give these women a job again. This law is also good for anyone with a sick child, a sick husband or wife, or even a sick parent.

2 Read the paragraph again. Underline the gerund subjects, circle the gerunds that follow prepositions, and <u>double underline</u> the infinitives that show purpose.

Writing Task

1 *Write* Use the paragraph in the Pre-writing Task to help you write about a group of people who fought for or are fighting for their rights. You can use the Internet to help you. Why was or is life difficult for this group? What rights was or is this group fighting for? Use gerunds as subjects and after prepositions, and use infinitives to talk about purpose.

2 *Self-Edit* Use the editing tips below to improve your paragraph. Make any necessary changes.

1. Did you use gerunds and infinitives to describe people's goals and reasons for those goals?
2. Did you use the third-person singular after subject gerunds?
3. Did you use gerunds after verb + preposition and adjective + preposition combinations?
4. Did you use infinitives with and without *in order* to show the purpose of an action?
5. Did you avoid the mistakes in the Avoid Common Mistakes chart on page 359?

Subject Relative Clauses (Adjective Clauses with Subject Relative Pronouns)

Sleep

1 | Grammar in the Real World

A How many hours a night do you sleep? Read the article about scientific research on sleep. Why do some people need only a few hours of sleep?

Sleep and Science

Sleep is important. We need it to live, but not everyone gets the same amount of sleep each night. There are many people **who need eight or more hours of sleep a night**.

5 However, there are also others **who are happy with only four or five hours**. Scientists call these people "short sleepers." Is this simply a lifestyle choice? Not necessarily. Researchers recently found a gene mutation[1] **that might**
10 **control our sleep**.

Recently, a research team studied a mother and her daughter **who are short sleepers**. They only sleep about six hours a night. The researchers analyzed the DNA[2] of the entire family, and they found a gene mutation in both the mother and daughter. The team already knew about this gene, the hDEC2 gene. It controls sleep in animals.
15 They made a guess: People **who have the mutation** might need less sleep than other people.

The researchers then created mice **that had the same hDEC2 gene mutation**. The mice **that had the gene mutation** slept less at night than mice **that didn't have the mutation**. After that, the researchers forced both kinds of mice to stay awake. The
20 mice **that did not have the mutation needed extra sleep**. The mice **that had the mutation did not**.

These researchers think genetics might be more important for our sleeping patterns than lifestyle. If you only sleep four or five hours a night, your lifestyle might not be to blame. Perhaps it's just in your genes!

[1]**gene mutation:** a change in the structure of a gene, the pattern of cell structure that we get from our parents |
[2]**DNA:** chemical in the cells of living things that controls the structure of each cell

B *Comprehension Check* Answer the questions.

1. What might control how much sleep we get?
2. What do scientists call people who do not need a lot of sleep?
3. Why did scientists study a mother and her daughter?
4. What did the experiment with mice show?

C *Notice* Find the sentences in the article and complete them.

1. There are many people _____ need eight or more hours of sleep a night.

2. Researchers recently found a gene mutation _____ might control our sleep.

3. The researchers then created mice _____ had the same hDEC2 gene mutation.

4. The mice _____ did not have the mutation needed extra sleep.

Look at the words you wrote. Circle the noun that each one refers to.

2 | Subject Relative Clauses

▶ Grammar Presentation

Relative clauses define, describe, identify, or give more information about nouns. Like all clauses, relative clauses have both a subject and a verb.

RELATIVE CLAUSE

SUBJECT   VERB

The team studied people **who** **slept only four to six hours**. *(who = people)*

2.1 Subject Relative Clauses

	RELATIVE CLAUSE			
	Subject Relative Pronoun	**Verb**		
The scientists studied people	**who**	**slept**	**only four to six hours.**	
The mice	**that**	**had**	**the gene mutation**	slept less at night.
It is a gene	**which**	**controls**	**sleep in animals.**	

2.2 Using Subject Relative Clauses

a. In a subject relative clause, the relative pronoun is the subject of the clause.	RELATIVE CLAUSE RELATIVE PRONOUN *There are people **who** only need about six hours of sleep.* RELATIVE CLAUSE RELATIVE PRONOUN *A mouse **that** had a mutated gene needed less sleep.*
b. The subject relative pronouns are *who, which,* and *that.*	
Use *who* or *that* for people.	*She's the researcher **who/that** heads the sleep project.*
Use *which* or *that* for things and animals.	*They created a mouse **which/that** had the same gene.*
c. Subject relative clauses combine two ideas.	*The scientists studied <u>mice</u>.* + *The <u>mice</u> had a gene mutation.* *The scientists studied <u>mice</u> **that** had a gene mutation.*
d. The verb after the relative pronoun agrees with the noun or pronoun before the relative pronoun.	*<u>People</u> **who** have the hDEC2 gene need less sleep.* *I know a <u>woman</u> **who** sleeps only four hours a night.*
e. A subject relative clause usually comes right after the word it modifies. It can modify any noun or pronoun in a sentence.	SUBJECT *<u>Someone</u> **who has the hDEC2 gene** sleeps less.* *The scientists studied <u>mice</u> **who had a mutated gene**.* *The women participated in a <u>study</u> **that ended last year**.*

▶ Grammar Application

Exercise 2.1 Subject Relative Clauses

Read the student summary of a science article. Circle the relative pronouns and underline the relative clauses.

Many researchers have done studies (that) look at sleep. This article is about a study

that compares the habits of good sleepers and bad sleepers. A group of scientists who

specialize in sleep research did the study. First, the scientists studied people who sleep

well. They learned about the habits that might make these people good sleepers. Then the

5 scientists studied people who do not sleep well. These short sleepers often have habits

which are very different from the habits of good sleepers. From this study, the researchers have developed the following tips for people who cannot sleep. First, do not drink caffeinated beverages like tea or coffee after noon. In addition, eat dinner at least three hours before going to bed, and, finally, get some exercise every day. These are three habits

10 of good sleepers. If you are a person who does not sleep well at night, try to start doing these things. They could help you change your sleep patterns.

Data from the Real World

Research shows that in informal speaking and writing, people use either *who* or *that* to refer to people.	A *Do you know the woman **who/that participated in the study**?* B *Yes. She's my aunt.*
In formal writing, people use *who* to refer to people and *that* or *which* to refer to things. *Which* is more formal.	*Participants **who had the hDEC2 gene** slept less.* *A report on the study **that/which showed a genetic basis for sleep patterns** appears in the journal* Genetics Today.

Exercise 2.2 *Who, That*, or *Which*?

Complete the article about sleep with the correct **formal** relative pronouns. Circle the noun that each relative pronoun refers to.

A Good Night's Sleep

Everyone needs a good night's sleep. This is important for staying healthy. However, (people) _____*who*_____ have trouble sleeping often worry about
(1)
their health. Troubled sleepers can get help from recent studies. Researchers

_____ study sleep have good advice for people with sleep problems. A
(2)
study _____ appeared recently showed some interesting results. Not
(3)
everyone needs the same amount of sleep. Most people need 8 to 8½ hours of

sleep a night. However, some people _____ have a special gene need less
(4)
sleep. People _____ have this gene probably cannot change their sleep
(5)
habits. They should not worry about sleeping less. However, sleep researchers

have some advice for people _____ do not have this gene.
(6)

People _____ have trouble sleeping should avoid caffeine after

(7)

noon. Some men and women _____ have trouble sleeping have found

(8)

it helps to exercise. Even walking 20 minutes every day can help. One idea

_____ has helped many people is for them to go to bed only when they

(9)

are tired. This might mean going to bed at 2:00 a.m. and waking up at 7:00 a.m.

Another strategy _____ has helped people is moving bedtime back 15

(10)

minutes each night until it is 8 hours before it is time to wake up.

Exercise 2.3 Using Subject Relative Clauses

A Complete the questions with a relative pronoun and the correct form of the verb.

1. Do you know someone _who/that_ _has_ (have) trouble sleeping? Who?

2. Do you know someone _____ _____ (sleep) nine
   hours most nights? Who?

3. Do you read websites or articles _____ _____ (give)
   tips on sleeping? Which websites or articles?

4. Do you have a friend _____ _____ (stay) up late?
   Who?

5. Do you have a relative _____ _____ (wake up)
   early most days? Who?

6. Do you have friends _____ _____ (take) naps?
   Who?

7. Do you have a favorite sleeping position _____ _____ (help)
   you get to sleep? What position is it?

8. Do you have tips _____ _____ (help) you get to
   sleep? What are they?

B *Group Work* Ask and answer the questions in A in a small group.
Compare answers.

A Do you have a favorite sleeping position that helps you get to sleep?

B Yes, I do.

C What position is it?

B I sleep on my back. What about you?

Exercise 2.4 Sentence Combining

A Combine the sentences from a web article on sleep position and personality. Make the second sentence a subject relative clause.

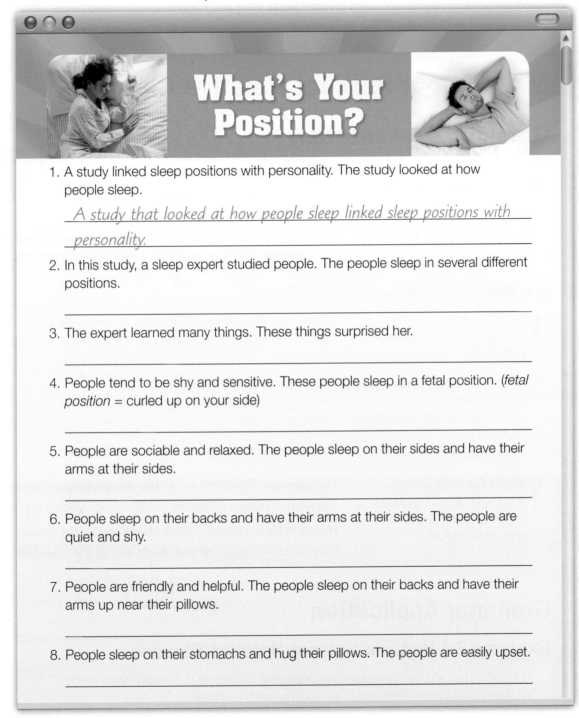

What's Your Position?

1. A study linked sleep positions with personality. The study looked at how people sleep.

   A study that looked at how people sleep linked sleep positions with personality.

2. In this study, a sleep expert studied people. The people sleep in several different positions.

   _____

3. The expert learned many things. These things surprised her.

   _____

4. People tend to be shy and sensitive. These people sleep in a fetal position. (*fetal position* = curled up on your side)

   _____

5. People are sociable and relaxed. The people sleep on their sides and have their arms at their sides.

   _____

6. People sleep on their backs and have their arms at their sides. The people are quiet and shy.

   _____

7. People are friendly and helpful. The people sleep on their backs and have their arms up near their pillows.

   _____

8. People sleep on their stomachs and hug their pillows. The people are easily upset.

   _____

B Underline the subject relative clauses in your new sentences. Circle the noun in the main clause that the relative pronoun refers to.

(A study) that looked at how people sleep linked sleep positions with personality.

C *Group Work* Take a survey of sleeping positions in your group. What is everyone's usual sleeping position and personality? Talk about your group. Give examples. Use subject relative clauses.

I don't think all people who sleep on their backs are quiet. For example, Marcelo sleeps on his back, and he's outgoing and friendly.

3 More About Subject Relative Clauses

▶ Grammar Presentation

<table>
<tr>
<td>Subject relative clauses can use a variety of verb forms.

They can also show possession.</td>
<td>People who have sleep problems can join the study.
People who are having sleep problems can join the study.
People who have had sleep problems can join the study.
Sally is a scientist whose discoveries have helped many people. (Sally's discoveries have helped many people.)</td>
</tr>
</table>

3.1 More About Subject Relative Clauses

<table>
<tr>
<td>a. Verbs in subject relative clauses can take a variety of verb forms.</td>
<td>The woman who <u>was participating</u> in the study was my aunt.
People that <u>have participated</u> in the study receive a payment.</td>
</tr>
<tr>
<td>b. The possessive form of who is whose. Whose + a noun shows possession in a subject relative clause.
A noun always follows whose.</td>
<td>NOUN   WHOSE + NOUN SUBJECT
The <u>scientist</u> whose work has helped many people won an award.</td>
</tr>
<tr>
<td>c. Whose can combine two sentences. Whose replaces the possessive form in the second sentence.</td>
<td>The woman is my neighbor. + ~~Her daughter~~ was in a sleep study.
The woman whose daughter was in a sleep study is my neighbor.

They are the scientists. + ~~Their study~~ was on the news last night.
They are the scientists whose study was on the news last night.</td>
</tr>
</table>

▶ Grammar Application

Exercise 3.1 Verbs in Subject Relative Clauses

🔊 Listen to a student podcast about sleeping. Complete the sentences with the relative pronoun and the correct form of the verb you hear.

Why do we sleep? This is still a mystery. Scientists <u>*who study*</u> (study) sleep are still
(1)
not completely sure of the reasons. They know some things about sleep, however. Here are

some facts:

- People _____ (be) asleep have active brains. Their brains are
  (2)
  most active during the "rapid eye movement," or REM, phase of sleep.

- Different animals sleep in different ways. For example, a dolphin
  _____ (sleep) may continue to swim.
  (3)

- Humans and animals _____ (lose) sleep need to make
  (4)
  it up later on.

- A person _____ (need) less than eight hours of sleep
  (5)
  should not worry about sleeping less than other people.

- There are animals _____ (sleep) very little. For
  (6)
  example, a horse only sleeps three hours a day. There are other

  animals _____ (sleep) a lot. For example, a small
  (7)
  animal called a ferret sleeps about 15 hours a day.

  Scientists _____ (study) sleep also have a few guesses
  (8)
about the reasons for sleep. There is a study _____ (show)
  (9)
REM sleep helps learning and memory. However, there are other studies

_____ (show) the opposite results. For example, certain drugs
  (10)
shorten REM sleep. A group of people _____ (take) these drugs
  (11)
showed no memory problems in a recent study.

  Most scientists agree on one thing. They need to do more research to solve the

mysteries of sleep.

Exercise 3.2 Sentence Combining with *Who, That,* and *Whose*

A Combine the sentences to complete a web article about interpreting (giving meaning
to) dreams. Make the second sentence a relative clause. Use *who, that,* or *whose*.

WHAT DO DREAMS MEAN?

What do your dreams mean? Interpreting dreams is an important part of
many cultures.

(1) *Some specialists whose goal is to understand dreams study*
   dream symbols.
   Some specialists study dream symbols. Their goal is to understand dreams.

(2) _____

_____

They believe dreams are about certain things. These things represent important ideas or feelings in our lives.

Here are some examples of dream symbols and their meanings;

▶ (3) _____

_____

People dream about losing a tooth. They are worried about something.

▶ (4) _____

_____

People may have a special wish for freedom. Their dreams are about flying.

▶ (5) _____

_____

People dream about falling. They have a fear of losing control of something.

▶ (6) _____

_____

People sometimes dream about a frightening dog. They have trouble with friends.

▶ (7) _____

_____

A dream can represent extreme emotions. The dream focuses on fire.

Some other meanings seem obvious. (8) _____

_____

For example, a person might also dream of fire. This person's room is too hot.

(9) _____

_____

In any case, most people do not see symbols in a simple way. These people analyze dreams.

Instead, they believe in looking at how the dreamer *feels* about the object in the dream.

B *Group Work* Discuss dream symbols in a group. Use the ones in A or your own ideas. Discuss possible interpretations for each symbol. Use subject relative pronouns. Present your ideas to the class. Use these questions to guide you.

- Which dream symbols are important in a culture you know well?
  Dream symbols that include animals are important in my culture.
- What are some interpretations of these symbols?
- Do you dream about any of these symbols? Which ones?
- What are some positive dream symbols?
- What are some negative dream symbols?
- Whose cultures have similar dream symbols?
- Do they have similar interpretations?

A *I think people who dream about teeth are worried about their appearance.*
B *Something good is going to happen to a person who dreams about a baby.*
C *In my friend's culture, a person who dreams about a dog will have bad luck.*

4 Avoid Common Mistakes ⚠

1. Use *who* or *that* for people and *which* or *that* for things.

   who / that
The scientists studied a woman ~~which~~ never sleeps.

   which / that
The research ~~who~~ proved the scientist's theory was interesting.

2. Do not use a subject pronoun after a subject relative pronoun.

Scientists study people who ~~they~~ sleep a short amount of time.

3. The verb after the relative pronoun agrees with the noun before the relative pronoun.

   have
People who ~~has~~ the hDEC2 gene need less sleep.

4. Do not omit the relative pronoun in a subject relative clause.

   who
Two women ∧ were "short sleepers" participated in a study.

5. Remember to spell *whose* correctly.

   whose
The scientist ~~who's / whoes~~ work has helped many people won an award.

Editing Task

Find and correct nine more mistakes in a web article about colors in dreams.

Dreaming in Color

Can dreams give us insights into our feelings? Some people who ~~they~~ analyze dreams believe this. There are dream analysts who's interest is the colors that they are in our dreams. In their opinion, these colors provide clues about our lives. For example, dreams about people which are wearing black

5 represent sadness. Dreams who have a lot of gray, brown, or tan in them can represent happiness. A dream who's main color is orange can represent boldness. Many people who analyzes dreams think green represents life or new beginnings. On the other hand, there are some people do not dream in color. These people dream in black and white.

10   Do you remember the colors that was in your dreams last night? The next time you dream, try to remember the colors. Write down the colors appear in your dream, and think about how they made you feel.

5 | Grammar for Writing 🖊

Using Subject Relative Clauses

Writers often use subject relative clauses to include more information in a sentence about who people are or what things do.

Subject relative clauses are common in scientific articles, product manuals, and other texts that involve definitions or technical explanations.

Remember:

- **Use subject relative clauses to define, describe, or identify nouns.**

  Afternoon naps that are not longer than 20 to 30 minutes are healthy. Longer naps can leave you feeling tired.

- **You can use subject relative clauses to give more information about any noun in a sentence.**

  An alarm clock that didn't work is an excuse that is common from students who arrive late to school because they overslept.

Pre-writing Task

1 Read the paragraphs below. What is the cause of the sleep problems the writer is writing about? What is the writer's solution?

One Useful Trick

People who have sleep problems need tricks that will help them sleep better. Some of these people have problems getting to sleep, while others have problems falling asleep again after they wake up in the middle of the night. One common cause of sleep problems is worrying. People whose problems keep them awake do not always have more problems

5 than other people. Instead, people whose worries keep them awake just cannot switch off their minds. Sometimes they think about important problems which are bothering them. Sometimes they think about appointments, chores, and meetings that are on their schedule for the next day.

One trick which can be very helpful is to make a "to do" list before going to sleep

10 every night. This list helps people feel better because they have a plan that will help them solve their problems the next day. People who do this remove the problems from their minds, and they sleep better.

2 Read the paragraphs again. Underline the subject relative clauses, circle the relative pronouns in the clauses, and draw an arrow to the nouns or noun phrases the relative clauses define, describe, or identify.

Writing Task

1 *Write* Use the paragraphs in the Pre-writing Task to help you write about a particular sleep problem and a solution to the problem. Write about the problem in the first paragraph and the solution in the second. What do you think is the cause of this problem? What is one possible solution?

2 *Self-Edit* Use the editing tips below to improve your paragraphs. Make any necessary changes.

1. Did you use subject relative clauses to write about a problem and solution to a sleep routine?
2. Did you use subject relative clauses to define, describe, or identify exactly the people and things you are writing about?
3. Did you use subject relative clauses in different positions in your sentences?
4. Did you avoid the mistakes in the Avoid Common Mistakes chart on page 371?

Object Relative Clauses (Adjective Clauses with Object Relative Pronouns)

Viruses

1 | Grammar in the Real World

A How do you feel when you get a cold or the flu? Read the article from a health website. Why is it so easy to get a virus?

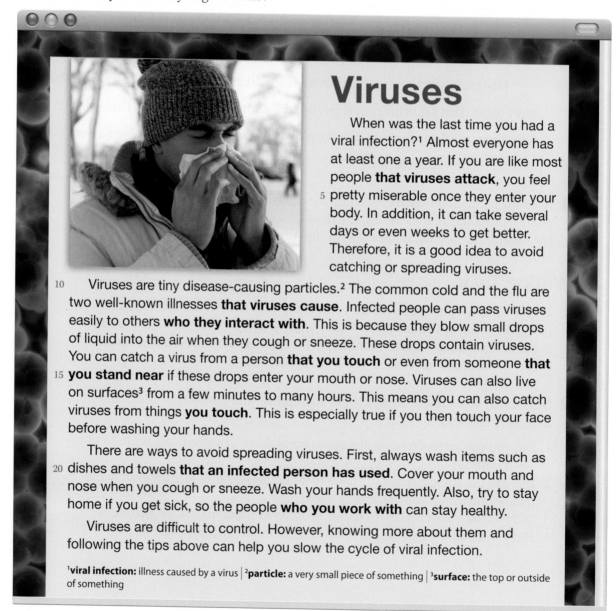

Viruses

When was the last time you had a viral infection?[1] Almost everyone has at least one a year. If you are like most people **that viruses attack**, you feel
5 pretty miserable once they enter your body. In addition, it can take several days or even weeks to get better. Therefore, it is a good idea to avoid catching or spreading viruses.

10 Viruses are tiny disease-causing particles.[2] The common cold and the flu are two well-known illnesses **that viruses cause**. Infected people can pass viruses easily to others **who they interact with**. This is because they blow small drops of liquid into the air when they cough or sneeze. These drops contain viruses. You can catch a virus from a person **that you touch** or even from someone **that**
15 **you stand near** if these drops enter your mouth or nose. Viruses can also live on surfaces[3] from a few minutes to many hours. This means you can also catch viruses from things **you touch**. This is especially true if you then touch your face before washing your hands.

There are ways to avoid spreading viruses. First, always wash items such as
20 dishes and towels **that an infected person has used**. Cover your mouth and nose when you cough or sneeze. Wash your hands frequently. Also, try to stay home if you get sick, so the people **who you work with** can stay healthy.

Viruses are difficult to control. However, knowing more about them and following the tips above can help you slow the cycle of viral infection.

[1]**viral infection:** illness caused by a virus | [2]**particle:** a very small piece of something | [3]**surface:** the top or outside of something

B *Comprehension Check* Answer the questions.

1. What are two illnesses that viruses cause?
2. How do viruses spread?
3. How long can viruses live on a surface?
4. What are three things you should do to protect yourself and others against viral infection?

C *Notice*   Look at the underlined words in these sentences from the article. Circle the nouns that the underlined words refer to.

1. The common cold and the flu are two well-known illnesses <u>that</u> viruses cause.

2. Infected people can pass viruses easily to others <u>who</u> they interact with.

2 | Object Relative Clauses

▶ Grammar Presentation

Object relative clauses describe, identify, or give more information about nouns. In an object relative clause, the relative pronoun is the object.

RELATIVE CLAUSE

OBJECT	SUBJECT	VERB

There are many diseases ***that*** *** viruses*** *** cause.***

2.1 Object Relative Clauses

	RELATIVE CLAUSE			
	Object Relative Pronoun	Subject	Verb	
You can infect people	that who / whom	you	meet.	
The virus	that which	the scientist	studied	was a type of flu.

2.2 Using Object Relative Clauses

a. In an object relative clause, the relative pronoun is the object of the clause.	RELATIVE CLAUSE ⌐OBJECT¬ *Cold and flu are illnesses* ***that*** *** viruses cause.***
b. The object relative pronouns are *who, whom, which,* and *that*. Use *that, who,* or *whom* for people.	RELATIVE CLAUSE ⌐OBJECT¬ *The professor* ***that*** *** I met yesterday*** *has the flu.*

2.2 Using Object Relative Clauses (continued)

Use *that* or *which* for things.

RELATIVE CLAUSE

OBJECT

She has a virus **that** **young people often get**.

---

c. Object relative clauses can combine two ideas.

That is the virus. + *Rob gave me the ~~virus~~.*
That is the <u>virus</u> **that** *Rob gave me.*

---

d. You can omit the relative pronoun in an object relative clause.

The doctor (who) she spoke with *had a cold himself!*
Wash **the things (that) you touch** *if you are infected.*

---

e. The object relative pronoun is followed by a subject and a verb.

SUBJECT VERB
I wash the towels **that** **she** **uses**.

SUBJECT VERB
The flu vaccine **that** **they** **use** *didn't work.*

---

f. An object relative clause usually comes right after the word it modifies. It can modify any noun or pronoun in a sentence.

SUBJECT
The <u>virus</u> **that she studied** *was a type of flu.*

OBJECT
She washed the <u>towels</u> **that she used**.

PRONOUN
He's the <u>one</u> **who I contacted on the phone**.

2.3 Comparing Subject and Object Relative Clauses

	Subject Relative Clauses	Object Relative Clauses
In a relative clause, the relative pronoun is . . .	the subject.	the object.
In a sentence, the relative pronoun modifies . . .	any noun or pronoun.	
In a sentence, the relative pronoun usually comes . . .	right after the word it modifies.	
In a sentence, the relative clause has . . .	a new verb.	a new subject and verb.
The relative pronoun can be omitted.	no	yes, except for *whose*
The relative pronouns include . . .	*who, which, that, whose.*	*who, whom, which, that, whose.*

2.4 Using Subject and Object Relative Clauses

Subject relative clause	*The* **doctor** *who treated her had a cold.*

SUBJECT
The **doctor** *had a cold.* + *The* **doctor** *treated her.*

Object relative clause	*The* **doctor** *who she visited had a cold.*

OBJECT
The **doctor** *had a cold.* + *She visited the* **doctor**.

Data from the Real World

Which is common in academic writing. It is much less common in informal language.	*The virus copies the host cell* **which** *it has invaded.*
In informal speaking and writing, *that* is more common in object relative clauses than *who* to refer to people. *Whom* is only used in rather formal situations.	A *Is she the scientist* **that you met at the lab**? B *Yes, she is.*

▶ Grammar Application

Exercise 2.1 Object Relative Clauses

A Read a passage from a history textbook about an epidemic (a disease that spreads quickly). Underline seven more relative clauses. Circle the relative pronouns. Three of the relative clauses do not have relative pronouns. Put a check (✓) above them.

In 1918 there was a global flu epidemic. It spread to almost every part of the world. The regions (that) the flu affected ranged from the Arctic to the South Pacific. In addition, the effects that
5   it had were devastating. The number of people this flu actually killed was between 50 and 100 million. However, the number of people that the virus infected was around 500 million. This was an epidemic scientists could not control. The virus spread very quickly, and it was very powerful. The people
10   who viruses usually affect are very old or very young. However, the people who this virus infected were healthy young adults. The 1918 flu was one of the worst natural disasters the world had ever seen.

B *Pair Work*   Compare answers with a partner. Which relative clauses do not have a relative pronoun?

Exercise 2.2 Combining Sentences

Combine the sentences using object relative clauses with *who*, *that*, and *which*.

1. Another name for the flu epidemic was the "Spanish flu." The world experienced this flu epidemic in 1918.

   Another name for the flu epidemic *that the world experienced in* 1918 was the "Spanish flu."

2. The people were mostly young adults. The flu killed them.

The people _____ were mostly young adults.

3. The people are typically elderly. The flu usually affects these people.

The people _____ are typically elderly.

4. The countries were very far apart. The flu affected countries.

The countries _____ were very far apart.

5. The 1918 flu was an unusual virus. Scientists could not control the virus.

The 1918 flu was an unusual virus _____ .

6. Strange flu viruses also occur today. Scientists do not understand these strange flu viruses.

Strange flu viruses _____ also occur today.

7. SARS, bird flu, and swine flu are recent examples of strange new viruses. Many people fear these viruses.

SARS, bird flu, and swine flu are recent examples of strange new viruses

_____ .

8. Scientists are interested in people. These strange new viruses affect these people.

Scientists are interested in people _____ .

Exercise 2.3 Using Object Relative Clauses

A *Over to You* Complete the sentences about getting sick. Use your own ideas. Write a correct relative pronoun, or Ø for no relative pronoun.

1. The thing _that /which/ Ø_ I usually do when I have a cold is _drink hot lemon juice with honey_ .

2. The thing _____ I usually do when I have

the flu is _____ .

3. I like the doctor _____ I go to when I get sick

because he / she _____ .

4. The best cold medicine _____ I know is

_____ .

5. _____ was the cold remedy

_____ my family used when I was a child.

6. _____ is the flu remedy

_____ my friend uses.

7. _____ is something _____ I avoid when I get sick.

B *Pair Work* Compare the sentences in A with a partner. Then tell the class about some of the interesting home remedies you discussed.

A *The thing that I usually do when I have a cold is drink hot lemon juice with honey. What about you?*

B *The thing that I usually do is . . .*

Exercise 2.4 Subject and Object Relative Clauses

A Complete the article about swine flu. Use the correct relative pronoun and the correct form of the verb in parentheses. Use Ø for no relative pronoun. If more than one pronoun is possible, write them all in the blank.

A New Flu

The flu is one of the most common diseases

___that / which / Ø___ viruses ___cause___ (cause).
    (1)   (2)

Sometimes the virus _____
                                (3)

_____ (cause) the flu isn't serious.
    (4)

Other times, it is. The number of people

_____ it _____ (attack)
       (5)   (6)

determines this. The number of places around

the world _____ it _____ (affect) also decides this. A
          (7)   (8)

disease _____ _____ (attack) a large number of people
      (9)   (10)

and areas is an epidemic. For example, the 1918 flu was an epidemic. In 2009, another

flu, swine flu, became an epidemic. Some people feel swine flu is still a serious threat.

Regions _____ swine flu still _____ (affect) include
         (11)   (12)

Europe, Africa, North and South America, the Middle East, and Asia. A lot of people

_____ _____ (have) swine flu have mild symptoms.
  (13)   (14)

Others _____ _____ (have) the disease have more serious
     (15)   (16)

symptoms. Swine flu became less serious after the 2009 outbreak, but it could return at

any time.

B *Pair Work* Compare answers in A with your partner. Which sentences have subject relative pronouns?

3 | More About Object Relative Clauses

▶ Grammar Presentation

Object relative clauses can use a variety of verb forms. They can also show possession.	He doesn't touch surfaces **that the patient touches**. He didn't touch the surfaces **that the patient touched**. He hasn't touched the surfaces **that the patient has touched**. The student **whose towel she used** had the flu. (It was the student's towel.)

3.1 More About Object Relative Clauses

a. *Whose* + a noun shows possession in an object relative clause.	WHOSE + NOUN The woman **whose husband** the doctor saw also needs an appointment.
A noun always follows *whose*.	WHOSE + NOUN The scientist **whose article** we read is giving a lecture at school.
Do not omit *whose*.	whose The scientist ̭article we read is giving a lecture at school.
b. *Whose* can combine two sentences.	The woman is sick. + The doctor saw ~~her~~ **children**. The woman **whose children** the doctor saw is sick.
Whose replaces the possessive form in the second sentence.	That is the scientist. + We read ~~his~~ **article**. That is the <u>scientist</u> **whose article** we read.

▶ Grammar Application

Exercise 3.1 Verbs in Object Relative Clauses

A ◀)) Listen to a podcast about the flu vaccine. Complete the sentences with the relative pronoun or Ø (for no relative pronoun) and the correct form of the verb in parentheses.

A vaccine is a substance _____*that*_____ a health practitioner
(1)

_____ (give) to help a person avoid getting a disease. There are
(2)

two types of flu vaccines. One is a shot _____ a practitioner usually
(3)

_____ (give) the patient in the arm. The other type is a nasal spray
(4)

_____ the practitioner _____ (spray)
(5)   (6)

directly into the patient's nose. Scientists develop new flu vaccines

every year. They study flu viruses _____ people
(7)

around the world _____ (had) the previous year.
(8)

Then they choose three critical viruses and make vaccines for

them. For example, in 2009, the viruses _____ they
(9)

_____ (choose) were the most likely to continue to
(10)

cause disease in 2010.

    People often don't like to get their flu shots. However, the

flu shot _____ scientists _____
(11)   (12)

(develop) for 2009 was in high demand in the United States. More

people than usual received that shot. According to doctors, getting a flu shot each year

is the most important thing _____ a person _____ (do) to
(13)   (14)

prevent the flu. Maybe their message is now being heard.

B 🔊 Listen again, and check your answers.

C *Pair Work* Compare answers with a partner. Which sentences did not have
relative pronouns?

Exercise 3.2 Sentence Combining

Combine the sentences about Louis Pasteur. Use *that, which, who(m), Ø,* or *whose.*

1. A biologist of the nineteenth century was Louis Pasteur. Doctors today still
   value his research.

   A biologist of the nineteenth century _whose research doctors today still value_

   was Louis Pasteur.

2. Pasteur was a scientist. We still use his vaccines.

   Pasteur is a scientist _____ .

3. Pasteur developed vaccines to prevent diseases. Farm animals often get the diseases.

   Pasteur developed vaccines to prevent the diseases _____

   _____ .

4. He also developed a vaccine to prevent a disease. People get the disease from dogs
   and other animals.

   He also developed a vaccine to prevent a disease _____

   _____ .

5. This is a disease. People get it from animal bites. The name of the disease is rabies.

   This is a disease _____ . The name of the disease is rabies.

6. Pasteur first tried his rabies vaccine on a young boy. A dog bit the boy.

   Pasteur first tried his rabies vaccine on a young boy

   _____ .

7. The vaccine worked. He cured the boy. The boy became his friend.

   The vaccine worked. The boy _____ became his friend.

8. Another disease is called anthrax. A lot of farm animals still get the disease.

   Another disease _____ is called anthrax.

Exercise 3.3 More Object Relative Clauses

A *Over to You* Answer the questions. Use object relative clauses.

1. In your opinion, what is the best thing that you can do to prevent the flu? Why?

   The best thing that you *can do to prevent the flu is get a flu shot. If you get a flu shot, you won't get the flu, and you won't give it to other people* .

2. What is the best thing that you can do to prevent the common cold? Why?

   The best thing that you _____

   _____ .

3. When you get the flu or a cold, what is the remedy that you use? Why?

   The remedy that I _____

   _____ .

4. What disease worries you the most? Why?

   The disease that I _____

   _____ .

5. What is the thing you worry about the most when you get sick? Why?

   When I get sick, the thing that I _____

   _____ .

B *Pair Work* Discuss your answers with a partner. What do you agree or disagree about?

A *The best thing that you can do to prevent the flu is get a flu shot. If you get a flu shot, you won't get the flu and you won't give it to other people.*

B *I disagree. Some people get very sick after they have a flu shot. I think the best thing that you can do to prevent the flu is get enough sleep and exercise.*

4 Avoid Common Mistakes ⚠

1. **Use *that / who / whom / Ø* to refer to people in object relative clauses; use *which / that* to refer to things.**

   that / who / whom / Ø
   The scientist ~~which~~ I remember reading about was Louis Pasteur.

2. **Do not confuse *whose* with *who*. *Whose* is possessive.**

   whose
   A person ~~who~~ computer is infected with a virus can use software to solve the problem.

3. **Use *whom* in object relative clauses only (and in rather formal situations).**

   who
   The man ~~whom~~ had the virus was very ill.

4. **Do not use an object pronoun at the end of an object relative clause.**

   The articles that I read ~~them~~ are about Louis Pasteur.

Editing Task

Find and correct eight more mistakes in the web article about computer viruses.

A New Kind of Epidemic

Are computer viruses similar to human viruses? In some ways, they are. A virus

that invades your computer sometimes behaves like a virus that infects your body.

Computer viruses became a serious problem in the 1990s. One of the first types of

that / Ø
virus ~~who~~ computer scientists created was a "worm." A worm is a computer virus that

5 a computer receives it without the user's knowledge. A user who computer is attacked

by a worm may lose data or suffer damage to his or her computer system.

The people which we must blame for the very first worm developed it in 1979.

Much like a human virus, the worm of 1979 gradually spread until it became an "epidemic." A virus who thousands of computers received very rapidly was the

10 famous "Melissa" virus of 1999. Luckily, someone developed a "vaccine" for this

virus, and it is no longer the cause of a computer virus epidemic.

However, people continue to create viruses of different kinds. For example, one

virus attacks people's electronic address lists and sends e-mails to everyone who

name is on a list. The people who you know them may be surprised when they get an

15 e-mail from you that is really an advertisement!

People who computers were infected with viruses needed protection, so

companies began to produce anti-virus software in the 1990s. Nowadays, a user

whom has good anti-virus software doesn't need to worry about a sick computer.

However, people create new viruses all the time. Viruses will continue to be a problem,

20 and new computer virus "vaccines" will need to be developed to fight them.

5 Grammar for Writing

Using Object Relative Clauses

Writers often use object relative clauses to include more information about the people, objects, and ideas that they are writing about.

Object relative clauses are common in formal academic writing and other texts where writers need to give specific definitions of things.

Remember:

- **You can use object pronouns to help you combine different pieces of information about something into one sentence.**

  My mother taught me home remedies. I use them.
  I use home remedies that my mother taught me.

Pre-writing Task

1 Read the paragraphs below. What remedies does the writer write about in the first paragraph? What prevention techniques does the writer write about in the second paragraph?

Being Sick and Staying Healthy

Everyone I know has been sick recently. The first symptom that everyone gets is a

sore throat. The next thing everyone complains about is achy muscles. The things that

I do to feel better are things which my mother and my grandmother taught me. For example, it is a good idea to drink plenty of liquids. For my throat, I drink a hot ginger

5 and honey tea that my mother used to make for me. It does not taste very good, and

sometimes it burns at first, but after drinking it, my throat always feels better. For aches

and pains, I use hot pads that I put in the microwave. I also take flu or cold medications

that I keep in my bathroom.

To avoid getting sick, I try to take care of myself. One of the most important things is

10 getting enough sleep. Most people I know do not sleep enough. The other helpful thing is

staying fit. Doctors, scientists, and other people whose opinion I respect say that exercise

is very important. They say that if you do not exercise regularly, you are more likely to

get sick.

2 Read the paragraphs again. Underline the object relative clauses and circle the object pronouns. Find the object relative clauses without object pronouns. What object pronoun could you add to each one?

Writing Task

1 *Write* Use the paragraph in the Pre-writing Task to help you write about an illness or health problem. In the first paragraph, write about the illness and the remedies you use to treat the symptoms. In the second paragraph, write about the things you do to prevent this illness. You can write about illnesses or problems such as:

- colds and flus
- frequent headaches
- toothaches

- stomach or back problems
- sunburns or other skin problems
- your own idea

2 *Self-Edit* Use the editing tips below to improve your paragraphs. Make any necessary changes.

1. Did you use object relative clauses to provide more information about the people, objects, and things you wrote about?
2. Did you use object relative clauses to combine different pieces of information?
3. Did you avoid the mistakes in the Avoid Common Mistakes chart on page 383?

UNIT
32

Conjunctions and Adverb Clauses

Special Days

1 | Grammar in the Real World

A What holidays do you celebrate each year? Which are your favorite days? Read the magazine article about "Black Friday" (the day after Thanksgiving). What's good and bad about Black Friday?

BLACK FRIDAY

Black Friday is the Friday after Thanksgiving Day in the United States. It is the start of the holiday shopping season, **so** it is an important day for
5 retailers.[1] It is called "Black Friday" **because** it is the day when retailers go "into the black." That is, they make a profit. Retailers can make 18 percent to 40 percent of their yearly sales in
10 the month between Thanksgiving and Christmas, **so** the holiday shopping season is crucial for them **and** the U.S. economy in general.

  Although Black Friday is not an
15 official holiday, many workers have the day off and start their holiday shopping. Shopping on this day is popular **because** retailers offer very low prices on items such as electronics.

20   There is a sense of excitement about Black Friday. Stores advertise their prices in advance and open their doors at 5:00 a.m. Shoppers often line up outside a store hours before it opens

so they can be the first ones in. Some   25
people even camp in the parking lot the
night before.

  However, Black Friday shopping
is not without its problems. **Even
though** the deals sound fantastic, they   30
are often not as good as they seem.
For instance, a store will advertise a
big screen TV at a very low price, **but**
there may be only one in the store.
Since there are not enough low-priced   35
items for everyone, sometimes people
get stressed **and** angry. Shoppers
occasionally get into arguments
and even fistfights. In addition,
since people are excited and stores   40
are crowded, there are sometimes
accidents on Black Friday.

  Some people avoid the problems of
Black Friday. They shop on the weekend
after, **or** they stay home and buy online.   45
Black Friday can mean crowds and bad
deals, **and yet** it remains one of the
busiest shopping days of the year.

[1]**retailer:** store owner

B *Comprehension Check* Answer the questions.

1. Why is the holiday shopping season important?
2. Why do people want to shop on Black Friday?
3. What are the problems with shopping on Black Friday?
4. What are some ways to avoid the problems of Black Friday?

C *Notice* Complete the sentences from the article. Circle the correct words.

1. It is the start of the holiday shopping season, **but** / **so** it is an important day for retailers.
2. For instance, a store will advertise a big-screen TV at a very low price,
   but / **because** there may be only one in the store.
3. Shoppers occasionally get into arguments **and** / **so** even fistfights.
4. They shop on the weekend after, **since** / **or** they stay home and buy online.

Think about the meaning of each word you circled. In which sentence above does
the word express these meanings?

a. a result ___1___   b. an addition _____   c. an alternative _____   d. a contrast _____

2 | Conjunctions

▶ Grammar Presentation

The conjunctions *and, or, but, so,* and *yet* can connect single words, phrases, or clauses.	WORD WORD *Black Friday causes problems for* <u>shoppers</u> ***and*** <u>stores</u>. PHRASE PHRASE *They shop* <u>on weekends</u> ***but*** <u>not on weekdays</u>. CLAUSE CLAUSE *He wanted to* <u>save money</u>, ***so*** <u>he shopped on Black Friday</u>.

2.1 Conjunctions

a. You can use *and* to connect related information and add ideas.	*The shoppers were tired **and** hungry.* (words) *People go out **and** spend money.* (phrases) *The store opened at 5:00 a.m., **and** shoppers were waiting outside.* (clauses)
b. You can use *or* to give alternatives or choices.	*You can shop today **or** tomorrow.* (words) *They camp in the parking lot **or** in front of the store.* (phrases) *You can shop today, **or** you can wait until tomorrow.* (clauses)

2.1 Conjunctions (continued)

c. You can use *but (not)* to connect contrasting ideas.	*The store is small **but** successful.* (words) *They liked the clothes **but** not the high prices.* (phrases) *She has invited Jim for the holiday, **but** she has never invited us.* (clauses)
d. You can use *so* to connect causes and results.	*The stores are crowded, **so** I'll stay home.* (clauses)
You can use *and* before *so* to show a result.	*Stores cut their prices, **and so** they make less money.* (clauses)
It is not common to use *so* to connect words and phrases.	

2.2 Using Conjunctions

a. Use a comma when you connect two long clauses. However, you do not need a comma when the clauses are short.	*This is an important day**, and** it is the busiest shopping day.* *Stores cut prices **and** people save money.*
b. When you connect two clauses and the subject is the same, you do not need to repeat the subject.	*People go shopping **and** (people) buy holiday gifts on this day.* *They save money **but** (they) don't realize the items aren't new.*
If the verb is the same, you do not need to repeat it.	*People can shop online **or** (can shop) at the mall.* *Shoppers start arguments **and** even (start) fistfights.* *Stores are cutting prices **and** (are) hoping to sell more.*
In addition, you often do not need to repeat prepositions after conjunctions.	*People are not at work on Thursday **and** (on) Friday.*
c. You can often use *but + not* to shorten contrasting clauses to words or phrases.	*They shop on Friday **but not** Thursday.* (= They shop on Friday, but they do not shop on Thursday.) *They liked the clothes **but not** the high prices.* (= They liked the clothes, but they did not like the high prices.)
Do not use *not* if the contrasting ideas are both affirmative.	*The store is small **but** successful.* (= The store is small, but it is successful.)

2.3 *Yet, And Yet*

a. *Yet* is a formal word. It has a similar meaning to *but*. *Yet* connects strongly contrasting ideas or surprising information.	*It is often cold, **yet** shoppers still sleep in doorways.* *The deals are often not good, **yet** people still go shopping.*
b. You can use *and* with *yet*.	*There is a downside, **and yet** it is a popular shopping day.*

▶ Grammar Application

Exercise 2.1 *And, Or, But, So,* and *Yet*

Complete a news article about the holiday shopping season. Circle the correct words.

Holiday Shopping in Our City

The malls are decorated **and**/**but** ready for the holiday shopping season.
(1)
The stores are hoping to attract a lot of customers **yet**/**and** make big profits
(2)
this year.

The holidays are a time for giving gifts, **or**/**and** the shopping season is
(3)
important for stores. Black Friday used to be the start of the shopping season,
but/**or** people are starting to shop earlier in November. We talked to some
(4)
retailers **so**/**and** analysts about their expectations for the holiday shopping
(5)
season this year.

"This year, stores are busy, **but not**/**but** as busy as last year," said one
(6)
retailer. "People are tired of the crowds, **but**/**so** they're shopping by telephone
(7)
but/**or** online," he added. "Unemployment in the city has gone up this year,
(8)
so/**and yet** people are still spending."
(9)
An analyst told us, "People are spending, **but**/**or** they are spending more
(10)
cautiously this year. The popular items are electronics **and**/**but** toys."
(11)
She added, "Stores are offering discounts **but**/**or** gifts with purchases.
(12)
They are staying open later on Saturdays **and**/**yet** Sundays."
(13)

Exercise 2.2 Repeated Subjects, Verbs, and Prepositions

Read an online interview with shoppers about Black Friday. If you do not need to repeat a subject or verb, cross it out.

Alex B., Detroit: (1) Black Friday can be a good thing or ~~Black Friday can be~~ a bad thing. (2) There are good deals and there are special offers. (3) For example, at a lot of stores, I can choose free shipping or I can choose a gift with my purchase. (4) I love the deals but I hate the crowds.

Maria S., Chicago: (5) People become over-excited and people become aggressive on Black Friday. (6) People push and people fight to get to the deals. (7) I stay home and I shop online, or I order things over the phone.

Wei P., San Francisco: (8) I can buy all of my gifts and I can save money, too. (9) We go shopping as a family and we enjoy our day out together.

Exercise 2.3 Using *And*, *Or*, *But*, and *So*

A *Pair Work* What do you know about Thanksgiving in the United States and Canada? When are the two holidays? How do people celebrate them? How did the holidays start? Make a list of facts with a partner.

B 🔊 Listen to a radio show about Thanksgiving in the United States and Canada. Complete the chart on the next page.

	Canada	The United States
1. What year was the first Thanksgiving Day?	1578	
2. Who started it (according to history books)?		
3. What month is it in?		
4. What day of the week is it on?		
5. What do people eat on Thanksgiving?		
6. What day of the week do they eat Thanksgiving dinner?		
7. What is the big shopping day?		

C Complete these sentences about Thanksgiving in the United States and Canada. Use the information in the chart to help you. Circle the correct conjunctions.

1. Thanksgiving is a holiday in _____the United States_____ (and) / but Canada.

2. Thanksgiving is in November in the United States, **but / so** the Canadian Thanksgiving is in _____ .

3. In the United States, Thanksgiving Day is always on a _____ , **or / but** in Canada, it's on a Monday.

4. In _____ , people get together with family **and / but** have a traditional Thanksgiving dinner.

5. People eat turkey **and / or** _____ .

6. In the United States, the meal is always on Thanksgiving Day, **but / so** in Canada, the meal can be on _____ .

7. Canadians can have Thanksgiving dinner on Saturday, Sunday, **or / but** _____ .

8. In the United States, Black Friday is the big shopping day, **but / and** in Canada, the big sales are on _____ .

Exercise 2.4 More Conjunctions

Group Work Make a list of favorite holidays and special days in your group. Talk about why the day exists, how people celebrate it, what they wear, what they eat or drink, where they go, and so on. Then discuss the similarities and differences among the days on your list. Use *and*, *but*, *or*, *so*, and *yet*.

A *People get together with family and eat a big meal on Thanksgiving and Christmas. People give gifts on Christmas, but they don't give gifts on Thanksgiving.*

B *People eat candy on Halloween, but they eat some healthy food on Thanksgiving.*

C *You don't get off work on Halloween, so it's not a big holiday.*

3 | Adverb Clauses

▶ Grammar Presentation

Adverb clauses show how ideas are connected. They begin with conjunctions such as *because*, *since*, *although*, and *even though*.

MAIN CLAUSE	ADVERB CLAUSE
	CONJUNCTION

*Many people have the day off work **even though it's not an official holiday**.*

3.1 Adverb Clauses

Adverb Clause		Main Clause
Because **Since**	**there is a big sale today,**	the stores are crowded.
Although **Even though**	**it is not a holiday,**	a lot of people have the day off.

Main Clause	Adverb Clause	
The stores are crowded	**because** **since**	**there is a big sale today.**
Many people have the day off	**although** **even though**	**it isn't a holiday.**

3.2 Using Adverb Clauses

a. Like most other clauses, an adverb clause must have a subject and a verb.	ADVERB CLAUSE SUBJ. VERB *People shop on Black Friday **because prices are lower**.*
b. An adverb clause on its own is not a sentence. It is a fragment.	*They have the day off work **although it's not a holiday**.* *They have the day off work. ~~Although it's not a holiday~~.*
c. An adverb clause can come before or after the main clause. Use a comma when the adverb clause comes first.	*Black Friday is an important day for retailers **because it is the start of the holiday shopping season**.* ***Because Black Friday is the start of the holiday shopping season**, it is an important day for retailers.*
d. *Although*, *even though*, and *though* connect contrasting ideas.	***Although it is not a holiday**, workers have the day off.* ***Even though some deals sound fantastic**, they are not.* ***Though prices are low**, the deals are often not good.*
e. *Because* and *since* introduce reasons or causes and connect them with results.	RESULT CAUSE *It's a popular day **since stores offer special deals**.* CAUSE RESULT ***Because prices are low**, the stores are crowded.* REASON RESULT ***Because stores are crowded**, many people stay home.*
You can use *since* when the reader or listener knows about the reason from general knowledge, or because you have explained it.	*Most stores cut their prices on Black Friday. **Since** prices are lower, it is a popular shopping day.*
f. *So* introduces results.	*The stores are crowded, **so** many people stay home.*
So can also introduce a purpose or reason.	*They camp in the parking lot **so** they can be first in the store.*
Do not start a sentence with *so*.	

Data from the Real World

Research shows that *since* is more common in formal writing than in speaking.

▶ Grammar Application

Exercise 3.1 *Because, Since, Although,* and *Even Though*

Complete the magazine article about "Cyber Monday" (the Monday after Thanksgiving in the United States). Circle the best conjunctions.

CYBER MONDAY

The holiday shopping season is important for the U.S. economy (since)/although a high percentage of retail sales occur between Thanksgiving
(1)
and Christmas. **Although / Because** Black Friday is an important day for
(2)
retailers, Cyber Monday has become equally important. Cyber Monday is the first Monday after Thanksgiving Day. It's called "Cyber Monday" **although / because** a lot of retailers have online sales on that day.
(3)
There are a number of reasons why so many people shop on Cyber Monday, **even though / because** they cannot touch or handle the items
(4)
they are buying. For one thing, it's convenient. **Even though / Because**
(5)
most companies have rules against online shopping, millions of people still shop online on Cyber Monday while they're at work and sitting in front of computers. Also, Cyber Monday deals are sometimes even better than Black Friday deals. **Although / Because** Monday is often the last chance for retailers
(6)
to get rid of all the items they had for Black Friday, they often cut prices on Cyber Monday. In addition, some people prefer to buy online **because / although**
(7)
shipping is usually free, and they don't have to carry heavy items home.

Since / Although most people think
(8)
of the Friday after Thanksgiving as the biggest shopping day in the United States, Cyber Monday is now almost as important for retailers as Black Friday.

Exercise 3.2 Adverb Clauses

Combine the sentences to make one sentence. Use *because, since, so, although, even though,* or *though.* Sometimes there is more than one correct answer.

1. Researchers study the psychology of giving gifts. Gift giving is an important part of life.

   Researchers study the psychology of giving gifts because/since gift giving
   is an important part of life.
   Gift giving is an important part of life, so many experts study the psychology
   of giving gifts.

2. Stores are crowded during the holiday shopping period. Some people decide not to give gifts.

   _____

   _____

3. Holiday shopping can be unpleasant and expensive. Sometimes people feel like they can't avoid gift giving.

   _____

   _____

4. Gift giving in the right situations can make our relationships with people stronger. It can be a nice reminder of how we feel about other people.

   _____

   _____

5. Gift giving varies from culture to culture. It's a good idea to learn about cultural rules for gift giving.

   _____

   _____

6. In some cultures, you open a gift as soon as you get it. You wait until the giver has left in other cultures.

   _____

   _____

7. A certain color can mean bad luck in some cultures. People will avoid using the color as a gift wrap.

   _____

   _____

8. Both men and women enjoy gifts. Researchers say that gift giving is more important for females.

   _____

   _____

Exercise 3.3 More Adverb Clauses

A Complete the questions about gift-giving habits with an appropriate conjunction.

1. Do you ever buy gifts for people _because_ you want to say "thank you"?

2. Do you ever feel you have to buy gifts _____ you can't really afford them?

3. Have you ever given a gift to someone _____ you felt you had to?

4. Have you ever taken a gift back to the store for a refund or exchange _____ you didn't like it?

5. Have you bought a gift for someone _____ you didn't like that person?

6. Have you bought a gift for someone _____ you wanted to say "I'm sorry"?

7. Have you ever given someone a gift _____ you had no reason?

8. Have you ever pretended to like a gift _____ you didn't like it?

B *Pair Work*   Ask and answer the questions in A with a partner. Do you have the same gift-giving habits?

A *Do you ever buy gifts for people because you want to say "thank you"?*

B *Yes, I sometimes buy a small gift for my neighbor when she waters my plants for me.*

4 Avoid Common Mistakes ⚠

1. Check the spelling of *although*.

Although
~~Althought~~ the stores are crowded, it's my favorite day to shop.

2. Do not link three or more clauses with *although*, *though*, or *even though*.

I like Black Friday. Although it is very tiring, it's a lot of fun.
~~I like Black Friday although it is very tiring it's a lot of fun.~~

3. Do not forget to use a comma after the adverb clause when it is first.

Although we think it is a modern celebration ˇ it is an ancient tradition.

Editing Task

Find and correct seven more mistakes in these paragraphs.

Although
~~Allthough~~ Mother's Day is an old holiday it may surprise you to know that

Father's Day is a modern holiday. Some people say the first modern Father's Day

was in 1908, althought most people agree it started in 1910. Father's Day was

born in Spokane, Washington, on June 19, 1910. Father's Day was partly the idea

5 of Mrs. Sonora Smart Dodd. Because her father was a single parent and raised six

children, she wanted to honor him. Although she suggested her father's June 5

birthday she did not give the organizers enough time to make arrangements. The

holiday moved from June 5 to the third Sunday in June. Father's Day is now a popular

holiday. Althogh people laughed at the idea of Father's Day at first it gradually

10 became popular.

Because retailers saw an opportunity to increase sales in the 1930s, they started

to advertise Father's Day gifts. People then felt that they had to buy gifts for their

fathers even though they realized this was commercialization, they still bought them.

Father's Day is an international holiday. Even though people celebrate it on different

15 dates it is an important day in many cultures.

5 | Grammar for Writing ✏️

Using Conjunctions and Adverb Clauses

> Writers often use conjunctions and adverb clauses to clearly show how ideas are connected to each other.
>
> Conjunctions and adverb clauses appear in almost every kind of text and are very common in academic essays, opinion articles, and other texts that give opinions or describe complex ideas.
>
> Remember:
>
> - **You can connect ideas in words, phrases, and clauses with the conjunctions *and, or, but, so*, and *yet*.**
>
>   *On Thanksgiving, people look forward to eating a lot, <u>yet</u> they also look forward to spending time with their families <u>and</u> friends.*
>
> - **You can show cause and result and connect contrasting ideas with adverb clauses beginning with *because, since, although*, and *even though*.**
>
>   *<u>Although</u> Halloween is a holiday for children, it is a favorite holiday of many adults.*

Pre-writing Task

1 Read the paragraphs below. Which holiday does the writer not like and why? Which holiday does the writer like and why?

The Least and Most Fun Holidays

Super Bowl Sunday is in late January or early February. On that day, two football teams play to see which team is the best team in the country. It is not a national holiday, yet most people think of it as a holiday. People gather together in living rooms or restaurants to watch the game together. The game lasts for several hours. People eat

5 a lot of burgers, hot dogs, pizza, potato chips, and other kinds of junk food on that day. I do not enjoy watching football, so I always get very bored at Super Bowl Sunday parties.

Halloween is on October 31, and it is one of my favorite holidays. Children dress up in costumes and walk from house to house asking for candy. It is a lot of fun answering the door and seeing the children and their costumes. Although this holiday

10 is really a children's holiday, there are always parties for adults to go to. Since most adults wear costumes at these parties, too, it is the one time of year that adults can act like children! Food is important on Halloween, too, but who does not like chocolate and candy?

2 Read the paragraphs again. Circle the conjunctions *and*, *but*, *or*, *so*, and *yet*, and underline the adverb clauses beginning with *because*, *since*, *although*, and *even though*.

Writing Task

1 *Write* Use the paragraphs in the Pre-writing Task to help you write two paragraphs about two special days. In the first paragraph, write about a day you don't enjoy. In the second paragraph, write about a day you enjoy. What do people do on these days? What do they eat? What do they wear? Why do you like or not like these days? Use conjunctions and adverb clauses.

2 *Self-Edit* Use the editing tips below to improve your paragraphs. Make any necessary changes.

1. Did you use conjunctions and adverb clauses to clearly explain how your ideas are connected to each other?
2. Did you connect words, phrases, and clauses with *and*, *but*, *or*, *so*, and *yet*?
3. Did you show cause and result or contrasting ideas with adverb clauses beginning with *because*, *since*, *although*, and *even though*?
4. Did you avoid the mistakes in the Avoid Common Mistakes chart on page 396?

Appendices

1. Capitalization and Punctuation Rules

Capitalize	Examples
1. The first letter of the first word of a sentence	*Today is a great day.*
2. The pronoun *I*	*After class, **I** want to go to the movies.*
3. Names of people	*Simon Bolivar, Joseph Chung*
4. Names of buildings, streets, geographic locations, and organizations	*Taj Mahal, Main Street, Mt. Everest, United Nations*
5. Titles of people	*Dr., Mr., Mrs., Ms.*
6. Days, months, and holidays	*Tuesday, April, Valentine's Day*
7. Names of courses or classes	*Biology 101, English Composition II*
8. Titles of books, movies, and plays	*Crime and Punishment, Avatar, Hamlet*
9. States, countries, languages, and nationalities	*California, Mexico, Spanish, South Korean, Canadian*
10. Names of religions	*Hinduism, Catholicism, Islam, Judaism*

Punctuation	Examples
1. Use a period (.) at the end of a sentence.	*I think I can pass this class**.***
2. Use a question mark (?) at the end of a question.	*Why do you want to buy a car**?***
3. Use an exclamation point (!) to show strong emotion (e.g., surprise, anger, shock).	*Wait**!** I'm not ready yet.* *I can't believe it**!***
4. Use an apostrophe (') for possessive nouns.	
Add *'s* for singular nouns.	*That's Sue**'s** umbrella.*
Add *s'* for plural nouns.	*Those are the student**s'** books.*
Add *'* or *'s* for nouns that end in *-s*.	*It is Wes**'** house. It is Wes**'s** house.*
Add *'s* for irregular plural nouns.	*Bring me the children**'s** shoes.*
Use an apostrophe (') for contractions.	*I**'ll** be back next week. He can**'t** drive a car.*
5. Use a comma (,):	
between words in a series of three or more items. (Place *and* before the last item.)	*I like fish**,** chicken**,** turkey**, and** mashed potatoes.*
after a time clause when it begins a sentence.	***Before** I play soccer**,** I do my stretching exercises.*
after a prepositional phrase when it begins a sentence.	***Next to** my house**,** there's a beautiful little park.*
after an adverb clause when it begins a sentence.	***Because** she got a job**,** she was able to get her own apartment.*
before *and, or, but,* and *so* to connect two or more main clauses.	*You can watch TV**, but** I have to study for a test.*

2. Stative (Non-Action) Verbs

Stative verbs do not describe actions. They describe states or situations. Stative verbs are not usually used in the present progressive, even if we are talking about right now. Some are occasionally used in the present progressive, but often with a different meaning.

Research shows that the 25 most common stative verbs in spoken and written English are:				
agree	dislike	hope	love	see
believe	expect	hurt	need	seem
care (about)	hate	know	notice	think
cost	have	like	own	understand
disagree	hear	look like	prefer	want

Other stative verbs are:				
be	feel	matter	recognize	sound
belong	forgive	mean	remember	taste
concern	look	owe	smell	weigh
deserve				

Using the present progressive of these verbs sometimes changes the meaning to an action.

*Can you **see** the red car?*   (= use your eyes to be aware of something)

*I'm **seeing** an old friend tomorrow.*   (= meeting someone)

*I **think** you're right.*   (= believe)

*Dina **is thinking** of taking a vacation soon.*   (= considering)

*I **have** two sisters.*   (= be related to)

*We're **having** eggs for breakfast.*   (= eating)

3. Irregular Verbs

Base Form	Simple Past	Past Participle	Base Form	Simple Past	Past Participle
be	was / were	been	keep	kept	kept
become	became	become	know	knew	known
begin	began	begun	leave	left	left
bite	bit	bitten	lose	lost	lost
blow	blew	blown	make	made	made
break	broke	broken	meet	met	met
bring	brought	brought	pay	paid	paid
build	built	built	put	put	put
buy	bought	bought	read	read [red]*	read [red]*
catch	caught	caught	ride	rode	ridden
choose	chose	chosen	run	ran	run
come	came	come	say	said	said
cost	cost	cost	see	saw	seen
cut	cut	cut	sell	sold	sold
do	did	done	send	sent	sent
draw	drew	drawn	set	set	set
drink	drank	drunk	shake	shook	shaken
drive	drove	driven	show	showed	shown
eat	ate	eaten	shut	shut	shut
fall	fell	fallen	sing	sang	sung
feed	fed	fed	sit	sat	sat
feel	felt	felt	sleep	slept	slept
fight	fought	fought	speak	spoke	spoken
find	found	found	spend	spent	spent
fly	flew	flown	stand	stood	stood
forget	forgot	forgotten	steal	stole	stolen
forgive	forgave	forgiven	swim	swam	swum
get	got	gotten	take	took	taken
give	gave	given	teach	taught	taught
go	went	gone	tell	told	told
grow	grew	grown	think	thought	thought
have	had	had	throw	threw	thrown
hear	heard	heard	understand	understood	understood
hide	hid	hidden	wake	woke	woken
hit	hit	hit	wear	wore	worn
hold	held	held	win	won	won
hurt	hurt	hurt	write	wrote	written

*pronunciation

4. Spelling Rules for Verbs Ending in -ing

1. For verbs ending in a vowel-consonant combination, repeat the consonant before adding -ing.

    get → getting   *swim → swimming*

2. However, if the verb has more than one syllable, repeat the consonant only if the final syllable is stressed.

    beGIN → beginning   BUT   *HAPpen → happening (no doubling of consonant)*

3. For verbs ending in a silent *e*, drop the *e* before adding -ing.

    move → moving   *drive → driving*

    For *be* and *see*, don't <u>drop</u> the *e* because it is not silent.

    be → being   *see → seeing*

    For verbs ending in -ie, change *ie* to *y* before adding -ing.

    die → dying   *lie → lying*

Verbs that end in -ing are also called *gerunds* when they are used as nouns. The same spelling rules above apply to gerunds as well.

5. Spelling Rules for Regular Verbs in the Simple Past

1. To form the simple past of regular verbs, add -ed to the base form of the verb.

    work → worked   *wash → washed*

2. For regular verbs that end in -e, add -d only.

    live → lived   *like → liked*

3. For regular verbs ending in a consonant + -y, change *y* to *i* and add -ed.

    study → studied   *hurry → hurried*

4. For regular verbs that end in a vowel + -y, add -ed.

    stay → stayed   *enjoy → enjoyed*

5. For regular verbs that end in a vowel-consonant combination, repeat the consonant before adding -ed. Exception: Do not double the last consonant for verbs that end with -w, -x, or -y.

    stop → stopped   *plan → planned*   BUT   *fix → fixed*

6. However, if the verb has more than one syllable, repeat the consonant only if the final syllable is stressed.

    preFER → preferred   BUT   *Visit → visited (no doubling of consonant)*

6. Verbs + Gerunds and Infinitives

Verbs Followed by a Gerund Only	
admit	keep (= *continue*)
avoid	mind (= *object to*)
consider	miss
delay	postpone
deny	practice
discuss	quit
enjoy	recall (= *remember*)
finish	risk
imagine	suggest
involve	understand

Verbs Followed by an Infinitive Only		
afford	hope	pretend
agree	intend	promise
arrange	learn	refuse
attempt	manage	seem
decide	need	tend (= *be likely*)
deserve	offer	threaten
expect	plan	volunteer
fail	prepare	want
help		

Verbs Followed by a Gerund or an Infinitive		
begin	like	start
continue	love	stop*
forget*	prefer	try*
hate	remember*	

*The meanings of these verbs are different when they are followed by a gerund or an infinitive. See Unit 28.

7. Verb and Preposition Combinations

Verb + *about*	Verb + *for*	Verb + *of*	Verb + *to*
ask about	apologize for	approve of	admit to
complain about	ask for	dream of	belong to
talk about	look for	think of	listen to
think about	pay for	**Verb + *on***	look forward to
worry about	wait for	count on	talk to
Verb + *against*	**Verb + *in***	decide on	**Verb + *with***
advise against	believe in	depend on	agree with
decide against	succeed in	insist on	argue with
Verb + *at*		plan on	bother with
look at		rely on	deal with
smile at			

8. Adjective and Preposition Combinations

Adjective + *of*	Adjective + *in*
afraid of	interested in
ashamed of	**Adjective + *for***
aware of	bad for
careful of	good for
full of	responsible for
sick of	**Adjective + *about***
tired of	concerned about
Adjective + *by*	excited about
amazed by	happy about
bored by	nervous about
surprised by	pleased about
Adjective + *at*	sad about
amazed at	sorry about
angry at	surprised about
bad at	upset about
good at	worried about
surprised at	**Adjective + *to***
Adjective + *from*	similar to
different from	
separate from	
Adjective + *with*	
bored with	
familiar with	
satisfied with	
wrong with	

9. Modal Verbs and Modal-like Expressions

Most modals have multiple meanings.

Function	Modal Verb or Modal-like Expression	Time	Example
Ability / Possibility	*can*	present, future	I **can** speak three languages. I **can** help you tomorrow.
	could	present, past	She **could** play an excellent game of tennis when she was young.
	be able to	past, present, future	I **won't be able to** help you tomorrow. I'**m not able to** help you today.
Permission less formal	*can* *could*	present, future	Yes, you **can** watch TV now. You **could** give me your answer next week.
more formal	*may*	present, future	You **may** leave now.
Requests less formal	*can* *will*	present, future	**Can** you stop that noise now? **Will** you please visit me tonight?
more formal	*could* *would*	present, future	**Could** you turn off your cell phone please? **Would** you please come for your interview this afternoon?
Offers	*can* *could* *may* *will*	present, future	I **can** help you paint your room. I **could** drive you to work next week. **May** I carry that for you? We'**ll** help you find your wallet.
Invitations	*would you like*	present, future	**Would you like** to come to my graduation tomorrow?
Advice less strong	*ought to* *should*	present, future	You really **ought to** save your money. She **shouldn't** go to school today.
stronger	*had better*	present, future	They **had better** be very careful in the park tomorrow.
Suggestions	*could* *might want to*	present, future	He **could** take a train instead of the bus. You **might want to** wait until next month.

Function	Modal Verb or Modal-like Expression	Time	Example
Preferences	*would like* *would prefer* *would rather*	present, future	I **would like** to take a trip next year. We **would prefer** to go on a cruise. They **would rather** eat at home than in a restaurant.
Necessity less formal	*have / has to* *need to*	past, present, future	We **had to** cancel our date at the last minute. She **needs to** quit her stressful job.
more formal	*have / has got to* *must*	past, present, future present, future	They**'ve got to** study harder if they want to pass. You **must** be more serious about your future.
Lack of Necessity	*don't / doesn't have to* *don't / doesn't need to*	past, present, future	I **didn't have to** renew my driver's license. You **don't need to** worry about your brother.
Prohibition	*can't* *must not* *may not*	present, future	You **can't** attend tonight without an invitation. You **must not** fish without a license. You **may not** board the plane before going through security.
Speculation / Probability	*could* *may* *might* *should*	present, future	He **could** be late because he missed his train. I **may** stay home. It **might** rain later because I see dark clouds. We **should** probably leave now.
	must	present only	She **must** be sick because she didn't come to work today.

10. Adjectives: Order Before Nouns

When you use two (or more) adjectives before a noun, use the order in the chart below.

Opinion	Size	Quality	Age	Shape	Color	Origin	Material	Nouns as Adjectives
beautiful	big	cold	ancient	rectangular	black	American	cotton	computer
comfortable	fat	free	new	round	blue	Canadian	glass	evening
delicious	huge	heavy	old	square	gold	Chinese	leather	rose
expensive	large	hot	young	triangular	green	European	metal	safety
interesting	long	safe			orange	Japanese	paper	software
nice	short				purple	Mexican	plastic	summer
pretty	small				red	Peruvian	stone	training
reasonable	tall				silver	Thai	wooden	
special	thin				yellow		woolen	
ugly	wide				white			

Examples:
I bought a beautiful, new, purple and gold Indian scarf.
There is a tall, young woman sitting next to that handsome man.
We're going to learn an interesting, new software program.
The museum has expensive glass jewelry.

11. Conditionals

The **factual conditional** describes general truths, habits, and things that happen routinely. The simple present is used in both clauses. You can use modals in the result clause, too.

      IF CLAUSE   RESULT CLAUSE

If you use the highway, the drive is much faster.   (general truth)

If you enter before 11:00 a.m., you can get a discount.   (general truth)

Use the imperative in the result clause to give instructions or commands.

If you don't like the oranges, give them to me.   (command)

The **future conditional** describes things that will happen under certain conditions in the future. The simple present is used in the *if* clause and a future form is used in the result clause. You can use modals in the result clause, too.

      IF CLAUSE   RESULT CLAUSE

If it rains tomorrow, they're going to cancel the game.

If I finish my homework early, I'll go to the movies.

If she works hard, she could get a promotion.

Conditionals *(continued)*

You can begin a conditional sentence with the *if* clause or the result clause. It doesn't change the meaning. Use a comma between the two clauses if you begin your sentence with the *if* clause.

RESULT CLAUSE   IF CLAUSE
They're going to cancel the game if it rains tomorrow.

     IF CLAUSE   RESULT CLAUSE
If it rains tomorrow, they're going to cancel the game.

12. Phrasal Verbs: Transitive and Intransitive

Transitive (Separable) Phrasal Verbs

Phrasal Verb	Meaning	Phrasal Verb	Meaning
add up	add together, combine	*give up*	quit
blow up	explode	*hang up*	end a phone call
bring back	return something or someone	*help out*	assist someone
bring up	(1) raise a child, (2) introduce a topic	*lay off*	lose a job, end employment
build up	accumulate	*leave on*	keep on (a light, clothing, jewelry)
call back	return a phone call	*let in*	allow someone to enter
call off	cancel	*look over*	examine
cheer up	make someone happy	*look up*	find information
clear up	resolve a problem or situation, explain	*make up*	create or invent (a story, a lie)
do over	do again	*pass out*	distribute (paper, a test, material, homework)
figure out	find an answer, understand	*pay back*	repay money
fill in	write in blank spaces	*pay off*	repay completely
fill out	complete an application or form	*pick up*	(1) go get someone or something, (2) lift
find out	look for or seek information, learn	*point out*	call attention to something
give away	donate, give for free	*put away*	(1) save for the future, (2) put in the correct place
give back	return		

Transitive (Separable) Phrasal Verbs *(continued)*

Phrasal Verb	Meaning	Phrasal Verb	Meaning
put back	return something to its usual place	*talk over*	discuss
put off	delay, postpone	*think over*	consider
put out	(1) extinguish, stop the burning of a fire or cigarette, (2) place outside	*throw away / throw out*	get rid of something; discard
put together	assemble	*try on*	put on clothing to see if it fits
set up	(1) arrange, (2) plan, (3) build	*turn down*	(1) lower the volume, (2) reject
shut off / turn off	stop (a machine, a light, a TV)	*turn on*	start (a machine, a light, a TV)
sort out	(1) organize, (2) solve	*turn up*	increase the volume
straighten up	(1) make something look neat, (2) stand tall	*wake up*	stop sleeping
take back	return something	*work out*	(1) solve, (2) calculate
take out	(1) remove, (2) obtain something officially	*write down*	write on paper

Intransitive (Inseparable) Phrasal Verbs

Phrasal Verb	Meaning	Phrasal Verb	Meaning
break down	(1) stop working, (2) lose control	*fall down*	fall to the ground
break up	end a relationship, separate	*fool around*	act playfully
come back	return	*get ahead*	succeed, make progress
come from	originate	*get along*	have a good relationship
come on	(1) hurry, (2) start	*get over*	recover from an illness or a shock
dress up	put on nice or formal clothes	*get up*	arise from bed
drop in	visit without advance notice	*give up*	stop
drop out	quit (school, a race, a club)	*go ahead*	start or continue
eat out	eat in a restaurant	*go away*	leave; go to another place

Intransitive (Inseparable) Phrasal Verbs *(continued)*

Phrasal Verb	Meaning	Phrasal Verb	Meaning
go on	continue	*run out*	(1) leave, (2) be completely used
go out	not stay home	*set in*	begin and continue for a long time
go up	rise, go higher	*show up*	appear
grow up	become an adult	*sign up*	register for a class or event
hang on	(1) wait, (2) keep going	*sit down*	sit; take a seat
hold on	(1) wait, (2) persist	*slip up*	make a mistake
look into	investigate	*speak up*	talk louder
look out	be careful	*stand up*	stand; rise
make up	end a disagreement	*stay up*	remain awake
move in (to)	(1) take your things to a new home, (2) begin living somewhere	*take off*	(1) leave on an airplane, (2) grow; be successful
move out (of)	leave a place you live in	*watch out*	be careful
run into	meet someone by chance or unexpectedly	*work out*	(1) exercise, (2) go as planned

13. Adjectives and Adverbs: Comparative and Superlative Forms

	Adjective	Comparative	Superlative
1. One-Syllable Adjectives a. Add *-er* and *-est* to one syllable adjectives.	cheap high large long new old small strong tall	cheaper higher larger longer newer older smaller stronger taller	the cheapest the highest the largest the longest the newest the oldest the smallest the strongest the tallest
b. For one-syllable adjectives that end in a vowel + consonant, double the final consonant and add *-er* or *-est*.	big hot sad thin	bigger hotter sadder thinner	the biggest the hottest the saddest the thinnest
Do not double the consonant *w*.	low	lower	the lowest

Adjectives and Adverbs: Comparative and Superlative Forms (continued)

2. Two-Syllable Adjectives a. Add *more* or *most* to most adjectives.	boring famous handsome patient	more boring more famous more handsome more patient	the most boring the most famous the most handsome the most patient
b. Some two-syllable adjectives have two forms.	friendly narrow simple strict quiet	friendlier more friendly narrower more narrow simpler more simple stricter more strict quieter more quiet	the friendliest the most friendly the narrowest the most narrow the simplest the most simple the strictest the most strict the quietest the most quiet
c. Remove the *-y* and add *-ier* or *-iest* to two-syllable adjectives ending in *-y*.	angry easy friendly happy lucky pretty silly	angrier easier friendlier happier luckier prettier sillier	the angriest the easiest the friendliest the happiest the luckiest the prettiest the silliest
3. Three or More Syllable Adjectives Add *more* or *most* to adjectives with three or more syllables.	beautiful comfortable creative difficult enjoyable expensive important independent relaxing responsible serious	more beautiful more comfortable more creative more difficult more enjoyable more expensive more important more independent more relaxing more responsible more serious	the most beautiful the most comfortable the most creative the most difficult the most enjoyable the most expensive the most important the most independent the most relaxing the most responsible the most serious
4. Irregular Adjectives Some adjectives have irregular forms.	bad far good	worse farther / further better	the worst the farthest / the furthest the best

Adjectives and Adverbs: Comparative and Superlative Forms (continued)

5. -ly Adverbs Most adverbs end in -ly. Add *more* or *most*. People usually only use *the* with superlative adverbs in formal writing and speaking.	dangerously patiently quickly quietly slowly	more dangerously more patiently more quickly more quietly more slowly	(the) most dangerously (the) most patiently (the) most quickly (the) most quietly (the) most slowly
6. One-Syllable Adverbs A few adverbs do not end in -ly. Add -er and -est to these adverbs.	fast hard	faster harder	(the) fastest (the) hardest
7. Irregular Adverbs Some adverbs have irregular forms.	badly far well	worse farther / further better	(the) worst (the) farthest / furthest (the) best

14. Academic Word List (AWL) Words and Definitions

The meanings of the words are those used in this book. ([U1] = Unit 1)

Academic Word	Definition
access (n) [U8] [U29]	easy way to enter
achieve (v) [U16]	do or obtain something that you wanted after planning and working to make it happen
administration (n) [U13]	the management or control of an organization
adult (n) [U8]	someone (or something such as a plant or animal) grown to full size and strength
affect (v) [U17] [U23] [U26]	have an influence on someone or something
analyze (v) [U8] [U30]	study something in a systematic and careful way
appropriate (adj) [U3]	right for a particular situation
appropriately (adv) [U3]	in a way that is right for a particular situation
area (n) [U12]	a particular part of a country, city, town, etc.
aspect (n) [U17]	a particular feature of or way of thinking about something
assess (v) [U21]	decide the quality or importance of something
assignment (n) [U3] [U20]	a particular job or responsibility given to you
available (adj) [U5]	ready to use or obtain
brief (adj) [U3]	short, concise, to the point
challenge (n) [U9] [U11] [U22]	something needing a great mental or physical effort in order to be done successfully
challenge (v) [U9] [U11] [U22]	test someone's ability or determination

Academic Word	Definition
chemical (n) [U2] [U10] [U13] [U15]	any basic substance that is used in or produced by a reaction involving changes to atoms or molecules
civil (adj) [U29]	of or relating to the people of a country
collapse (v) [U11]	fall down suddenly, or to cause to fall down; to be unable to continue or to stay in operation
comment (n) [U8]	an opinion or remark
commission (n) [U13]	an official group of people who get information about a problem or perform other special duties
communicate (v) [U3] [U14] [U18]	give messages or information to others through speech, writing, body movements, or signals
communication (n) [U14]	the exchange of messages or information
community (n) [U20]	all the people who live in a particular area, or a group of people who are considered as a unit because of their shared interests or background
computer (n) [U1] [U2] [U4] [U6] [U19]	an electronic device that can store large amounts of information and organize and change it very quickly
constantly (adv) [U24]	nearly continuously or frequently
consumer (n) [U22]	a person who buys goods or services for their own use
contact (v) [U20]	have communication with someone, or with a group or organization
convince (v) [U22]	cause someone to believe something or to do something
couple (n) [U23]	two people who are married or who spend a lot of time together, especially in a romantic relationship
create (v) [U3] [U5] [U12] [U16] [U28] [U30]	cause something to exist, or to make something new and imaginative
creative (adj) [U9] [U22] [U26]	producing or using original and unusual ideas
credit (n) [U7] [U25]	a method of buying goods or services that allows you to pay for them in the future; *academic meaning:* acknowledgment or praise
crucial (adj) [U32]	extremely important because many other things depend on it
culture (n) [U24] [U28]	the way of life of a particular people, especially shown in their ordinary behavior and habits, their attitudes toward each other, and their moral and religious beliefs
cycle (n) [U28] [U31]	a process that repeats
decline (n) [U23]	a decrease in amount or quality
design (v) [U4] [U12]	make or draw plans for something
discriminate (v) [U29]	treat people differently, in an unfair way
discrimination (n) [U13] [U29]	treating people differently, in an unfair way
distribute (v) [U15]	divide something among several or many people, or to spread something over an area
distribution (n) [U15]	the division of something among several or many people, or the spreading of something over an area

Academic Word	Definition
document (n) [U7]	a paper or set of papers with written or printed information
dominate (v) [U26]	control a place or person, want to be in charge, or be the most important person or thing
economic (adj) [U23]	connected to the economy of a country
economy (n) [U23] [U32]	the system of trade and industry by which the wealth of a country is made and used
editor (n) [U8]	a person who corrects and makes changes to texts or films before they are printed or shown, or a person who is in charge of a newspaper, magazine, etc., and is responsible for all of its reports
environment (n) [U18] [U19]	the air, water, and land in or on which people, animals, and plants live
environmental (adj) [U12]	related to the air, water, and land in or on which people, animals, and plants live
estimate (n) [U12]	a judgment or calculation of approximately how large or how great something is
ethical (adj) [U13]	good, correct
expert (n) [U21] [U23] [U24]	a person having a high level of knowledge or skill in a particular subject
feature (n) [U16] [U18]	a noticeable or important characteristic or part
finally (adv) [U3] [U20]	at the end, or after some delay
finance (n) [U25]	the management of money, or the money belonging to a person, group, or organization
flexible (adj) [U28]	able to change or be changed easily according to the situation
focus (v) [U17]	direct attention toward something or someone
gender (n) [U26]	the male or female sex
goal (n) [U9] [U16] [U17] [U25]	an aim or purpose
grade (n) [U26]	a school class or group of classes in which all children are of a similar age or ability; *also:* a score on a test
identity (n) [U7]	who a person is, or the qualities of a person, thing, or group that make them different from others
illegal (adj) [U13] [U29]	against the law
image (n) [U6]	a picture, especially one seen in a mirror, through a camera, in a photo, on TV, or on a computer
income (n) [U25]	money that is earned from doing work or received from investments
instance (n) [U32]	a particular situation, event, or fact
instruction (n) [U19]	advice and information about how to do or use something
interact (v) [U1] [U31]	communicate with or react to each other
issue (n) [U13]	a subject or problem that people are thinking and talking about

Academic Word	Definition
item (n) [U31] [U32]	a particular thing considered as one among others of its type
job (n) [U6] [U9] [U12] [U13] [U21] [U29]	the regular work that a person does to earn money
legal (adj) [U13]	connected with or allowed by the law
link (n) [U8]	a word or image on a website that can take you to another document or website; *academic meaning:* a connection
major (adj) [U27]	more important, bigger, or more serious than others of the same type
medical (adj) [U19]	of or relating to medicine, or the treatment of disease or injury
migrate (v) [U12]	move from one place to another
migration (n) [U11]	movement from one place to another
motivate (v) [U16]	cause someone to behave in a certain way, or to make someone want to do something well; give a reason for doing something
motivating (adj.) [U16]	causing someone to behave in a certain way or to do something well; giving a reason for doing something
negative (adj) [U23]	not happy, hopeful, or approving
network (n) [U27]	a group of computers that are connected and can share information; a group of people who share ideas
networking (n) [U1] [U8] [U27]	the process of meeting and talking to a lot of people, especially in order to get a lot of information that can help you
normally (adv) [U18]	usually or regularly
occupational (adj) [U13]	relating to or caused by a person's work or activity
occur (v) [U11] [U28]	happen
percent (n) [U8] [U32]	for or out of every 100
period (n) [U17]	a length of time
positive (adj) [U3] [U6] [U17] [U23]	without any doubt; certain; good
predict (v) [U23]	say that an event will happen in the future
prioritize (v) [U25]	put things in order of importance
priority (n) [U25]	something that is considered more important than other matters
process (n) [U5] [U15]	a series of actions or events performed to make something or achieve a particular result, or a series of changes that happens naturally
process (v) [U15]	prepare, change, or treat food with chemicals to make it last longer; deal with something according to a specific set of actions
processing (n) [U15]	the preparation, change, or treatment of food with chemicals to make it last longer; the act of dealing with something according to a specific set of actions, such as processing an insurance claim
professional (n) [U3]	a person who has a job that needs skill, education, or training

Academic Word	Definition
professional (adj) [U3] [U23]	having the qualities of skilled, trained, and educated people
project (n) [U21]	a piece of planned work or activity that is completed over a period of time and intended to achieve a particular aim
psychologist (n) [U16]	someone who studies the mind and emotions and their relationship to behavior
psychology (n) [U26]	the scientific study of how the mind works and how it influences behavior
purchase (n) [U25]	something that you buy or the act of buying something
range (n) [U8]	the level to which something is limited, or the area within which something operates
reaction (n) [U8]	a behavior, feeling, or action that is a direct result of something else
recover (v) [U19]	get better after an illness or a period of difficulty or trouble
relax (v) [U25]	become or cause someone to become calm and comfortable, and not worried or nervous
relaxed (adj) [U26]	comfortable and informal
research (n) [U16] [U19] [U30]	a detailed study of a subject or an object in order to discover information or achieve a new understanding of it
researcher (n) [U11] [U26] [U30]	someone who does a detailed study of a subject or an object in order to discover information or achieve a new understanding of it
respond (v) [U3]	say or do something as a reaction to something that has been said or done
response (n) [U6]	something said or done as a reaction to something; an answer or reaction
revolution (n) [U5]	a sudden and great change, especially the violent change of a system of government
role (n) [U27]	the duty or use that someone or something usually has or is expected to have
schedule (n) [U1] [U28]	a list of planned activities or things to be done at or during a particular time
secure (adj) [U7]	safe
security (n) [U7] [U17]	protection from risk and the threat of change for the worse
similar (adj) [U10]	looking or being almost the same, although not exactly
site (n) [U1] [U7] [U8] [U27]	a place where something is, was, or will be
source (n) [U27]	someone or something from which you obtain information; origin or beginning of something
specific (adj) [U3] [U28]	relating to one thing and not others; particular
strategy (n) [U14]	a plan for achieving something or reaching a goal
stressed (adj) [U32]	worried by a difficult situation; being physically tested, like a car part to make sure it is strong
style (n) [U14]	a way of doing something that is typical to a person, group, place, or time

Academic Word	Definition
task (n) [U9] [U24]	a piece of work to be done
team (n) [U10] [U28] [U30]	a group of people who work together, either in a sport or in order to achieve something
technique (n) [U14]	a specific way of doing a skillful activity
technological (adj) [U19]	relating to, or involving, technology
technology (n) [U1] [U19] [U27]	the methods for using scientific discoveries for practical purposes, especially in industry
text (n) [U3]	written or printed material
theory (n) [U11]	something suggested as a reasonable explanation for facts, a condition, or an event
topic (n) [U27]	a subject that is written about, discussed, or studied
traditional (adj) [U5]	established for a long time, or part of behavior and beliefs that have been established
transport (v) [U15]	take things, goods, or people from one place to another
trend (n) [U12] [U23]	direction of changes or developments
volunteer (n) [U20]	someone who does something for other people, willingly and without being forced or paid to do it
volunteer (v) [U9] [U20]	do something for other people, willingly and without being forced or paid to do it

15. Pronunciation Table International Phonetic Alphabet (IPA)

Vowels	
Key Words	**International Phonetic Alphabet**
cake, mail, pay	/eɪ/
pan, bat, hand	/æ/
tea, feet, key	/iː/
ten, well, red	/e/
ice, pie, night	/aɪ/
is, fish, will	/ɪ/
cone, road, know	/oʊ/
top, rock, stop	/ɑ/
blue, school, new, cube, few	/uː/
cup, us, love	/ʌ/
house, our, cow	/aʊ/
saw, talk, applause	/ɔː/
boy, coin, join	/ɔɪ/

Vowels (continued)	
put, book, woman	/ʊ/
alone, open, pencil, atom, ketchup	/ə/

Consonants	
Key Words	**International Phonetic Alphabet**
bid, job	/b/
do, feed	/d/
food, safe	/f/
go, dog	/g/
home, behind	/h/
kiss, back	/k/
load, pool	/l/
man, plum	/m/
need, open	/n/
pen, hope	/p/
road, card	/r/
see, recent	/s/
show, nation	/ʃ/
team, meet	/t/
choose, watch	/tʃ/
think, both	/θ/
this, father	/ð/
visit, save	/v/
watch, away	/w/
yes, onion	/j/
zoo, these	/z/
beige, measure	/ʒ/
jump, bridge	/dʒ/

Glossary of Grammar Terms

action verb a verb that describes an action.
> I **eat** breakfast every day.
> They **ran** in the 5K race.

adjective a word that describes or modifies a noun.
> That's a **beautiful** hat.

adjective clause see **relative clause**.

adverb a word that describes or modifies a verb, another adverb, or an adjective. Adverbs often end in *-ly*.
> Please walk **faster** but **carefully**.

adverb clause a clause that shows how ideas are connected. Adverb clauses begin with conjunctions such as *because*, *since*, *although*, and *even though*.
> **Although it is not a holiday**, workers have the day off.

adverb of degree an adverb that makes other adverbs or adjectives stronger or weaker.
> The test was **extremely** difficult.   They are **kind of** busy today.

adverb of manner an adverb that describes how an action happens.
> He has **suddenly** left the room.

adverb of time an adverb that describes when something happens.
> She'll get up **later**.

article the words *a/an* and *the*. An article introduces or identifies a noun.
> I bought **a** new MP3 player. **The** price was reasonable.

auxiliary verb (also called **helping verb**) a verb that is used before a main verb in a sentence. *Do, have,* and *be* can act as auxiliary verbs.
> **Does** he want to go to the library later?   **Have** you received the package?

base form of the verb the form of a verb without any endings (*-s* or *-ed*) or *to*.
> **come**   **go**   **take**

clause a group of words that has a subject and a verb. There are two types of clauses: **main clauses** and **dependent clauses** (*see* dependent clause). A sentence can have more than one clause.
> MAIN CLAUSE   DEPENDENT CLAUSE   MAIN CLAUSE
> I woke up when I heard the noise. It was scary.

common noun a word for a person, place, or thing. A common noun is not capitalized.
> **mother**   **building**   **fruit**

comparative the form of an adjective or adverb that shows how two people, places, or things are different.
> My daughter is **older than** my son. (adjective)
> She does her work **more quickly** than he does. (adverb)

conjunction a word such as *and, but, so, or,* and *yet* which connects single words, phrases, or clauses.

*We finished all our work, **so** we left early.*

consonant a sound represented in writing by these letters of the alphabet: ***b, c, d, f, g, h, j, k, l, m, n, p, q, r, s, t, v, w, x, y,*** and ***z.***

count noun refers to a person, place, or thing you can count. Count nouns have a plural form.

*There are three **banks** on Oak Street.*

definite article *the* is a definite article. Use *the* with a person, place, or thing that is familiar to you and your listener. Also, use *the* when the noun is unique – there is only one (*the sun, the moon, the Internet*).

***The** movie we saw last week was very good.*

***The** Earth is round.*

dependent clause a clause that cannot stand alone. Some kinds of dependent clauses are adverb clauses, relative clauses, and time clauses.

***After we return from the trip**, I'm going to need to relax.*

determiner a word that comes before a noun to limit its meaning in some way. Some common determiners are *some, a little, a lot, a few, this, that, these, those, his, a, an, the, much,* and *many.*

***These** computers have **a lot** of parts.*

*Please give me **my** book.*

direct object the person or thing that receives the action of the verb.

*The teacher gave the students **a test**.*

factual conditional describes something that is generally true in a certain situation. The *if* clause describes the condition and is in the simple present. The result clause is in the simple present as well.

***If** it's late, I don't stay online for a long time.*

formal a style of writing or speech used when you don't know the other person very well or where it's not appropriate to show familiarity, such as in business, a job interview, speaking to a stranger, or speaking to an older person who you respect.

Good evening. I'd like to speak with Ms. Smith. Is she available?

future a verb form that describes a time that hasn't come yet. It is expressed in English by *will, be going to,* and present tense.

*I'**ll meet** you tomorrow.*

*I'**m going to visit** my uncle and aunt next weekend.*

future conditional describes something that will happen under certain conditions in the future. The *if* clause describes the condition and is in the simple present. The result clause uses a future form of the verb.

***If** I do well on this final exam, I'**ll get** an A for the course.*

gerund the *-ing* form of a verb that is used as a noun. It can be the subject or object in a sentence or the object of a preposition.

*We suggested **waiting** and **going** another day.*

*Salsa **dancing** is a lot of fun.*

*I look forward to **meeting** you.*

habitual past a verb form that describes repeated past actions, habits, and conditions using *used to* or *would*.

*Before we had the Internet, we **used to** go to the library a lot.*

*Before there was refrigeration, people **would** use ice to keep food cool.*

helping verb *see* **auxiliary verb**.

imperative a type of clause that tells people to do something. It gives instructions, directions to a place, and advice. The verb is in the base form.

***Listen** to the conversation.*

***Don't open** your books.*

indefinite article *a/an* are the indefinite articles. Use *a/an* with a singular person, place, or thing when you and your listener are not familiar with it, or when the specific name of it is not important. Use *a* with consonant sounds. Use *an* with vowel sounds.

*She's going to see **a** doctor today.   I had **an** egg for breakfast.*

indirect object the person or thing that receives the direct object.

*The teacher gave **the students** a test.*

infinitive *to* + the base form of a verb.

*I need **to get** home early tonight.*

infinitive of purpose *in order* + infinitive expresses a purpose. It answers the question *why*. If the meaning is clear, it is not necessary to use *in order*.

*People are fighting **(in order) to change** unfair laws.*

informal a style of speaking or writing to friends, family, and children.

Hey, there. Nice to see you again.

information question (also called **Wh- question**) begins with a *wh-* word *(who, what, when, where, which, why, how, how much)*. To answer this type of question, you need to provide information rather than answer *yes* or *no*.

inseparable phrasal verb a phrasal verb that cannot be separated. The verb and its particle always stay together.

*My car **broke down** yesterday.*

intransitive verb a verb that does not need an object. It is often followed by an expression of time, place, or manner.

*The flight **arrived** at 5:30 p.m.*

irregular adjective an adjective that does not change its form in the usual way. For example, you do not make the comparative form by adding *-er*.

good ➞ *better*

irregular adverb an adverb that does not change its form in the usual way. For example, you do not make the comparative form by adding *-er*.

badly ➞ *worse*

irregular verb a verb that does not change its form in the usual way. For example, it does not form the simple past with *-d* or *-ed*. It has its own special form.

go ➞ *went*   *ride* ➞ *rode*   *hit* ➞ *hit*

main clause (also called **independent clause**) a clause that can be used alone as a complete sentence.

*After I get back from my trip, **I'm going to relax**.*

main verb a verb that functions alone in a clause and can have an auxiliary verb.

*They **had** a meeting last week.*

*They have **had** many meetings this month.*

measurement word a word or phrase that shows the amount of something. Measurement words can be singular or plural.

*I bought **a box** of cereal, and Sonia bought **five pounds** of apples.*

modal a verb such as *can, could, have to, may, might, must, should, will*, and *would*. It modifies the main verb to show such things as ability, permission, possibility, advice, obligation, necessity, or lack of necessity.

*It **might** rain later today.*

*You **should** study harder if you want to pass this course.*

non-action verb *see* **stative verb**.

noncount noun refers to ideas and things that you cannot count. Noncount nouns use a singular verb and do not have a plural form.

*Do you download **music**?*

noun a word for a person, place, or thing. There are common nouns and proper nouns (*see* **common noun, proper noun**).

COMMON NOUN   PROPER NOUN
*I stayed in a **hotel** on my trip to New York.*   *I stayed in the **Pennsylvania Hotel**.*

object pronoun replaces a noun in the object position.

*Sara loves exercise classes. She takes **them** three times a week.*

particle a small word like *down, in, off, on, out,* or *up*. These words (which can also be prepositions) are used with verbs to form **two-word verbs** or **phrasal verbs**. The meaning of a phrasal verb often has a different meaning from the meaning of the individual words in it.

past participle a verb form that can be regular (base form + *-ed*) or irregular. It is used to form the present perfect and the passive. It can also be an adjective.

*I've **studied** English for five years.*

past progressive a verb form that describes events or situations in progress at a time in the past. The emphasis is on the action.

*They **were watching** TV when I arrived.*

phrasal verb (also called a **two-word verb**) consists of a verb + a particle. There are two kinds of phrasal verbs: separable and inseparable (*see* **particle, inseparable phrasal verb, separable phrasal verb**).

VERB + PARTICLE
*They **came back** from vacation today.* (inseparable)
*Please **put** your cell phone **away**.* (separable)

plural noun a noun that refers to more than one person, place, or thing.

students   women   roads

possessive adjective *see* **possessive determiner.**

possessive determiner (also called **possessive adjective**) a determiner that shows possession (*my, your, his, her, its, our,* and *their*).

possessive pronoun replaces a possessive determiner + singular or plural noun. The possessive pronoun agrees with the noun that it replaces.

My exercise class is at night. **Hers** *is on the weekend.* (hers = her exercise class)

preposition a word such as *to, at, for, with, below, in, on, next to,* or *above* that goes before a noun or pronoun to show location, time, direction, or a close relationship between two people or things. A preposition may go before a gerund as well.

I'm **in** *the supermarket* **next to** *our favorite restaurant.*

The idea **of** *love has inspired many poets.*

present perfect a verb form that describes past events or situations that are still important in the present, actions that happened once or repeatedly at an indefinite time before now, and to give the number of times something happened up to now.

Lately scientists **have discovered** *medicines in the Amazon.*

I've **been** *to the Amazon twice.*

present perfect progressive a verb form that describes something that started in the past, usually continues in the present, and may continue in the future.

He **hasn't been working** *since last May.*

present progressive a verb form that describes an action or situation that is in progress now or around the present time. It is also used to indicate a fixed arrangement in the near future.

What **are** *you* **doing** *right now?*

I'm **leaving** *for Spain next week.*

pronoun a word that replaces a noun or noun phrase. Some examples are *I, we, him, hers,* and *it* (see **object pronoun, subject pronoun, relative pronoun, possessive pronoun, reciprocal pronoun, reflexive pronoun**).

proper noun a noun that is the name of a particular person, place, idea, or thing. It is capitalized.

Central Park *is in* **New York City***.*

punctuation mark a symbol used in writing such as a period (.), a comma (,), a question mark (?), or an exclamation point (!).

quantifier Some quantifiers are *much, many, some, any, a lot, plenty,* and *enough.*

reciprocal pronoun a pronoun (*each other, one another*) that shows that two or more people give *and* receive the same action or have the same relationship.

Mari and I have the same challenges. We help **each other***.* (I help Mari and Mari helps me.)

reflexive pronoun a pronoun (*myself, yourself, himself, herself, ourselves, yourselves, themselves*) which shows that the object of the sentence is the same as the subject.

I taught **myself** *to speak Japanese.*

regular verb a verb that changes its form in the usual way.

live → live**s**

wash → wash**ed**

relative clause (also known as **adjective clause**) defines, describes, identifies, or gives more information about a noun. It begins with a relative pronoun such as *who, that, which, whose,* or *whom.* Like all clauses, a relative clause has both a subject and a verb. It can describe the subject or the object of a sentence.

People ***who have sleep problems*** *can join the study.* (subject relative clause)

There are many diseases ***that viruses cause.*** (object relative clause)

relative pronoun a pronoun *(who, which, that, whose, whom)* that connects a noun phrase to a relative clause.

People ***who*** *have sleep problems can join the study.*

There are many diseases ***that*** *viruses cause.*

sentence a complete thought or idea that has a subject and a main verb. In writing, it begins with a capital letter and has a punctuation mark at the end (. ? !). In an imperative sentence, the subject *(you)* is not usually stated.

This sentence is a complete thought. ***Open your books.***

separable phrasal verb a phrasal verb that can be separated. This means that an object can go before or after the particle.

Write down *your expenses.*

Write *your expenses* ***down.***

simple past a verb form that describes completed actions or events that happened at a definite time in the past.

They ***grew up*** *in Washington, D.C.*

They ***attended*** *Howard University and* ***graduated*** *in 2004.*

simple present a verb form that describes things that regularly happen, such as habits and routines (usual and regular activities). It also describes facts and general truths.

I ***play*** *games online every night.* (routine)

The average person ***spends*** *13 hours a week online.* (fact)

singular noun a noun that refers to only one person, place, or thing.

He is my best ***friend.***

statement a sentence that gives information.

Today is Thursday.

stative verb (also called **non-action verb**) describes a state or situation, not an action. It is usually in the simple form of the present or past.

I ***remember*** *your friend.*

subject the person or thing that performs the action of a verb.

People *use new words and expressions every day.*

subject pronoun replaces a noun in the subject position.

Sara and I are friends. ***We*** *work at the same company.*

superlative the form of an adjective or adverb that compares one person, place, or thing to others in a group.

*This storm was **the most dangerous** one of the season.* (adjective)

*That group worked **most effectively** after the disaster.* (adverb)

syllable a group of letters that has one vowel sound and that you say as a single unit.

There is one syllable in the word lunch *and two syllables in the word* breakfast. (*Break* is one syllable and *fast* is another syllable.)

tense the form of a verb that shows past or present time.

*They **worked** yesterday.* (simple past)

*They **work** every day.* (simple present)

third-person singular refers to *he, she,* and *it* or a singular noun. In the simple present, the third-person singular form ends in *-s* or *-es.*

***It looks** warm and sunny today.*   ***He washes** the laundry on Saturdays.*

time clause a clause that shows the order of events and begins with a time word such as *before, after, when, while,* or *as soon as.*

***Before** there were freezers, people needed ice to make frozen desserts.*

time expression a phrase that functions as an adverb of time. It tells when something happens, happened, or will happen.

*I graduated **in 2010**.*   *She's going to visit her aunt and uncle **next summer**.*

transitive verb a verb that needs an object. The object completes the meaning of the verb.

*She **wears** perfume.*

two-word verb see **phrasal verb**.

verb a word that describes an action or a state.

*Alex **wears** jeans and a T-shirt to school. Alex **is** a student.*

vowel a sound represented in writing by these letters of the alphabet: ***a, e, i, o,*** and ***u.***

***Wh-* question** see **information question**.

***Yes / No* question** begins with a form of *be* or an auxiliary verb. You can answer such a question with *yes* or *no.*

*"**Are** they going to the movies?"*   *""**No**, they're not."*

*"**Can** you give me some help?"*   *"**Yes**, I can."*

Index

Art Credits

Illustration